A GUIDEBOOK TO REHABILITATION AND HUMAN SERVICES MANAGEMENT
Fine Tuning for Excellence

A GUIDEBOOK TO REHABILITATION AND HUMAN SERVICES MANAGEMENT
Fine Tuning for Excellence

By

STEVEN E. SIMON, PH.D.

Chief
Vocational Rahabilitation and Counseling Division
Veterans Administration Regional Office
Cleveland, Ohio
and
Assistant Professor (Part-time)
Kent State University
Kent, Ohio

CHARLES C THOMAS • PUBLISHER
Springfield • Illinois • U.S.A.

Published and Distributed Throughout the World by

CHARLES C THOMAS • PUBLISHER
2600 South First Street
Springfield, Illinois 62794-9265

© *1989 by* CHARLES C THOMAS • PUBLISHER

ISBN 0-398-05582-3

Library of Congress Catalog Card Number: 89-30372

With THOMAS BOOKS *careful attention is given to all details of manufacturing
and design. It is the Publisher's desire to present books that are satisfactory as to
their physical qualities and artistic possibilities and appropriate for their particular
use.* THOMAS BOOKS *will be true to those laws of quality that assure a good
name and good will.*

Printed in the United States of America
SC-R-3

Library of Congress Cataloging-in-Publication Data

Simon, Steven E.
    A guidebook to rehabilitation and human services management : fine
timing for excellence / by Steven E. Simon.
        p.   cm.
    Bibliography: p.
    Includes index.
    ISBN 0-398-05582-3
    1. Human services—United States—Management.   I. Title.
HV95.S54   1989
361'.0068—dc19   89-30372
                                                                            CIP

To Gail, Bonnie, and Matt

PREFACE

The purpose of this book is to provide a foundation for supervising and managing in rehabilitation and other human services settings. It is written to meet the needs of the new manager, or as a first text for those aspiring toward a management career. It is intended that the book be used as a primary or supplementary text in introductory graduate and undergraduate human services management courses. It may also be used as a supplement to in-service training of rehabilitation and human services managers in agency settings. Although the book is oriented most toward management in vocational rehabilitation settings, examples and literature coverage is inclusive of most counseling, social work, psychology and some medical related service areas.

The major premise of the book is that new human services managers need a balanced foundation in both the theoretical and practical sides of management, **prior to or at the time they begin practice.** Unfortunately, most managers begin this aspect of their careers with training and experience mainly in direct services. Most have no formal education in management. It is my belief that such a scenario contributes to inability to achieve the results and consequently the continuing resources needed for agencies and their programs to survive or remain effective.

Skilled management and leadership will assume increasing importance in an economic environment characterized by competition for scarcer resources in the public and private not-for-profit sector. As with competition in private sector business, the best led and managed organizations will survive. Since management and leadership skills differ sharply from those needed for direct service, aggressive action is needed on the part of universities, political leaders, professional organizations, consumers and current leaders to assure that future leaders are adequately trained.

As implied above, the book focuses on both the theoretical and practical aspects of management. As a management practitioner for most of my career, I am sensitive to the day to day functional needs of managers.

However, also having experience as an academician, I am aware of the need to integrate important theoretical fundamentals from rehabilitation, organizational psychology, other human services and general management literature into practice. In maintaining a practitioner's perspective, I have tried to include topics regarding down to earth, day to day concerns of managers. Time management techniques, how to manage employee leave abuse and how to deal with conflict resolution are examples. When theory and research have been presented, I have attempted to make the connection to management practice with examples, suggestions and step by step guidelines. However, to make this information more directly applicable, it is intended that it be used in the classroom or in-service training setting with real or simulated situations as a stimulus for discussion. To assist with this, I have included exercises at the end of each section that can be used by instructors to provide experiential learning in key areas covered in the readings. Most of these exercises have been successfully used with graduate students. It is also suggested that the reading material be integrated into discussions of real situations contributed by students and instructors.

Philosophically, the book stresses the importance of mastering six basic management functions as a prerequisite to running effective human services systems: planning, organizing, controlling, coordinating, communicating, and organization development and change. From my perspective, it is the manager's role to use these functions to continually fine tune his or her work unit or organization toward optimum functioning. Optimum functioning implies a well balanced, synergistic system that results in excellent services, satisfied clients, a satisfied, committed workforce, and high productivity and efficiency in carrying out the agency mission. The organization development and change function provides the basis for using all of the other functions to perpetually fine tune.

The book is organized into eight sections. The introductory section includes a chapter on "The Human Services Manager," and a chapter which attempts to define general principles for operating an effectively functioning organization. This is followed by seven sections covering the management functions. Each section covers a function through several chapters. However, due to it's extensiveness, the controlling function is divided into two sections. The book culminates with a model for "fine tuning" as part of the organization development and change function.

After teaching introductory rehabilitation administration for several years, I am particularly sensitized to the unfamiliarity of the management approach and terminology to those who have focused on direct service helping careers. I have thus tried to improve the ease of reading and understanding this sometimes foreign material, and it's value for reference purposes, by using a question and answer format. For easy reference and overview, the CONTENTS includes a listing of all questions for each chapter and major topic area.

Many people have assisted in the writing of this book. I would like to acknowledge the managers, program administrators and vocational rehabilitation staff with whom I have worked in the Veterans Administration over the past twenty years. These relationships have contributed greatly to my perspective on management.

I would particularly like to acknowledge those who spent many hours in providing assistance, advice and guidance throughout preparation of the manuscript. G. Thomas Yungman of the Vocational Rehabilitation and Education Service in VA Central Office, James Malley of the Hartford VA Regional Office and Terry Etling of the Ohio Rehabilitation Services Commission contributed many useful suggestions. Martha Walker of Kent State University and Ernest Biller of Ohio State University did reviews in the early stages of the book and provided invaluable advice based on their own book publishing experiences. Armand Lauffer of the University of Michigan provided extensive suggestions regarding practical applications, that were incorporated into the final manuscript. Henry Millat of the Cleveland VA Regional Office was instrumental in supplying legal and technical insights with respect to the topic of employee selection.

I would also like to acknowledge my wife, Gail Simon of New Directions for editorial reading, and Patricia Seifert of the Cleveland Clinic for technical reading, editorial and administrative assistance in preparing the final manuscript. Finally, I wish to thank all of my students who read and critiqued early versions of the manuscript. Their "careful," but spontaneous and candid comments helped to make the book more pertinent to future student needs.

Steven E. Simon
Cleveland, Ohio

CONTENTS

system control relate to these concepts? Is it possible to overcontrol a system? In summary then, how can we characterize effective systems management?

Have there been any large scale studies of human services organizations that shed light on effective management? Are there any large scale studies of other types of organizations that also have general relevance to human services agencies? What then, on the basis of these studies, can human services managers hope to achieve with their work units? Can we generalize much beyond the need for effective communications? What about accountability? How important is that? What is the significance of accountability to the human services manager's role? Are there any other important factors based on these studies?

What then can we conclude are some general principles important to running a good organization?

What is the structure of formal planning in human services agencies? Does it matter who is involved in the formal planning process?

How do we define the mission of an agency? What are the characteristics of a good mission statement? Mission statements look easy to develop. Is this true?

What are goals? What is the difference between goals and objectives? Why are goals and objectives so important? Is there a correct way to structure goals and objectives? Writing general goals seems to be a common practice. Is this effective? What areas should

What are specialized structures? When should specialized structures be established? What are some major types of specialized structures? What is the matrix structure? What is a parallel structure? What are quality circles? What is an ad hoc task force? What are integrative committees and individuals? What is a formal committee? What are informal problem solving groups? What are mixed innovative groups? Specialized structures seem to have value, but don't they unnecessarily take up a lot of time that could be used more effectively for other purposes—like direct service and management?

To what parts of the organization does the informal structure apply? What are the main functions of the informal group? What is the nature of the informal structure within the organization? What are some informal roles? What is the nature of the status hierarchy? What are norms and how do they impact on the group? Do professional groups have a unique structure? Does the informal professional group structure have any special impact on management? How can managers make effective use of the informal structure? What can be done to create informal groups and structure that supports management? How can managers use the informal structure to bring about change?

What is the purpose of macro control? What is the nature of macro control?

What are some macro models of control, and how do they work? What is management centered control? What are the implications of management centered control for an organization? Does management centered control ever work effectively in human services agencies? What is group centered control? What are the implica-

xvi *A Guidebook to Rehabilitation and Human Services Management*

tions of group centered control for an organization? How can group centered control be used effectively? What is a good example of this? What is employee centered control? How does employee centered control relate to group centered control? How can management engineer a work environment that supports employee centered control? What is money centered control? When can money centered control be used in a human services agency?

What are special rewards? What is the purpose of special rewards?
Which are more effective, intrinsic or extrinsic rewards? What is
required for effective distribution of extrinsic rewards? What types
of employee evaluation systems best support the effective use of
extrinsic rewards? What is the significance of the relationship
among rewards, employee satisfaction, performance and turnover?

administrative use to human services organizations? How is computerized data typically communicated? Is on-line access to a computer always necessary? What is "user friendliness" and how does this impact on communication of computerized data? What role should managers play in computerization? Are managers typically resistant to using computers?

ment by objectives? Is the management control project approach transferable to other human services settings? How can this approach improve the overall efficiency and effectiveness of human services agencies? What are the research findings on the management control project? What additional suggestions can be made for managers who wish to implement the management control project approach?

A GUIDEBOOK TO REHABILITATION AND HUMAN SERVICES MANAGEMENT
Fine Tuning for Excellence

Section I

INTRODUCTION

OVERVIEW

Human services managers play a special and important role in organizations and in the lives of others. They influence how their organizations will function and how well clients will be served. They can exert a major positive impact depending upon how well they manage.

The first two chapters of this section discuss the job of the human services manager and present a perspective for understanding organization systems. This clarifies the manager's role, and provides a general approach to analyzing and successfully managing a human services organization. Such information forms a philosophical basis for action, and a results oriented foundation toward which the management functions discussed throughout this book may be applied.

Chapter 1 suggests both a management and leadership role for human services managers in carrying out six basic functions: planning, organizing, controlling, coordinating, organization development/change and communicating. Day to day functions including personnel management and supervision related tasks, production management, marketing and purchasing, public relations, and evaluation/research activities are described.

In Chapter 2, systems concepts are explored. Effective systems management suggests the need to use energy efficiently through assuring optimum levels of control, facilitating synergy among system components, and paying attention to all important classes of outputs. Studies of organizations suggest the importance of effective communications among managers and employees within the fabric of a positive organization culture. Employees should also clearly understand the values, goals and policies of the organization. In addition, a focus on quality of services, results, client satisfaction and accountability appears important to effective human services organization performance.

Chapter 1

THE HUMAN SERVICES MANAGER

What is a human services manager?

For our purposes, the term manager is used generically. It refers to any person who has the responsibility of leading, supervising, managing or administering a work unit of a human services organization. A work unit may be a small group of employees in an agency, such as a work evaluation unit, or it may be as large as an entire private or government agency. A human services organization, in this context, is one that provides direct helping services to clients, usually of a professional nature. Examples are agencies that provide psychological, social and rehabilitation services and benefits. Management, in this context, does **not** refer to case or caseload management.

What is the human services manager trying to accomplish?

It is the responsibility of human services managers to establish, maintain, develop and sustain work units that efficiently assist clients in achieving desired outcomes, and that meet organizational, legal, professional and related requirements. This description implies that managers are responsible for seeing that results are achieved with clients, but within the constraints of the service delivery systems in which they function. However, managers may also seek to change work units and environmental forces, thus modifying the constraints.

What is required to do this?

A manager must have the ability to control the internal operations of a work unit and interact effectively with the environment outside of the work unit. The manager must be able to run the work unit on a day to day basis, usually through the efforts of his or her staff. This must be done at reasonable cost, with methods and results that are acceptable to consumers, resource providers, policy makers, legislators and others. The work unit must also be operated in a manner consistent with legal,

4

ethical, agency and professional standards. The manager must also be able to accomplish internal change, when that is needed to meet needs, requirements or improve efficiency or results.

The manager must be effective in communicating with the environment in order to acquire enough resources to carry out the mission of the work unit, to keep the work unit alive, or to provide better services. For example, an agency director must be able to influence funders regarding the need for enough staff to accomplish good results. He or she may also need to assess what services are needed in the community, market the agency's services, and influence legislators regarding necessary laws. This, in turn, will effect how much business the agency generates and even whether or not it will exist. The director may also need to attend to procuring services through other agencies for clients, to assure continuity of treatment and rehabilitation. Since all agencies have their own priorities, achieving precise coordination is often difficult. Although these examples apply to an agency director, the situation regarding external management is analogous for managers at all levels.

In summary, in order to achieve effective results, managers must focus on internal and external concerns while effecting both maintenance and change as needed.

Is there a difference between managing and leading?

Although the above definition of a manager includes both, it is useful to make a distinction between terms. Management implies an emphasis on current stability, efficiency, standards and controls, i.e., keeping daily routines running smoothly. On the other hand, leadership implies a focus on creativity, risk taking and change (Broskowski, 1984). A review by Latta (1987) regarding leadership in rehabilitation organizations suggests that leaders are able to conceptualize and communicate (through behaviors) a long range vision of what "should be". The term leadership also implies the ability to actualize this vision through a compelling personal influence on the organization and its culture (such as through the use of charisma).

What are the major functions of human services managers?

Human services managers must usually accomplish six major functions in carrying out their roles. These include:

Planning
Organizing
Controlling
Coordinating
Organization Development/Change
Communicating

Planning helps determine the direction of the work unit. Organizing establishes the internal structure needed to carry out what is planned, most efficiently and effectively. Controlling assures that plans are implemented in the manner intended and that feedback (evaluation) is used to improve the work unit's performance. Coordinating is necessary to synchronize the work unit's services with the services of other work units, inside or outside of the organization, in a manner consistent with client needs. Organization development/change assures that work unit modifications needed for optimal performance will be diagnosed and made, and that other required changes will be made or influenced. Communicating underlies effective achievement of the other management functions, including the assurance of adequate resources to keep the work unit alive and well.

These functions are a little abstract. What do managers really do?

A study by Matkin, Sawyer, Lorenz and Rubin (1982) sheds some light on this in the rehabilitation administration area. The information should also generalize to other human services management fields. The study surveyed 426 randomly selected members of the National Rehabilitation Administration Association, with a 57% response rate. Ten work role factors were identified as follows:

General Personnel Management — This includes supervisory management of staff, such as recruiting, interviewing, selecting employees, evaluating, disciplining, and dealing with employee conflicts.
Professional Management — This includes tasks involved in direct supervision of professional staff.
Fiscal Management — Preparing budgets, managing accounting systems, doing financial analyses, identifying resources and making/implementing financial decisions is included.
Production Management — This area involves contract procurement related tasks and carrying out duties related to assuring adequate productivity.

Program Planning and Evaluation — This entails community needs assessments, establishing goals, policies and objectives, and conducting program evaluation and related activities.

Public Relations — This includes dealing with public education and information regarding the agency. It involves such activities as relating to boards of directors, preparing grant applications, legislative relationships, testifying, public speaking and writing.

Marketing Service — This involves marketing and sales for the facility and soliciting volunteers for the agency from the community.

Labor Relations — This includes maintaining effective labor-management relations in the agency.

Purchasing — This involves purchasing goods and supplies for the facility.

Research — This entails conducting research relative to the activities performed in the agency.

Do all managers carry out all of these roles?

No. In fact, the same study found that different levels of managers and managers in facilities such as rehabilitation centers vs. state/federal rehabilitation agencies differed in the roles they performed most. Also, some roles, such as production management, research, marketing service and labor relations were rated as minor aspects of their jobs, by most managers.

What are the advantages of being a human services manager?

The roles and functions of managers often seem foreign to professionals who have completed their training in direct service. However, most practicing managers in human services come from such backgrounds. Thus, a whole new body of information and behavior needs to be learned to function effectively as a manager. Is it worth it?

From the perspective of a helping professional, being a manager gives us the power to help larger groups of people. Although the manager's role is indirect, how a manager controls a work unit influences the treatment or rehabilitation of a far greater volume of clients than providing individual services. As a manager, we influence servicing values, methods and results, usually through others. Most of our direct service and communication skills are utilized, but as a tool to influence events on a larger scale.

From a purely practical standpoint, management jobs command higher salaries and greater status than direct service jobs in agency settings. These often become important long term career considerations to human services professionals.

Chapter 2

MANAGING EFFECTIVE ORGANIZATION SYSTEMS

Now that we know what human services managers are trying to accomplish, are there any general principles for effectively doing that?

There is no one best way to run a work unit. Based on its mission, history, culture, employee composition, structure and environment, what is best for one work unit may not be best for another. However, there are some generalities about how organizations function and about the characteristics of particularly well or poorly functioning organizations, that can form the basis for managing an effective work unit. These come from the study of general systems and from some studies of characteristics of effective organizations.

What is the general systems approach?

The systems approach suggests that generalizations can be made regarding the structure and functions of different types of systems. In other words, different systems, such as a human being or a plant or a business organization or a planet, all have similarities in organization and behavior. An understanding of these similar characteristics helps us generalize knowledge from one type of system to another.

What is the practical value of this information in running a human services organization?

It gives the manager a foundation for understanding the principles of all systems. Thus, it may help to understand why things are happening the way they are and what needs to be done to change them. For example, if a small rehabilitation agency is expanding and the nature of the work is changing rapidly due to legislative changes, a sense of disorganization and chaos may be evident. Poor services may be provided and there may be many complaints. A manager well versed in the systems approach would recognize that a state of homeostasis or equilibrium had been lost, which must be restored as soon as possible. Without quick restoration, too much staff energy might be needed to deal with the effects of the chaos (e.g., complaints) and not enough time on serving clients. Without appropriate action, chaos would be likely to increase to the point that severe damage might be done to the agency. This might hurt the agency's reputation enough to reduce the existing level of clientele, resulting in a shrinking of resources. Thus, instead of expanding and growing, the agency would be deteriorating.

GENERAL SYSTEMS PRINCIPLES

What is a system?

A system is an entity which usually has the purpose of accomplishing predetermined functions. These functions are achieved through integrated interaction of interdependent elements. The action or interaction of any of the elements impacts on the functioning of the total system.

In plain language, what happens in one part of a system usually influences what happens somewhere else in the system, and to the total system. If we think in terms of the human body, for example, it is easy to see the interdependency of one part to another. Rarely does something occur in one part that does not have an effect on some other part.

The same is true with organizational systems. For example, a decision to fire an employee, or serious conflict among employees usually has an effect on others and on the work. An awareness of this interdependency and its effects requires that the manager consider the possible repercussions of all decisions and actions.

What are the important structural aspects of a system?

Inputs — These are variables which act upon other variables, or which are acted upon. Inputs usually come from outside the system. Clients, staff, funds to operate the agency, and equipment are examples of inputs.

Processes — These are the activities within the system that convert inputs to outputs, by importing and transforming energy. For example, interactions take place between staff and clients, and clients engage in work activities, leading to treatment or rehabilitation results.

Outputs — These represent the results of system processes. In some instances in human services, results reflect the processes of many systems. For example, a client may find a job through the help of friends rather than through the direct assistance of the rehabilitation agency serving him or her. However, the agency may have been instrumental in encouraging the client to develop a network among friends.

Subsystems — These are systems within the overall system. Each subsystem has inputs, processes and outputs that contribute to the process and outputs of the total system. For example, a human services agency has an **operating** subsystem which is responsible for the processing of services delivered to clients. This is the main subsystem and is responsible for carrying out the agency mission. However, in order for the operating subsystem to function efficiently, there may be a **personnel** subsystem to assure that employee recruitment takes place, labor-management issues are resolved and employee benefits are administered. There may also be a **maintenance** subsystem to assure that facilities are cleaned, equipment is repaired, and that security is maintained. All subsystems must be managed to coordinate efficient achievement of the overall agency's desired outputs.

Environment — This is everything outside of the system. The environment is particularly important since it is the source of all resources necessary for the system to operate, such as staff, funds and equipment.

Suprasystem — This is the larger system to which a system belongs (and of which it is thus a subsystem). For example, every human services agency belongs to a community, state or national system.

What is the significance of outputs for a human services system?

Some outputs represent the main reason the system exists and are one basis for assessing how well the system is achieving it's primary purposes. Other outputs represent important byproducts of system functioning that impact on ability to achieve the primary purposes. Thus, outputs can be a basis for planning (e.g., setting performance goals, objectives or standards) and evaluation, for the total system and for its different processes.

Are there different types of outputs?

There are several important types of outputs. First, outputs may be classified as intermediate or final. **Intermediate** outputs are those that occur during system processes, but which do not represent the final result. For example, a counseling session may result in a small amount of progress for a client. However, this would only represent an intermediate step on the way to the desired final result of adjustment in a suitable job. The desired final result, in this instance, would be a **final** output.

Final is a relative term and simply infers that this is the end result that the agency seeks based on the services provided at that time. Typically, many intermediate outputs may be achieved before a final output occurs.

Are there different types of intermediate and final outputs?

Yes. Intermediate and final outputs may be viewed as being productive or affective.

What are productive outputs and what is their relevance?

Productive outputs imply that an achievement or gain has occurred. Thus, when productive outputs can be measured and compared against inputs, agency productivity and related performance can be assessed. Productive outputs in human services work units include:

Outcomes — These are instances of achieved client status, for example, achievement of reduced anxiety after a series of psychotherapy sessions, or obtaining a job after rehabilitation services. In each instance, a particular outcome has been achieved as the result of a process.

Staff Outputs — These are units of completed staff efforts on behalf of the agency mission. Examples are completion of a counseling session (intermediate output) or completion of all services (final output) to a client by a **staff member.** The important point here is that staff outputs represent units of work **completed by a staff member,** regardless of the outcome. It is a representation of completed work efforts which may include numerous specific activities. Staff outputs can often be associated with time spent or time necessary to complete different types of helping processes with clients. Thus, staff outputs can sometimes be used to measure how efficiently staff time is being used or to determine how much staff time is needed to provide a known quantity of service.

Benefits — These are client gains (or losses) usually expressed in monetary terms. For example, a rehabilitation client may achieve a gain in income as the result of a rehabilitation program.

What are affective outputs?

Affective outputs are those associated with client or employee feelings as the result of system processes.

What are some relevant examples?

Client satisfaction is a typical example. This refers to the affective status of the client resulting from his or her evaluation of the satisfactoriness of services rendered through the system. This is a particularly important output since it may impact on how the agency is perceived. Client satisfaction is used as a part of many evaluation systems that assess program, agency and staff performance.

Organization climate and **employee satisfaction** are examples of important employee related affective outputs. Organization climate refers to the overall perception of agency personnel about the characteristic ways of working that have evolved in an organization (Olmstead and Christensen, 1973). A positive organization climate and employee satisfaction encourage commitment by employees to an agency. This may have such advantages (to the agency) as improving performance and reducing levels of absenteeism and turnover.

How can outputs serve as a basis for setting goals, objectives or standards for performance in a system?

If we can identify the types of outputs that we are trying to achieve from the system and its subsystems, we can then aim for specified levels of performance. This is done through establishing specific goals, objectives and/or performance criteria and standards. For example, for an entire agency, the productive outputs **number of rehabilitated clients** (which is a type of outcome) and **number of cases completed** (which is a type of staff output) might be considered relevant criteria. The affective outputs **client satisfaction level** and **employee satisfaction level** might also be relevant. Achievement of reasonable levels of these outputs might indicate that the agency is achieving its mission effectively. Thus, once types of output and measurement criteria are selected, goals and objectives can be set, or standards for expected continuing performance can be established.

What types of outputs should agencies strive for?

Organizational literature suggests at least some emphasis on the ones already mentioned: Productive, client satisfaction and organizational climate or employee satisfaction.

Which of those should be emphasized most?

The systems approach would suggest a balanced emphasis. In other words, while we should be very concerned with productive results, we cannot ignore or underemphasize what is happening to employees within the organization. In effect, as suggested in the definition of systems, everything impacts on everything else. Thus, we must pay reasonably equal attention to all classes of outputs.

What are some principles of how systems work?

Important principles of practical value involve entropy, homeostasis and control.

What is entropy?

Entropy is the universal tendency of systems to move toward disorder and death. This is perhaps the most important systems principle for a manager to keep in mind. When a system or it's environment is not tended to, or problems are ignored and not diagnosed, systems tend to move toward their destruction.

Can the process be reversed?

Ultimately, most systems will die, but it is possible to at least temporarily reverse or retard this process. **Negative entropy** is the movement of a system away from entropy. System growth, and development toward optimum efficiency and effectiveness are consistent with negative entropy.

What is an open system and how does that relate to entropy?

An **open system** is one that takes in energy from the environment and gives back energy to the environment. If a system does not exchange energy with the environment, it will die. For example, an animal that does not eat or take in oxygen can only sustain itself for a short period. Similarly, an organization that does not take in resources (e.g., clients, staff, funds) from its environment will soon cease to exist. This underlines the importance for the manager of interacting effectively with the environment. If he or she does not maintain effective communications and relationships with important others outside of the work unit (e.g., contractors, referral sources, funders), or if he or she loses contact with important information available outside of the work unit (e.g., new technology or methods), this is likely to contribute to entropy.

What is homeostasis and how does that relate to entropy?

Homeostasis is a state of system balance or equilibrium. This occurs when internal and external forces are balanced and the system maintains its basic character. For example, when an agency has been operating in a stable manner, seeing the same types of clients, using the same methods, maintaining a stable staff and receiving the same funding for a long period of time, we might say that a state of homeostasis has been achieved. However, when changes begin to occur, such as loss of funding sources, changes in laws governing the agency, a new director with demands for changes in servicing methods and productivity levels, then the former level of homeostasis is lost until a new level is reached. In the interim, things become more chaotic, and a great deal of energy is spent in dealing with the chaos. Energy spent on non system sustaining activities (such as returning chaos to order) supports movement toward entropy. If too much energy is spent in that manner the agency may deteriorate, as illustrated in an earlier example. However, if the energy expended results in only a temporary setback on the way to a higher level of homeostasis, then movement toward negative entropy will have been achieved.

How does system control relate to these concepts?

Control is required to maintain a particular state of homeostasis, or to purposefully change the level and nature of homeostasis effectively. As part of the entropic process, systems tend to lose their desired levels of equilibrium unless control is exerted. Thus, managers must obtain feedback that loss of equilibrium is occurring and they must take the needed actions to get the system back on track (in a manner analagous to how a thermostat works). Ongoing control mechanisms for this include feedback (information gathering and monitoring), evaluation of the information, and regulation. Regulation involves the managers response to change something (take corrective action) or maintain the status quo based on evaluation of the information received.

Control is also achieved through **fixed** or **adaptive** mechanisms of systems. These mechanisms are often needed as expansion takes place. They tend to serve as structural devices that help maintain a sense of organization. Included are:

Structural differentiation —This is the specialization of roles and functions. For example, as an agency gets larger, it may be more efficient to have departments specialize in certain areas of service (e.g., work evaluation, work adjustment, counseling, psychological evaluation) than have a group of employees doing all functions under a single supervisor.

Standardization —This involves the use of self regulatory devices such as procedures, policies, rules, regulations and other standard practices.

These tend to avoid chaos by standardizing acceptable practices for employees.

Coordination — This involves arranging tasks and roles to synchronize effectively in the desired direction (Georgopoulis, 1975). For example, written guidelines may define how and when a client will be referred from treatment to vocational rehabilitation services in a hospital.

Integration — This is a method of collaboration among different components or subsystems in a system. Usually these components have very different values and priorities (such as a surgical unit and social service unit in a hospital). Integration involves creating social unity through shared norms and values (Georgopoulos, 1975), so that coordination can be improved. This is a more advanced control mechanism than coordination and may involve a person, such as a manager who is the integrator, or groups of employees from each component who work together toward this purpose. Integration also often occurs through informal relationships among such units.

Is it possible to overcontrol a system?

Yes. As implied earlier undercontrol may lead to loss of homeostasis and entropy. However, overcontrol can also lead a system toward entropy. For example, if there are too many rules and procedures in a human services agency, the system may not be able to respond appropriately to the individual needs of some clients. Services may be provided that are unnecessary or the rules may not allow for providing what is needed. This may lead to wasted staff time, dissatisfied clients and inability to achieve the agency mission. However, as agencies get larger, such levels of control are viewed as necessary to keep services uniform, consistent with laws and easy to evaluate by regulatory groups. This is a paradox that very large agencies face.

In summary then, how can we characterize effective systems management?

Effective system management requires understanding the interdependency of system components and taking action accordingly. It also requires defining the desired system outputs and managing to achieve them in a balanced manner. In addition, maintaining open systems, and identifying and using control mechanisms such that optimal levels of control are achieved, supports movement toward negative entropy. Generally, the more efficiently energy is used in a system, the longer it will remain alive and well. Thus, management decisions and actions should be directed toward that end.

STUDIES OF CHARACTERISTICS
OF EFFECTIVE ORGANIZATIONS

Have there been any large scale studies of human services organizations that shed light on effective management?

Yes. A national study of social welfare and rehabilitation workers was completed by Olmstead and Christensen in 1973. This study surveyed 1662 workers from 31 public agencies nationwide, using questionnaire and interview methods. Although the study has technical weaknesses, some results are significant.

It was found that seven factors contributed to criteria of agency performance, agency competence, individual performance, absenteeism, turnover and employee satisfaction. These factors are summarized in Table I. The most critical factor appears to be the nature and quality of agency communications. This refers to the effective transmission of information, on a day to day basis, of everything that employees need to know in order to do their jobs. The authors found that lack of information results in frustration that effects all aspects of agency operations. In addition, it was clear that while higher level managers may presume that communication is adequate, employees may not perceive this to be the case. From the standpoint of its effects on employee relations and performance, the most important factor is the perception of employees. In other words, if employees perceive poor communications, then that may require attention in order to avoid negative consequences, regardless of managerial perceptions.

Many of the other factors in this study relating to the criteria are dependent upon effective communications. For example, for agency goals and policies to take on significance, they must be effectively communicated on a continuing basis. In addition, communication is the singular medium through which supervision takes place. Thus, the nature and quality of communication determines the effectiveness of supervision.

TABLE I

NATIONAL STUDY OF SOCIAL WELFARE AND REHABILITATION WORKERS
FACTORS CONTRIBUTING TO PERFORMANCE RELATED CRITERIA

Agency Goals — Defined as specific, concrete ends sought within a specified time period. Goals must be clear, perceived as feasible and awareness of goals should exist at all levels.

Agency Policies — Defined as broad statements of intent. Policies must be communicated so that they are understood at all levels.

Communications — Blockages should be avoided in chain of command communications.

Supervision — Should be oriented toward emotional and technical support, maintaining work group solidarity, facilitating work group goal accomplishment, representing the work group to higher organization levels and non-directive.

Agency Structuring of Activities — Less structuring is suggested, more freedom and trying to find optimal levels of structure.

Work Environment Stability — Suggests moderating anxieties about turbulence/change by planning and communication about reasons for and implications of change.

Size and Dispersion of Agencies — Smallness is better. Avoid large, centralized locations.

Are there any large scale studies of other types of organizations that also have general relevance to human services agencies?

Peters and Waterman's (1982) study of excellent companies as reported in the book **In Search of Excellence** falls in this category. This study analyzed forty-three private business and service companies twenty or more years old. These organizations were selected as exemplary on the basis of financial measures as well as opinions by an informed group of observers of the business scene. The study did not include any human service organizations, but the findings should have applicability. A summary of the major characteristics of the excellent companies is included in Table II.

The authors found that the best functioning companies are effective at both rational, quantitative analysis as well as being strongly and genuinely concerned for the humanistic/people side of business. Less successful companies often demonstrate "paralysis by analysis" or a tendency to substitute overanalysis for action. They are concerned with cost reduction rather than quality. They tend to be conservative with respect to experimentation, values take a back seat to numbers, they are procedures oriented and they tend to use negative reinforcers and punishment as employee motivators.

TABLE II
PETERS AND WATERMAN STUDY:
MAJOR CHARACTERISTICS OF EXCELLENT COMPANIES

One:	A bias for action: a preference for doing something—anything—rather than sending a question through cycles and cycles of analyses and committee reports.
Two:	Staying close to the customer—learning his preferences and catering to them.
Three:	Autonomy and entrepreneurship—breaking the corporation into small companies and encouraging them to think independently and competitively.
Four:	Productivity through—creating in all employees the awareness that their best efforts are essential and that they will share in the rewards of the company's success.
Five:	Hands-on, value driven—insisting that executives keep in touch with the firm's essential business.
Six:	Stick to the knitting—remaining with the business the company knows best.
Seven:	Simple form, lean staff—few administrative layers, few people at the upper levels.
Eight:	Simultaneous loose–tight properties—fostering a climate where there is dedication to the central values of the company combined with tolerance for all employees who accept those values.

Eight Basic Principles from *In Search of Excellence* by Thomas J. Peters and Robert H. Waterman, Jr. Copyright © 1982 by Thomas J. Peters and Robert H. Waterman, Jr. Reprinted by permission of Harper & Row Publishers, Inc.)

In contrast, the highest performers focus on making employees feel like winners. This is done through nurturing positive internal cultures that foster a sense of commitment to the organization, its values and its customers. The emphasis is on positive reinforcement, experimentation (regardless of small failures), teamwork, an emphasis on self direction by employees toward goals of the organization and goals driven by values of strong leaders.

These organizations genuinely stress customer service and satisfaction, and quality. They tend to keep their staffs lean, and relationships are informal and personal. They support innovation through voluntary, loosely structured or spontaneous short term problem solving groups. A bias exists towards getting results through quick action, with little time wasted on non-essentials. Large amounts of ideas and information are transmitted in these informal environments often characterized by a "fun" atmosphere. Although sometimes appearing chaotic, this type of environment seems to encourage motivation, commitment, innovation and thus the ability to achieve what is needed to make an organization run effectively.

What then, on the basis of these studies, can human service managers hope to achieve with their work units?

At the very least, good communications seem necessary. However, this is not a simple matter. Maintaining good communications involves creating and maintaining a constructive interactive atmosphere within the work unit. This is an environment in which accurate and open information exchange can take place. It is also an environment in which the nature of management/employee communications motivate people to work toward the goals of the agency with the minimum possible amount of explicit management control. In other words, because employees understand and can accept the expectations of management and because they feel that their needs are met through the work and work environment, then the work of the agency takes place more efficiently. It is an atmosphere in which communications focus on trust, honesty and openness in a problem solving mode. Solutions to problems tend to produce winners rather than winners and losers.

Over time, such an atmosphere produces a culture, with employees highly motivated toward the values of the organization. With appropriate external rewards (e.g., adequate salary and benefits), such employees should tend to stay with the agency longer. Over the long run, the agency will be more efficient and effective because less energy must be spent on management (e.g., hiring, firing, extensive training, close supervision) and more efforts can be spent on direct service by a smaller but experienced, motivated staff.

Thus, effective communications is an important and complex phenomenon that seems to underlie how well an organization functions. However, good communications is inclusive of more than just accurate, timely information exchange. It includes a tone and character that motivates people at all levels to relate to one another, to clients and to the external environment in a manner that produces the most positive results. Managers who can achieve and maintain this type of environment can more easily carry out other essential functions such as planning, organizing, controlling and dealing with change. Thus, they have a strong foundation for fulfilling their roles effectively.

Can we generalize much beyond the need for effective communications?

It seems evident that certain other factors will almost always support high performance. Employees who clearly know the agency's direction (goals, policies, values) are in a better position to do what is expected than those who do not. Thus, agency leaders need to establish clear direction and be sure that employees know about it. Also employees need to be clear on the nature of their individual roles and functions. Role ambiguity may lead to unnecessary stress, dissatisfaction and possible ineffectiveness (Huse, 1975).

Focus on quality of services, results and client satisfaction, rather than procedures, forms and documentation should also support high performance. This is not to say that the latter should be ignored. In fact, attention to these matters is often essential to assure program justification, funding or accreditation, quality control, or to make certain that agency policies and laws are being carried out. However, particularly with pressures for accountability, staff and leaders can lose sight of the human services mission and shift the **main** focus to program or agency justification and procedural issues.

What about accountability? How important is that?

Accountability is absolutely essential to the continued existence of programs and agencies. Profit making agencies must be accountable to their clients. Otherwise, their flow of income will stop. Non-profit and government agencies must be accountable to their consumers, communities, funding agencies and lawmakers. Otherwise, their funds will cease to exist. This is entirely reasonable, since an agency should serve some significant purpose and carry out its function efficiently and effectively in order to successfully compete for usually scarce funds. Accountability requires the ability to demonstrate and adequately communicate how effectively, efficiently and productively an individual, work unit or agency is meeting needs and/or carrying out its intended purposes.

What is the significance of accountability to the human services manager's role?

Considering the background of most human services managers (direct service), there may be a tendency to focus on the humanistic/people side of agency operations. As the Peters and Waterman study showed, this is something that is lacking in less successful businesses. However, we must remember that the **most** successful businesses are effective at **both** rational, quantitative analysis and people concerns.

In human services, we may run the risk of a tendency to be people oriented while avoiding quantitative analysis. This may place us in a situation similar to the business that suffers from an overemphasis on cost analysis and little emphasis on employee or customer factors. The point is that a balance must exist. The human services manager must be concerned with the quantitative side of the agency because that is how, from a practical standpoint, accountability is established and communicated— from employee to manager, from director to board of directors, from agency head to Governor, from program director to Congress and so on. Communication of that information also often forms the basis for effecting and measuring changes in performance at all agency levels.

Are there any other important factors based on these studies?

Yes. One more may be significant. Both of these studies suggest that small is better than large in terms of work unit size. This is also supported by systems thinking. Generally, the smaller the work unit, the less energy that must be expended on control. Also, smaller work units are not as likely as larger ones to get bogged down in fixed controls, such as rules and procedures, that inhibit flexibility. In addition, smaller units are much more conducive to maintaining unblocked, high quality communications. Thus, managers should probably consider decentralizing strategies as work units become larger.

GENERAL PRINCIPLES FOR
RUNNING A GOOD ORGANIZATION

What then can we conclude are some general principles important to running a good organization?

First, we need to be aware of and take actions based upon our understanding of system dynamics. It is our responsibility to know when our systems are becoming entropic, and why, from a systems perspective; and to be able to diagnose what actions are needed to restore the openness, control and direction that we seek. We also need to recognize the significance of balanced attention to the outputs that we identify as important, and to maintaining efficient interdependence among system components.

Second, the significance of good communications within and outside the agency is clearly evident. Managers should be able to create and support a climate in which communications are clear, timely, accurate, and relevant at all levels. The nature of the communication process should support a problem solving approach to interpersonal communications and an atmosphere of employee self motivation.

Third, managers should assure that the work unit direction and values are clear to all employees and to significant others outside the work unit. In addition the main operational focus should be on quality and productive results, with reasonable attention paid to client and employee satisfaction. Managers should be cognizant of the need for objective accountability measures and not underemphasize the need to pay attention to this aspect of work unit administration.

Lastly, managers should consider the significance of work unit size as a factor in achieving the climate needed for excellent work unit performance.

INTRODUCTION EXERCISE 1
SYSTEMS CONCEPTS

(Group or Individual)

THE DEMISE OF UNITY HOUSE

Unity House was a psychiatric rehabilitation center that recently terminated all services after six years of operation. It was located in a major metropolitan area with no other similar facilities, but with an apparent need for psychiatric rehabilitation services.

Unity House began with a Board of Directors from the business and mental health communities. A director with a background in direct services in psychiatric rehabilitation was hired from out of state. Initial funding was received from a State rehabilitation agency grant. After the first year of operation, some funds were received from the United Way and from a two year grant from the State mental health agency. After the third year of operation, no grants were available and most funds needed to be self generated.

The Unity House program began with seven staff: the Director, three masters degree counselors, a workshop supervisor with an industrial background and no rehabilitation experience, a consulting psychiatrist and a secretary. During the first three years of operation, the facility expanded from ten to forty full time clients. During this period, one additional staff person, a work evaluator, was added.

There was no clear differentiation of staff roles at Unity House and everyone reported to the Director. The management environment could best be described as "loose." Staff often felt uncertain of the Director's expectations, there were frequent disagreements among staff about who was responsible for what and some staff felt that they just could not do everything that was expected. The counselors and workshop supervisor were particularly at odds because of the differences in how they viewed the clients, and staff roles. The counselors were very accepting of all client behaviors, while the workshop supervisor felt the counselors were too "soft." The Director believed it was important to maintain as informal and unstructured an atmosphere as possible because he felt that professionals do not appreciate a great amount of structure, rules and procedures. With the low salary structure at Unity House, he was afraid turnover would worsen if he moved in that direction.

During the first few years of the program, referrals from the State rehabilitation agency were increasing since the community desperately needed this type of facility. However, State rehabilitation counselors were feeling that results of sending clients to this facility were no better than fair. This was sometimes expressed to Unity House counselors, who blamed poor results on the types of clients referred. The Director rarely met with State rehabilitation officials or counselors and was considered by many as difficult to reach. He rarely returned phone calls and was often defensive about the program. He was clinically oriented in his approach, perceived as rigid in thinking and not inclined toward being too concerned about what others were thinking. In fact, he was known to be rather aloof from the community in general. Most of his energy was spent on professional supervision to staff, conflict resolution among staff, and some diagnostic and treatment work with agency clients.

Throughout its existence, Unity House did not measure its results. There was no formal program evaluation system with the exception of a measure of client satisfaction. The Director was most concerned about this and did whatever he felt necessary to avoid client complaints, even though the staff often believed this to be inappropriate to rehabilitation goals.

There was often a great deal of tension and dissatisfaction among staff at the agency. Turnover was above thirty percent a year during the third and fourth years of operation. During the fifth year, when a comprehensive rehabilitation center in the community began accepting psychiatric clients, all three counselors left Unity House, and new referrals dropped thirty percent. At about the same time, a review of Unity House by the United Way indicated little evidence that sufficient results were being achieved, nor that an efficient, productive enough operation was being run to justify any continuing funding. With the United Way funds cut, loss of clients and revenue from the State rehabilitation agency, and loss of staff, the Board fired the Director. Within four months they hired someone new. However, the new services at the other rehabilitation center were becoming well respected. The center was able to demonstrate significant positive outcome statistics and their director made this known to the community through the media and through the State rehabilitation agency Director. Their counselors also held regular meetings with State rehabilitation counselors to obtain feedback and suggestions regarding future services. As a result, referrals increased. Referrals to Unity House continued to decline and services ceased within six months after the new Director was hired.

QUESTIONS

1. Were Unity House's outputs balanced?
2. How synergistic was the Unity House system?
3. What was the level and adequacy of system control?
4. To what extent was environment taken into consideration by the Director and Board of Unity House?
5. What universal process gradually overtook this facility?
6. What were some inputs, processes and outputs of this system?
7. What adaptive mechanisms should have developed as this system expanded?
8. How could energy have been used more efficiently in running this facility?

Section II

PLANNING

INTRODUCTION AND OVERVIEW

Planning provides direction for an organization and it's components. It is important to those who must achieve and evaluate results. Without planning, we do not know to what ends we are working and whether we are successful.

For human services, the **agency/program management cycle** in Figure 1 depicts the relationship of planning to implementing and evaluating. Together, these processes form a cycle for conceptualizing how agencies can fine tune achievement toward their missions. Planning leads to implementation, which in turn is followed by evaluation. The purpose of evaluation is to determine whether what was planned, for example, the goals and objectives or program standards, were actually achieved. Evaluation may also assess the effectiveness of how implementation took place. Thus, evaluation findings may lead to changes in plans; or changes in how organizations are run or how programs are carried out. Evaluation and its relationship to planning is discussed in detail in Section V.

Planning in organizations is done at both formal and informal levels. As a formal process, planning tells those who are managing and doing the work, and others, what the work unit (and total organization) is about, what it is trying to achieve, and how that will be done. As we know from the studies cited in Chapter 2, communicating work unit direction, whether through values, goals, policies or through other means, is related to high performance.

As discussed in Chapter 3, **formal planning** includes setting goals and objectives to be achieved over the long term or within specified time frames; determining strategies for their achievement; and developing operating policies. It may also include establishing **ongoing** standards for organization, specific work unit or program performance as a component of program evaluation systems. In addition, it involves assessment of servicing needs, resources and other factors, so that continuing plans

27

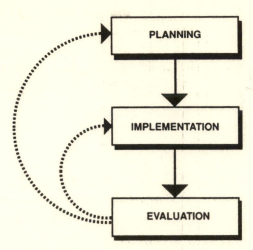

Figure 1—Agency/Program Management Cycle.

are realistic and attainable. Finally, budgeting is required to provide financial support for carrying out the plan.

The formal planning process must be **flexible** to assure appropriate responses to changing conditions. For example, we may set a yearly productivity goal of one hundred rehabilitated cases for a work unit, and perhaps a few strategies as to how that may be achieved. However, during the year we find that money has become available for several new computers that would save twenty percent of existing counselor time. At that point, it might be appropriate to decide to computerize, even if that means planning for extensive training over the next few months, scrapping some of the other strategies and maybe not even reaching the productivity goal. Over the long run, computerization may be best and the money may not be available again. If that is done, then short term plans will also be needed to carry out this strategy and still meet other priorities.

Routine planning occurs in a less formal manner. It involves the day to day and month to month operation of work units, including how to achieve performance and other goals from a practical perspective. This can include anything from planning how to get staff to consistently carry out a new procedure to planning a reorganization of office furniture. Even though formal plans may exist, **much of the practical planning in daily management occurs on an informal basis.**

The importance of routine planning is often understated in management texts. However, the manager's effectiveness in this area can be important in determining whether formal plans will be achieved and whether daily priorities will be accomplished. Effective routine planning allows for proactive management and control of ones situation. It is extremely common for human services managers to complain "I'm always fighting fires—I never have time to manage." This is an expression of loss of control, a situation intolerable to an effective manager. Loss of control and management effectiveness are usually contradictory.

As discussed in Chapter 4, effective routine planning is facilitated through the use of delegation and time management. These techniques help the manager avoid stress, disorganization and chaos in carrying out daily management tasks.

Chapter 3

FORMAL PLANNING

What is the structure of formal planning in human services agencies?

G enerally, it is useful to have a plan for the total agency, called the strategic plan. The **strategic plan** includes an agency mission statement; a set of long range goals and objectives consistent with the mission; strategies for each goal or objective; and agency policies.

Once the strategic plan is developed, each work unit within the agency uses that information to develop operational plans, i.e., short and long term goals and objectives, strategies, and policies, based on its own function in relation to the total organization. What results is analogous to a waterfall. What is planned for the entire agency flows down to each level and unit. Thus, if all of the work units achieve their goals and objectives, the agency will achieve its goals and objectives. It will then be achieving its mission.

Goals and objectives tend to be structured toward achievement within time frames. However, agencies, their work units or specific programs may also have ongoing goals, objectives and/or standards. For example, goal oriented program evaluation systems (Spaniol, 1977) in public or non profit agencies may include such components as a basis for establishing and periodically measuring whether performance expectations in pertinent program areas are being achieved. Program evaluation and it's relationship to planning are discussed further in Chapter 12.

Does it matter who is involved in the formal planning process?

Planning can involve only top level management, all levels of managers or all levels of employees in the organization. **Who** is involved usually varies based on the management philosophy, management style, history and culture of the organization.

It is essential that the plan be clearly linked to action, since planning for planning's sake is useless. Those involved in the process may have an impact on how easily or completely implementation takes place. For example, when more employees participate, there may be a tendency toward greater understanding and commitment than when plans are imposed by an agency head or top management group without prior consultation. This may be particularly true with professional or other employees who expect to be involved in agency decisions that impact on them. The less understanding of and commitment to an agency plan that exists prior to its implementation, the more management energy and resources that will be needed to assure that the plan is followed. For example, when commitment and understanding are low, extensive training, close supervision and frequent performance reviews may be needed to clearly communicate the plan and keep people focusing on it.

AGENCY MISSION

How do we define the mission of an agency?

The mission is an expression of the agency's unique aim. It is a statement of what the organization is about; one that provides a sense of direction and significance to agency members (Donnelly, Gibson and Ivancevich, 1987).

What are the characteristics of a good mission statement?

A mission statement should be specific, achievable, motivational and it should focus on client needs (Donnelly, Gibson and Ivancevich, 1987). An example of a mission statement for a comprehensive rehabilitation center is: "To provide comprehensive rehabilitation services, which lead to enhanced community functioning through employment and independent living, for physically disabled individuals who reside within a thirty mile radius of Kent, Ohio."

Mission statements look easy to develop. Is this true?

No. Although an agency's mission sometimes seems obvious, mission statement development by groups of individuals often reveals disagreements that require resolution and clarification. This occurs even among long time organization members and leaders.

GOALS AND OBJECTIVES

What are goals?

They are statements of expected achievements or levels of performance. For example, the statement, **productivity in 1988 will increase by 10%**

over 1987 productivity, is an expression of an expected level of achievement.

Goals are not statements of what is routinely done. For example, **eligible physically disabled clients in our geographic region will be served,** is not a goal. It is a statement of what a particular work unit does rather than what level of performance it aspires to achieve.

The above distinction is critical to effective goal development.

What is the difference between goals and objectives?

These terms are often used interchangably, or they may be defined in different ways. For our purposes, goals are more general than objectives. Objectives are viewed as sub-goals to a particular goal. However, both goals and objectives have the same characteristics.

Why are goals and objectives so important?

Aside from factors already discussed, research on goal setting (Latham and Yukl, 1975) indicates that performance tends to be higher in situations in which goal setting takes place (vs. no goal setting).

Is there a correct way to structure goals and objectives?

Yes. **Specificity** and **measurability** are important. Also **difficult** goals and objectives tend to lead to higher performance, as long as they are accepted (as achievable) by those trying to reach them.

In addition, goals and objectives should be **clearly stated,** they should include **time frames** for achievement and they should focus on either intermediate or final **results. Prioritizing** may also be helpful.

Writing general goals seems to be a common practice. Is this effective?

General goals do nothing more than state a direction. They give little specific guidance regarding expectations and there is no way to know whether such goals have been achieved. It may be appropriate, however, to have general goals if they include specific, measurable objectives. In that way it is clear that such goals will be achieved when all of their objectives are achieved. For example, a goal and its objectives might be:

Goal: Clients will demonstrate improved pre-vocational skills as the result of rehabilitation program attendance.

    Objective 1: On the average, productivity of clients served will increase by 20% over the standard three month work adjustment period.

> **Objective 2:** At least 60% of clients served in the unit will enter a skills training program or employment when exiting pre-vocational services.

What areas should goals and objectives cover?

This will vary depending upon the level of the agency at which the goals and objectives are being established. Goals and objectives should concentrate on performance areas essential to meeting the purposes of the specific work unit, to supporting achievement of goals and objectives of the next higher level work unit in the agency, and to reaching the overall agency mission more effectively and efficiently. In order for any work unit to effectively establish goals, it is necessary to know the agency goals, and goals of the next higher level work unit.

At the agency level, goals and objectives should relate directly to effective, efficient mission achievement. Specific areas may include:

Productivity — In a generic sense, this includes productivity, efficiency, effectiveness (of results), quality and timeliness of services. These terms are defined and discussed in Chapter 11.

Client Satisfaction

Organization Climate — Generically, this includes areas related to maintaining a committed, motivated and qualified work force. Employee satisfaction, absenteeism, turnover rates, employee development and related areas are included.

Agency or Program Development — This includes new program development, consolidation or reorganization. It also includes marketing related goals such as, **increase the proportion of disabled county residents served by this agency by 10% within 5 years.**

Research

Once goals and objectives are established at the agency level, other work unit's goals and objectives can be set. However, at each level some goals should also be set that relate specifically to performance areas that the work unit wishes to or needs to improve. For example, in a state vocational rehabilitation agency, a local office might have a productivity goal and several other goals related to the overall agency goals. However, this office may have very high turnover that needs to be reduced. Thus, a goal dealing specifically with that issue would be included in the formal plan for that office, even though the whole agency does not have a goal in that area.

How many goals and objectives should a work unit have?

There is no specific number. However, it seems easier for managers and staff to remember and maintain control over smaller numbers of goals and objectives. When people forget what the goals are or must collect too much data to determine whether goals are being met, the goals become meaningless. This can be ameliorated to some extent by computerization when goals/objectives and data on their achievement can be fed back on a regular basis to relevant staff.

STRATEGIES

What are strategies?

Strategies are approaches to reaching goals and objectives. They are the methods that will be used. They answer the question "**what** will we do to go about reaching the performance required for this goal or objective?"

Students of human services management often confuse strategies with goals and objectives. The key point is that goals and objectives deal with defining an expected **level of performance** or a **result,** often different from what currently exists; or an expected achievement. Strategies then define what needs to be done (actions) to achieve that level of performance, result or achievement. For example:

Goal: Increase the number of clients served through this office by 15% within the next year.

Strategies:

1. Visit all local hospitals at least once during the year and explain the services that we offer.
2. Develop a colorful brochure and send to all possible referral sources.
3. Obtain a listing of all people in the county with disabilities and send out brief letters and a brochure about our program.

Note that the strategies state what will be done so that the goal may be achieved. They do not refer to a level of performance that will be achieved.

POLICIES

What are policies?

Policies are relatively permanent general guidelines for carrying out action toward the goals and objectives in a work unit. For example, in a mental health clinic, all clients will be seen for an intake interview; eligibility will be determined; and if appropriate, an individual treatment plan will be developed. Also, all services will be provided in accordance with professional ethical standards.

How do policies differ from procedures?

Procedures are the specific methods for carrying out the work. They are a more specific extension of policies in that they define how the work will be done in accordance with policy. For example, in the above example, procedures would include the specific method for documenting the treatment plan.

PLANNING ASSESSMENT

What should be assessed during the planning process?

An evaluation of potential clients and service needs is important, as well as an assessment of available resources. In addition, legislative information, and feedback from consumers, staff and funding sources is of value. Program evaluation information is also important, since this provides after the fact information on the effectiveness of previously implemented plans and current programs. For example, through program evaluation it may be determined why a particular program is not performing well. Current planning might then include new strategies for improvement.

How does planning assessment really help?

If potential clients or servicing needs are not accurately known, it is difficult to set realistic goals, objectives and strategies. If we are uncertain of our resources, such as funds for staff or for equipment and building space, then we also cannot be certain of the levels at which to set our goals and objectives, or what strategies are feasible. We must also know about the status of legislation in order to know whether our plans are consistent with the law. We may even wish to know whether we can influence new legislation since that may impact on planning. Feedback from consumers, staff and funding sources also provides information internally and from the environment that must be considered in planning for change or maintenance.

What methods can be used for planning assessment?

Some specific methods include needs assessment, forecasting and operations research techniques.

Needs Assessment

What is needs assessment?

This is a procedure used to gather information in order to better understand the needs, demands and priorities for services, in order for planning to take place.

How does needs assessment differ from program evaluation?

Needs assessment determines what needs to be done. **Program evaluation** determines whether the activities that were designed to do that were successful. Needs assessment tends to be done before program implementation, while program evaluation is often done during or after program implementation. However, as illustrated above, program evaluation sometimes serves the purposes of needs assessment.

What is a suggested process for carrying out a needs assessment?

The following steps are suggested:
1. Define the problem or concerns.
2. Identify the information sources and assessment techniques.
3. Collect and analyze the information.
4. Assess and consider resources and limitations, e.g. facilities, personnel, operating funds, procedures, legislation and organizational priorities.
5. Determine conclusions regarding servicing needs, priorities, programs needed and resources available or possible.
6. Decide on any actions to be taken.

For a comprehensive description of the needs assessment process, see Auvenshine and Mason (1982).

Forecasting

What is the purpose of forecasting methods?

In human services, forecasting methods are useful for predicting future workload levels and budget requirements.

What are some suggested forecasting techniques for planning assessment?

The simplest technique is "informed" guessing (which managers probably use most). However, there are more sophisticated methods. These include mathematical approaches such as the **moving average, regression analysis** and **exponential smoothing.**

The moving average involves predictions based on averaging a series of values. Subsequent predictions are based on dropping the oldest value of the series and adding the newest. For example, if we are predicting workload based on a four quarter moving average, we would do the following:

quarter 1—600 cases
quarter 2—300 cases
quarter 3—500 cases
quarter 4—300 cases

To predict quarter 5, we would take the average of quarters 1 through 4. To predict quarter 6, we would take the average of quarters 2 through 5 (i.e., drop quarter 1 and add quarter 5). For further discussion of this method, see Feldman, Sorensen and Hanbery (1981).

Regression techniques involve the use of statistical methods for prediction. They include simple linear regression, time series analysis, multiple regression and more complex methods. Usually, the complexity of variables involved in prediction preclude the sole use of simple techniques in prediction. However, these often provide a starting point from which values can be adjusted based on subjective knowledge. For example, if we can show that number of applicants for job placement services is statistically correlated with county unemployment rates, then we can at least roughly project future volume of applicants using linear regression, if we have an estimate of the future unemployment rate. Such statistical projections can then be modified based on other available information.

Exponential smoothing is described by Hanbery and Cattanach (1972). It is slightly more complex than moving averages but fewer items are required to make predictions. In this technique prior estimates are compared with actual values in formulating future estimates.

Is it really necessary to use quantitative techniques?

There may be a tendency for human services managers to avoid quantitative techniques. However, these can add to predictive accuracy, if used effectively. Also, when dealing with funding sources, using quantitative techniques may add to the credibility of the human services manager's forecasts.

Operations Research Techniques

What is operations research?

Operations research is an area of knowledge involving the use of mathematical and statistical models and techniques for solving production and operations problems in organizations. These techniques are most often used for planning and control purposes.

What operations research techniques can apply to human services planning?

Linear programming, network analysis and queuing analysis show some promise for use in human services systems. **Linear programming** is a method for allocating scarce resources to achieve objectives in some optimal way. It can help to minimize a function, such as costs; or maximize a function, such as a type of service outcome within a definable set of constraints. For example, in the **assignment model** of linear programming, we may be able to establish a method of assigning cases to staff that will minimize total costs of processing while maximizing the total payoff (e.g., positive client outcomes).

Network analysis is a set of techniques designed to find the shortest path through a network. In human services work, this may help identify the sequence of services that moves clients toward improved functioning with maximum effectiveness, maximum speed or minimum cost. For example, is it most cost effective to route certain vocational rehabilitation clients through a work evaluation, work adjustment, skills training and job placement sequence vs. short term work readiness training followed by placement into supported employment?

Queuing analysis is designed to determine the point of service availability at which the costs of clients waiting (for service) justifies hiring additional staff, or opening new facilities. It can also be used to find the decline in client intakes that would justify decreasing personnel or closing facilities.

Operations research techniques seem very complicated. Are they really of benefit to human services agencies?

Operations research techniques are somewhat experimental for use in human services. They tend to be used most in business and industry. However, they can be of value, particularly in large agencies.

Is it necessary to hire a specialist in this area?

While a specialist or consultant may be helpful, existing staff with quantitative capabilities and a computer should be able to make use of these methods. For further details on using specific operations research techniques in human services situations, see Yates (1980).

BUDGETING

How is budgeting used in the planning process?

A budget is needed to plan costs for carrying out proposed goals, objectives and strategies, and for achieving program standards. It is also needed to assure adequate monetary resources for accomplishing routine agency activities.

Is all budgeting done during the planning process?

No. Budgets are also used for control purposes. This provides a basis for assuring that funds spent are consistent with planned expenses.

Are all budgets prepared in a similar manner?

No. There are different types of budget systems. Government agencies differ from private agencies, and agencies within these categories differ from one another.

What are some major types of budgets?

The **master budget** is one type. It contains the operations budget and the financial budget. The **operations budget** includes services activities, cost of services and the administrative budget. The **financial budget** may include cash receipts and disbursements, the budgeted statement of financial position and the budgeted statement of changes in financial position.

The **capital budget** is a second type. This is a long range budget prepared for major capital acquisitions such as buildings and equipment (Feldman, Sorensen & Hanbery, 1981).

What are some major budget systems?

The Planning-Programming-Budgeting System (PPBS) and Zero Based Budgeting (ZBB) are both planning oriented systems that have been used in government and other settings. **PPBS** involves stating program objectives, then weighing the costs and benefits of alternatives for the effective achievement of the objectives. This system has found little use in recent years, however, due to reasons such as a tendency to encourage preoccupation with quantification, measurement and overanalysis.

ZBB requires reviewing each program completely during every budget cycle. In order for continued funding, each program's activities must be rejustified. The intent in this system is to eliminate outdated or ineffective programs so that resources may then be used more effectively. As with PPBS, ZBB has the disadvantage of requiring a great deal of continuing analysis, with questionable results (Tyer and Brabham, 1981).

Since budgets are partially based on forecasts which may not be accurate, can budgets be flexible?

Although some budgets are set on a yearly basis, flexible budgeting methods exist. For example, the **continuous, rolling** or **moving** budget is updated at fixed intervals such as one month or one quarter at a time. The **flexible** or **variable** budget allows for changes based on actual volumes of service or activity achieved (Feldman, Sorensen & Hanbery, 1981).

How does one prepare a budget?

This will differ from agency to agency. In general, amounts of projected revenue are identified, payments for services and supplies are estimated, and salary expenses and disbursements are estimated, by month. This data is combined into several budget statements which indicate projected expenses, cash available, financial condition etc. at particular times during the year. For a complete step by step description of agency master budget preparation, see Feldman, Sorensen & Hanbery (1981).

What are some typical problems in planning and executing budgets?

Inaccurate forecasts and unanticipated events are the most frequently occuring problems. For example, budgets can be cut if promised funds become unavailable. If forecasts for workload size are inaccurate, more or less funds may be needed. New laws may also create programs for which adequate funds are unavailable. Any of these circumstances may create problems of inability to provide services, and over or underspending.

Chapter 4

ROUTINE PLANNING

What is routine planning?

Routine planning is what a manager does on an everyday basis to assure that his or her job gets done effectively and without unnecessary delay. It entails managing crises and emergencies, short term changes and other arising situations that require foresight and thoughtful action. It also involves the management of how one's time use is organized on a daily basis. It is the type of activity needed to avoid continual "fire fighting."

Is effective routine planning difficult to achieve?

Yes. Many managers complain that too much work, excessive time pressures, too few staff and poorly trained staff contribute to this. Entering such a managers office is like visiting a disorganized paper factory. Interestingly, however, one can observe that there are some managers in similar situations who almost seem as though they have nothing to do. When you enter their offices you first notice that their desk is empty, there are few papers littering the office and they seem relaxed and ready to deal with **your** problem. The difference between these two types of managers relates to their modes of handling routine planning.

What accounts for differences in how one handles routine planning?

Two major factors are probably personality and skills. For example, personality characteristics and life styles which support a **present** rather than **future** orientation to problems, or which support less than well organized approaches to life situations, may interfere with effective routine planning. This may be especially evident when stressful or work overload situations exist. Also, in some instances, managers may thrive on the excitement of crises. Yet management around this life style may not be consistent with effective routine planning.

Important routine planning skills for managers include delegation and time management methods. However, whether and how well these skills are used, often seems to depend on personality factors. This is not to say that people cannot improve their skills. However, a disorganized person who takes a time management skills course does not automatically become organized. For such a person, it takes a great deal of discipline and practice even to implement just a few new techniques. However, changing just a few habits may make a significant difference.

DELEGATION

What is delegation?

Delegation is the assignment of work, usually to a subordinate employee. When delegating work assignments, the manager retains final accountability for the work.

Delegation can occur at different levels of responsibility. For example, a manager may delegate an entire project and hold the employee responsible for results. However, delegation could also be as simple as assigning someone to do only data collection for the project.

Why is delegation important?

Delegation is usually a **must** for managers because it is a "safety valve" for freeing up needed time. Also, it is an activity over which the manager has substantial control. An advantage that many managers have (over direct service personnel) is that they have a staff that can be called upon for this purpose. For example, when a manager has five staff, if he or she had to delegate the entire management job, each staff member would only need to increase workload by $\frac{1}{5}$. Usually, a manager need not delegate more than about $\frac{1}{4}$ of his or her total tasks (for any substantial time period) in order to free up needed time. With five staff or even much less, the time that might be spent on management tasks by others is insignificant in relation to the advantages to the work unit when the manager has sufficient time for routine planning or other necessary functions.

This seems reasonable. However, when work is assigned to direct service staff doesn't it take away time from their work with clients?

Yes, but even when a work unit is understaffed and workload is high, it is more important to have a manager who has time to plan for handling the work and who can handle crises effectively, than to have a small fraction of additional total direct service time. The benefits of a more organized approach to total servicing should outweigh the benefits of a very slight increase in percentage of direct service time available.

What are some other advantages of delegation?

Delegation keeps staff more in touch with the problems of management. This may help in understanding why things are done the way they are. A better appreciation of management by direct service staff may help reduce complaints and improve management-staff relationships and communication.

Delegation also helps provide a different perspective to managers. People who are doing direct service or other tasks are usually closest to the work and its methods. Their solutions to or ideas regarding problems may be more accurate than those of managers. The **feedback** obtained through delegation may thus lead to better problem solving, as well as a feeling that "we are being listened to" by employees. This should support improved work unit communications, as well as feelings of enhanced power by employees. The latter has been associated with more effectively functioning organizations (Tannenbaum, 1968).

Delegation also may support feelings of trust and involvement on the part of employees. This encourages increased commitment to what management is trying to achieve. Finally delegation is an excellent staff development tool for future managers and an opportunity to assess management skills and potential of subordinate employees. This aspect may be motivating to staff who realize that success on delegated assignments may be a springboard to a management career or to higher level positions.

What should I do if I have no staff who can be trusted to do a delegated job correctly?

Most staff can do some delegated work correctly. For example, when necessary, delegation could consist of only the simpler, time consuming parts of tasks (e.g., data collection or compilation).

Sometimes, training in delegated tasks may be necessary and the manager may feel "it would be quicker if I did it myself". That may be true. However, if it is a recurring project and someone is available who could handle it, it should be worthwhile to take the time to train, **even if other work gets backed up temporarily**. The idea is to think long term.

If only one person is available who can be trusted to handle more important delegated work or major projects, it may be important to delegate some of that person's work to others so that he or she can be delegated the managerial work. Whatever the method, it is critical for a manager to find ways to delegate, since this is a major time saving tool.

Why don't managers delegate more?

They may be uncomfortable giving others **their** work, they may not want to offend staff, they may not trust staff, they may not want to give up control, or they may feel that staff are already too overloaded with work. Managers sometimes also enjoy doing some of the routine work, like collecting data, doing calculations, typing, using the computer or even the copy machine. However, all of these factors must be weighed against the disadvantages of not being able to manage the work unit as effectively as possible.

What are some principles of effective delegation?

Per Laird and Laird (1957):
1. Responsibility for the task should be shared with the subordinate.
2. The subordinate should be given sufficient authority.
3. Either share decision making or leave that to the subordinate.
4. Give the subordinate the freedom he or she thinks is needed to complete the delegated task.

In addition, it is suggested that sufficient checking of the completed product be done by the manager. If problems exist, the work should be returned to the subordinate for correction after providing feedback on the nature of the problems and their solution.

TIME MANAGEMENT METHODS

What is time management?

Time management, in this context, refers to how a manager organizes and uses time. Effective time management refers to using time efficiently. Effective time managers are able to achieve more or accomplish more work in the same period of time than less effective time managers.

What are some important time management methods?

The following methods, if put to consistent use, can save substantial time:

Prioritizing — Maintain three incoming bins or boxes labeled priority #1, #2, and #3. Classify all incoming work into three priorities by order of importance and time frame, and place the work materials or a note to yourself in the appropriate box. For example, two new items come to your attention on Monday morning; a report due to your supervisor by Friday, and a memo on chronic tardiness that you wish to send to all your employees. The report will require a great deal of research and writing and must be in on time. You decide that the report is a #1 priority and the memo is a #2 priority. You then place the report materials in box #1 and a note to yourself about the memo in box #2. On Wednesday, you review your materials in each box and find that you have completed almost all of the report and the rest could wait until Friday morning. However, you want to get the memo out as soon as possible. So, you move the memo to box #1 and the report to box #2. After prioritizing each time, work on those items with the highest priority until you complete them. Then go on to the next priority.

In reality, many things are coming in and going out of your office daily. The priority system is best for projects that will take more than a few minutes. Items that will take just a few minutes, like reviewing and signing a routine employee request, **should be done immediately.** This is important, because if action is deferred, you will need to waste as much time rereading the request or reviewing an issue as it would have taken you to dispose of it in the first place. So, when handling new items, dispose of what you can right away.

With a priority system such as the above, it will be necessary to review and rearrange priorities from time to time. Every few days or once a week may be enough.

Dealing with Unforeseen Events — Many events come up during the day that cannot be controlled or anticipated. For example, a client emergency arises requiring supervisor assistance, the Director calls a sudden meeting that lasts an hour or a complaining client gets through to you on the telephone. From a time management perspective, we can plan that a certain proportion of our day will be **routinely spent on unforeseen events.** Thus, when planning prioritized work, we must figure on spending about 1/2 of the day or less on that, and the rest on the unexpected. If we actually spend less on the unexpected, the extra time is a gift.

Designating Quiet Times — It is usually acceptable practice to designate times during the day when we will not accept most interruptions. For example, we may make it known that phone calls received during this time will be returned later and that employees will not be seen. This allows time to make sufficient progress on projects without interruption. Interruptions are time wasters since one's train of thought is lost and time is required to reestablish project focus.

Explanations to a secretary or clerical staff can help in assuring that external demands are handled sensitively during these periods. For example, a client may be told "Mr. Williams is unavailable now, but he will be happy to return your call later today. Can he reach you at about 3:00 this afternoon?" There will of course be times when the quiet time will need to be interrupted, such as when your supervisor wants to see you, or calls a meeting. This should be the exception rather than the rule.

Aren't there more time management techniques?

Yes. In fact many books have been written on this topic and time management seminars are given daily. The above methods are very basic, but if they are not being used they could save substantial time. Two sources for more information on time management are:

Lakein, A.: **How to Get Control of Your Time and Your Life.** New York, P. W. Wyden, 1973.
Scott, D.: **How to Put More Time in Your Life.** New York, Signet, 1980.

PLANNING EXERCISE 1
STRATEGIC AND OPERATIONAL PLAN DEVELOPMENT

(Group or Individual)

Choose a familiar agency or institution and do the following:
1. Write a mission statement
2. For the entire agency or institution, write a portion of a strategic plan to include:
   a. Two long range goals, with two objectives for each goal.
   b. Two strategies for each goal and its associated objectives.

3. Select one organizational sub-unit of the agency or institution and write a portion of a one year operational plan to include:
   a. Two goals, with two objectives for each goal.
   b. Two strategies for each goal and its associated objectives.

RULES

- Do not take the above information from an existing agency or institution plan. Devise your own.
- Your mission statement, goals, objectives and strategies should be structured per information in Chapter 3. For example, be sure that you achieve the waterfall effect; that the mission is consistent with the four characteristics stated; that objectives are in relevant areas, reflect expected levels of achievement, are specific, measurable, clearly stated and contain a time frame; and that strategies reflect statements of what will be done to help achieve the goal and objectives.

PLANNING EXERCISE 2
DELEGATION

(Group)

1. Divide class into groups of four.
2. Assign roles randomly as follows:
   a. Supervisor of case managers in a small social service agency.
      This supervisor's job consists of providing individual supervision to the three case managers (ten hours per week), collecting data for and writing monthly reports to higher level management (three hours per week), handling some more difficult cases (four hours per week, assisting in resolving complaints and inquiries from clients and the general public (ten hours per week), planning and conducting program evaluation (two hours per week), answering letters from congressmen (three hours per week), attending agency Director's meetings (four hours per week) and doing miscellaneous clerical tasks (e.g., reproducing copies of documents, filing etc.) (four hours per week). With the current amount of time needed, virtually no time is available to deal with planning and the supervisor feels discouraged and like a "fire-fighter."
   b. Casemanager A
      Casemanager A has fifty cases, while a reasonable size workload

for most is about forty cases. However, A's productivity, quality and timeliness of work is very good, suggesting that she has the capacity to handle this or a higher workload. She feels a little overloaded and is aware that her caseload is higher than others. She has management aspirations, has good writing skills and works well with numbers and details.

  c. Casemanager B

  Casemanager B has thirty-five cases, while forty is considered a reasonable size caseload. B is a slow deliberate worker whose quality of work is good because he is so thorough. However, even with a smaller than average caseload, he cannot schedule cases as timely as desirable, because of the amount of time he spends in working with each case. He believes that his caseload is too large considering what he believes needs to be done with clients. B is very effective in developing rapport with people, even the most hostile clients. He is toward the end of his career and looks forward to retirement.

  d. Casemanager C

  C handles a caseload of forty, which is considered an appropriate size workload. His quality, timeliness and productivity are acceptable. However, his motivation to do more than the minimal needed to avoid complaints seems low. He will do what is assigned in a minimally acceptable manner. He will complete extra assignments although he complains about them and feels taken advantage of. He has very efficient clerical skills (for a professional counselor).

TASK

  The supervisor in each group will delegate as much work as is feasible to his/her workers. The goal is to free at least ¼ of his or her current available time (ten hours per week) for planning and related management tasks. Workers should be involved in the process through group or individual discussion and negotiation, per the supervisor's discretion.

  At the conclusion of the exercise, the supervisor will list the tasks and amount of hours delegated to each casemanager, as well as the total amount of hours of work delegated. Each supervisor will rate his or her level of comfort with the decisions as follows:

Uncomfortable   1   2   3   4   5   6   7   8   9   10   Comfortable

Class discussion should focus on amount of tasks/time delegated and feelings of both supervisors and supervisees in each group.

Section III

ORGANIZING

INTRODUCTION AND OVERVIEW

The organizing function of managers involves establishing structures of task and authority relationships. The purpose is to achieve coordinated efforts among employees and work units within the organization. In this role, the manager is essentially a "conceptual" engineer.

Effective organization permits efficient use of staff energy. This is done by creating structural channels and arrangements that aid communication, clarify decision making authority and power relationships, and prevent unnecessary overlap of job functions.

In carrying out the organizing function, managers develop position descriptions and design formal structures. They also establish specialized structures, and manage informal structures.

Position descriptions are the building blocks of formal structures. They state the job responsibilities (tasks) for each position, the **depth** or amount of freedom the jobholder has in performing the job, and to whom the employee in the position is responsible. Position descriptions form a logical basis for grouping together jobs to form work units. They also help reduce **role ambiguity,** which as noted in Chapter 2, can be a source of stress, dissatisfaction and employee ineffectiveness. A sample position description is shown at the end of Section III.

As discussed in Chapter 5, the **formal structure** establishes how work units, power and authority relationships are organized. This is reflected in the written **table of organization,** which groups work units and lines of authority in the appropriate sequence. Tables of organization are illustrated in Figures 2, 3 and 4 in Chapter 5.

Chapter 6 discusses specialized and informal structures. **Specialized structures** include ways of arranging individual or work unit relationships to meet a particular need or to serve a special purpose. They are creative methods managers can use to innovate, improve services or

51

performance, and solve problems that are not as well handled through the formal structure.

The management of informal structures is a special management role within the organizing function. **Informal structures** are naturally developing groups, and configurations of power and leadership outside the formal structure. For example, apart from the formal organization of a counseling department (supervisor, and counselors who report to the supervisor), an informal structure exists in which counselors view one of their peers as their leader. This person may be the spokesperson to the supervisor when problems exist, or he or she may be the person others go to for technical help or advice — rather than the supervisor. Informal structures may work to the benefit or detriment of the manager and thus they must be handled effectively.

Chapter 5

FORMAL STRUCTURE

What should the formal structure accomplish?

It should establish a design for:

Flow of communications throughout the organization
Differentiation of decision making responsibility
Coordinated task accomplishment and work processes
Power and authority within the organization

Overall, the formal structure should be constructed so that coordinated effort toward organization goals is achieved in the most efficient manner.

What factors should be considered in establishing an efficient formal structure?

It is important to consider the nature of the employees, the work and the environment. For example, a situation may exist in which most employees are well trained professionals, the work is not amenable to standardized methods because it requires individual judgement (e.g., psychotherapy), and the environment is changing rapidly (e.g., changing laws and client needs). Under these conditions, a structure that facilitates individual autonomy; and rapid, open communications, unhampered by a long **chain of command** may be most efficient. (Chain of command refers to the line of authority in an organization, e.g., director to department head to unit chief to direct service worker.)

In addition, the formal structure should support and be consistent with the organization's control needs. For example, agencies that employ many semiskilled and paraprofessional employees may need to have more supervisors. Typically, organizations with employees less prepared to function independently, need more levels of management to assure that the work is carried out effectively.

Ideally, we would like to create agencies that require the least amount of supervisory or management control to achieve their purposes. When that is the case, more resources can be expended on direct services and related functions. This results in the most efficient use of energy.

TYPES OF FORMAL STRUCTURES

What are the major types of formal structures?

Taller and flatter pyramidal (pyramid like) structures (see Figures 2 and 3).

What is a tall structure?

Tall structures are characterized by multiple layers of departments and units. Jobs tend to be highly specialized and managers have short **spans of control**, i.e., numbers of employees supervised. There are also usually many rules and procedures.

Organizations with tall structures tend toward **centralized authority**, i.e., authority and major decision making concentrated at the top and flowing downward. What we commonly refer to as **bureaucracies** tend to fall in the category of tall organizations.

There is a tendency to view bureaucracies in a negative sense. Are tall, bureaucratic structures always inefficient or ineffective?

No. In fact, under certain conditions, they are the most efficient design. For example, this would be true in an industrial environment where employees are unskilled or semiskilled, employees expect to be closely supervised and do not seek autonomy, the technology is routine and stable, and it is most efficient to develop procedures for most job tasks.

Is this ever the most efficient or effective structure for a human services agency?

Sometimes. This may be the case in situations where an agency operates in a fairly structured environment, such as a welfare agency or a state rehabilitation agency. In such instances, benefits may be distributed on the basis of laws which require regulations and procedures to be followed in a uniform manner, to assure equity in service delivery. This may require large numbers and types of policy making staff as well as more managers and auditors to assure that the policies and procedures are implemented correctly. Also, in such agencies, personnel are often hired

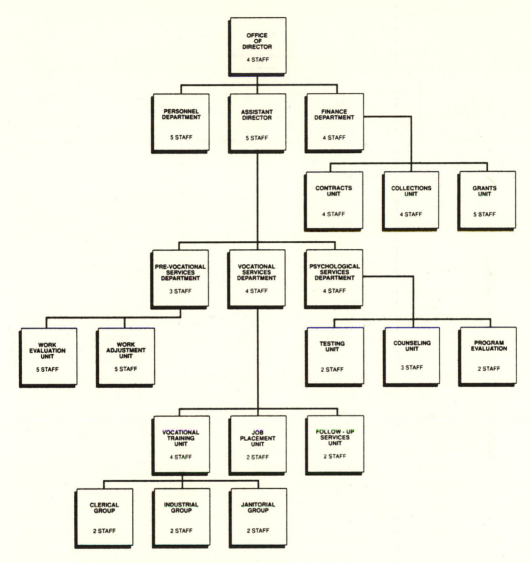

Figure 2 — Table of Organization — Taller Structure.

at low levels of professional preparation. They thus require more technical supervision than those normally trained to function more independently in a professional specialty. For example, an agency that hires social workers or counselors with bachelors' degrees will usually need to provide more casework supervision than one that hires masters' or doctoral level personnel.

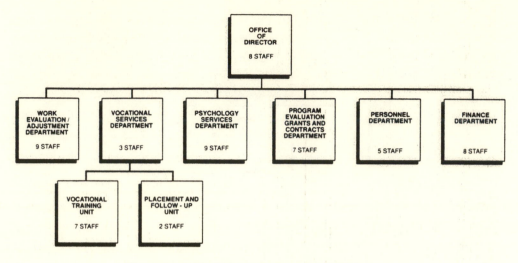

Figure 3 — Table of Organization — Flatter Structure.

What is a flat structure?

Flat structures are characterized by few layers of departments and units. This gives the table of organization the appearance of a flat pyramid. Jobs tend to be more general in task content and managers have larger spans of control than in tall structures. There may be specialization, but tasks are performed with a view toward the entire organization mission, rather than as isolated specialties. There are also usually fewer rules and procedures, and the management hierarchy is not clearly the focus of problem solving and decision making. Interactions and decision making tend to occur as much through lateral as through vertical communications. Thus, authority tends to be more **decentralized** as compared with tall structures.

Under what conditions are flat structures effective?

Flat structures are often most effective in rapidly changing environments where open communications are needed among all levels of staff. For example, in a highly competitive and changing field, such as the computer industry, the creativity and responsiveness necessary to compete would require this type of research atmosphere. A tall structure, with a long chain of command and many rules and procedures would neither allow for the necessary creativity or quick response to rapid change in the industry.

Other factors conducive to flat structures include organizations employing highly trained or educated workers with high self-esteem and growth needs. Such employees often can and expect to work more autonomously than less skilled workers. Flat structures are also appropriate when non routine or rapidly changing technology exists, procedures cannot be developed for most job tasks (or specific procedures would not improve effectiveness), and when there are few or stable legal requirements and standards necessary to carry out the work.

For human services agencies, which is better, tall or flat structures?

This goes back to the earlier question regarding factors to consider in establishing an efficient formal structure. The employees, work, and environment are important determining factors. It is important to point out that tallness or flatness can occur along a continuum, e.g., very tall to very flat with many interim variations. In fact, an agency can be very tall with some of the characteristics of flat organizations, such as decentralized authority; or flat with characteristics of tall organizations, such as high task specialization. A contingency approach allows for designing the agency to fit its circumstances and environment. Table III illustrates some of the factors that may be related most appropriately to the characteristics of a continuum of tall to flat structures.

What can be done when an agency has a particular structure, e.g., very tall, yet it has some of the factors related to another type of structure (like highly educated employees) or needs that are inconsistent with the existing structure (like open communications)?

In these situations, the structure of particular work units or groups of work units can be modified. For example, in a tall, multilevel government agency that has multiple medical, administrative and other programs, a mental health counseling unit can be structured for open communications and shared decision making in an otherwise highly centralized system. Also, substructures are possible within the total structure of such organizations which allow for the flexibility and responsiveness that might be obtained in a flatter organization. Substructures are discussed in Chapter 6,

TABLE III
FACTORS RELATED TO TALL AND FLAT STRUCTURES

Type of Structure

Flat——Tall

Related Factors

Employee Technical Skills
High——Low

Employee Self Esteem
High——Low

Employee Growth Needs
High——Low

Work Technology
Non Routine————————————————————————————————————Routine
Rapidly Changing————————————————————————————————Stable

Standard Procedures
Infeasible—————————————————————————————————————Feasible
Reduces Quality————————————————————————————————Improves Quality
Reduces Efficiency———————————————————————————————Improves Efficiency
or Productivity   or Productivity

Legal Requirements
Few———Many

External Agency Environment
Rapidly Changing————————————————————————————————Stable

DEPARTMENTALIZATION

What is departmentalization?

As organizations increase in size, individual positions are combined into work unit groupings, or departments. This helps to organize the work into logical segments and control the chaos that would exist if all jobs were treated as single entities. Very small agencies do not need departmentalization. However, as size increases above a few staff, separate departments become the more efficient way to run the agency. Departmentalization is reflected in the table of organization.

What are the ways an agency may be departmentalized?

Ways for departmentalizing relevant to human services agencies include (Broskowski, 1984; Donnelly, Gibson and Ivancevich, 1984):

Geographic — This includes work units that are based on geographic location. For example, if clients must be served throughout an entire state, local offices providing a full range of services may be located in areas of highest population density. This is referred to as **geographic decentralization** (which should be distinguished from decentralization of authority discussed earlier).

Type of Clients — For example, type of client problem (marital, educational/vocational) or age (child, adult) may be the basis for departments.

Type of Product — This might include departments based on products completed, e.g., typing pool, psychometric testing.

Function or Discipline — These work units may be based upon professional discipline such as internal medicine, nursing, rehabilitation counseling and psychology; or it may include specialties such as personnel, marketing or accounting which involve several disciplines.

Process — This is a grouping of jobs by technical operations or by time frame of processes. For example, work adjustment, work evaluation, inpatient or outpatient services departments are organized by technical processes. Examples of departments involving time frame of processes include intake, treatment, rehabilitation and follow-up units.

Can an agency departmentalize using more than one of the above methods?

Yes. In fact, many large agencies use different methods at different levels. Figure 4 illustrates functional departmentalization at the central office level of a large agency, with geographic departmentalization at the operational level. Such mixtures help to meet the multiple needs that large agencies must serve.

When organizations have very different types of departments, like a department of medicine and a department of rehabilitation counseling, isn't it difficult to achieve coordination?

Yes. This is often the case because the departments may have very different priorities, interests and levels of knowledge about one another. This situation is called high **differentiation**.

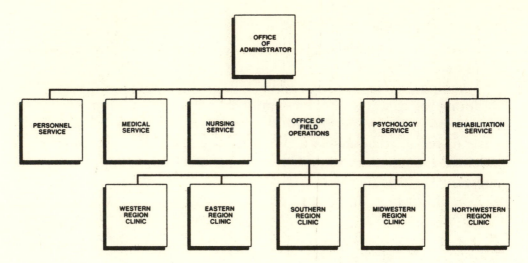

Figure 4—Functional and Geographic Departmentalization.

How can that be managed constructively without changing the whole organization structure?

Lawrence and Lorsch (1967) studied this problem extensively and found that when high differentiation exists, it is usually necessary to have high **integration** among such departments. Integration often requires special mechanisms to bring about the coordination that will not take place naturally. For example, managers from the differentiated units may act as integrators, liaisons from each unit to the other may serve this purpose, or regular staff meetings among units to discuss mutual clients may be used. The need for and methods of integration should always be considered when establishing bases for departmentalization in human services organizations. Integrative methods are discussed further in Chapters 6 and 14.

Chapter 6

SPECIALIZED AND INFORMAL STRUCTURES
SPECIALIZED STRUCTURES

What are specialized structures?

These are ways of restructuring parts of the organization to overcome shortcomings resulting from pyramidal structures, or to otherwise improve effectiveness or efficiency. For example, specialized structures may help to quickly create innovations, solve problems, improve work processes or create integration among work units. They may also help to improve motivation and commitment of employees. Specialized structures may involve the entire organization or only some work units and individuals. They may be either temporary or permanent.

When should specialized structures be established?

Whenever the need for their specific purpose becomes evident to managers.

What are some major types of specialized structures?

Matrix structure
Parallel structures
Quality circles
Ad hoc task forces
Integrative committees and individuals
Formal committees
Informal problem solving groups
Mixed innovative groups

What is the matrix structure?

This structure involves lateral integration or assignment of one or more staff from departments at the same level of the organization. The purpose is usually to establish a structure for temporary teams to work on complex projects that require a rapid response to some changed circumstance. In a pyramidal structure, particularly a taller structure, such a response might not be possible under normal circumstances. For example, a matrix structure might bring together the expertise of staff from a social work, vocational rehabilitation, rehabilitation medicine, program evaluation and contracts/grants department in a rehabilitation hospital to develop a new program to respond to newly passed legislation regarding persons with severe disabilities. It may be necessary to quickly establish the program before competing programs are developed in the community. Using the matrix design, one staff person would be assigned to the team by each department until the project is completed. A team leader would be assigned from among project workers. One problem with this design, however, is that assigned members of the team often retain responsibility to the manager in their regular department as well as to the project team leader. This may result in confusion and conflict.

In human services agencies, matrix structures may also be used as relatively permanent structures which allow for comprehensive services to be provided in different geographical locations. For example, a centralized facility with comprehensive medical services in one location may choose to establish satellite units in several locations, each of which includes one specialist from each department (e.g., internal medicine, psychiatry, laboratory services). Thus, in this situation, the matrix design provides a basis for an efficient and more responsive approach to treatment than could be provided at a single, large location.

What is a parallel structure?

Parallel structures involve both **lateral** and **vertical integration**, or assignment of one or more staff from departments at both the **same** and **different** levels of the organization. The purpose is to establish **permanent** teams that focus on innovation and change in large bureaucratic structures. For example, a group which is representative of several levels and functions within an agency may work as advisors to top management in determining ways to improve quality, productivity or quality of work life in the organization.

Parallel structure groups are involved in advisory activities of a planning, implementation and evaluation nature. In contrast to temporary matrix structures which focus on one project, parallel structures are involved in continuous processes of data gathering, diagnosis, generation of alternatives, making recommendations, monitoring and facilitating implementation. Members spend about 15–20% of their time on parallel organization activities. As with matrix structures, members also usually report to two managers. The major advantage of parallel structures is that it places a permanent focus on innovation in organizations that might normally be slow to innovate. (Moore, 1985)

What are quality circles?

These are groups of about four to fifteen employees **from a work unit.** Members meet on a regular basis to identify and solve work problems, and to study how quality and productivity of the work unit may be improved. In Japan, these groups often develop spontaneously with workers from the same unit plus their first line supervisor. In America, there appears to be a tendency for more formalization, including use of special facilitators and participation of union representatives.

Quality circles may be both **laterally** and **vertically integrated.** In effect, a quality circle is a parallel structure within a particular functional area. For example, a quality circle might form within the rehabilitation department of a hospital.

What is an ad hoc task force?

Peters and Waterman (1982) describe the characteristics of the effective ad hoc task force. This is a small group of organizational members who come together to accomplish a specific purpose. Usually the group consists of less than ten members, and only those who are most important to solving the problem. Members can come from any part of the organization. The duration of the effective ad hoc task force is short, and membership is voluntary. There seems to be a sense of impatience among members about getting the problem solved, e.g., "I'd be happy to serve, but it better result in something because I don't have time to waste."

The task force is put together quickly with very few formalities, follow-up by management is quick and documentation is unnecessary. The focus of these task forces is on a "no nonsense" approach to producing **solutions.** Peters and Waterman suggest that the typical task force lacks these action oriented qualities and thus they **add** to the problems of large organizations. Thus, it is incumbent upon managers to be very cautious in how task forces are structured.

What are integrative committees and individuals?

These have already been discussed briefly as tools in dealing with highly differentiated departments. They are temporary or permanent structures that improve or solve coordination problems between and among work units. For example, a manager of a rehabilitation services department may have an excellent work and social relationship with the manager of the benefits payment department. This may facilitate resolution of any differences that would occur in coordination of services and benefits to clients. Other possibilities would include establishing a small benefits payment unit in the rehabilitation services department or developing a permanent committee of members of each department to solve continuing problems.

What is a formal committee?

This is a policy making committee that serves in an advisory capacity to management at a particular level in the organization. It is similar to a parallel structure in that it is relatively permanent and may be laterally and vertically integrated. However, the formal committee is not concerned with innovation or change as its main purpose. It is most concerned with carrying out a necessary organization function, with broad participation by leaders of those who are impacted. Examples are committees which recommend policy on equal employment opportunity, affirmative action, agency files management, security and safety.

What are informal problem solving groups?

These are spontaneously developing sub-groups which solve operating problems within a work group, without the direct assistance or intervention of management. For example, case discussion groups may develop spontaneously regarding strategies of dealing with difficult counseling cases. In other instances, members of a work group may spontaneously discuss and solve an administrative problem that they know is of concern to their supervisor, e.g., increasing productivity. This type of group serves as an integrative mechanism between the organization's formal and informal structures. If nurtured effectively by management, and if staff-management relations with high mutual commitment and high quality communications exist, these groups are able to facilitate efficient management.

What are mixed innovative groups?

These are groups of **influential** leaders from both formal and informal groups within the organization, who are brought together on a temporary or permanent basis to introduce or implement an innovation. Voluntary participation is most desirable. This type of group is particularly effective where broad organizational acceptance of the innovation is desired. For example, in establishing an employee assistance program (EAP) in a large agency, a planning committee might be established consisting of the union president, the assistant agency administrator, the EAP administrator, an influential member of the agency EEO planning committee and the personnel director. After the program is established, a continuing advisory body consisting of similar influentials, perhaps including EAP service consumers, would meet regularly to make policy and evaluate the EAPs performance.

Specialized structures seem to have value, but don't they unnecessarily take up a lot of time that could be used more effectively for other purposes—like direct service and management?

It is true that they are often time consuming. However, in many instances, they are also the best way to achieve excellent results. This may be particularly true when agency structural characteristics get in the way of innovating or getting things done quickly. Also, when employees are involved in successful ventures that empower them to influence positive change, their levels of commitment to achieving the goals of management increases. This should contribute to the type of positive organizational culture described by Peters and Waterman in the excellent companies.

INFORMAL STRUCTURE

To what parts of the organization does the informal structure apply?

The informal structure is most evident among groups of employees and their immediate supervisors. For example, this would include a unit supervisor and all of his or her employees; or a department head, and all of his or her subordinate supervisors and support staff; or an agency director, and all of his or her department heads and support staff. Components of the informal structure, such as informal roles, also permeate the entire organization as well as the sphere of influence outside the organization (e.g., political groups and coalitions), and may be useful (or detrimental) to managers at any level in influencing decision making and change.

What are the main functions of the informal group?

The informal group tends to help members meet personal needs. It may strive to resist changes in the formal structure, such as management attempts to implement new procedures. It also tends to provide social satisfaction to group members, it serves as a communication channel through the "grapevine" and it serves as a medium for social control of work groups (Kazmier, 1974).

What is the nature of the informal structure within the organization?

The structure consists of a set of roles that employees implicitly play, positions that each employee occupies in a status hierarchy, and norms which govern group behavior.

What are some informal roles?

Roles include informal leaders, gatekeepers, innovators and resistors (Walz and Benjamin, 1977). **Informal leaders** are very influential with employees in the group. They are usually well respected by their colleagues and may set the tone for employee responses to events that occur in the work setting. **Gatekeepers** are employees who occupy an important position in the path of information flow, for example, the secretary to a work unit manager or the manager's assistant. These are the people who have direct access to the formal leader and who are in a position to control the flow of information to that person. Gatekeepers can provide or withhold important information which may influence management decisions.

Innovators are group members who are quickly responsive to new ideas. They tend to be knowledgeable, vocal, risk takers, outspoken and considered different by their peer group. They are often not too influential, although they may be helpful in disseminating awareness of new ideas or innovations. **Resistors** tend to be logical, critical, conservative, protective of the status quo and negative toward change.

What is the nature of the status hierarchy?

Informal groups assign an implicit level of status to each member. This may be important to some members who achieve high status within the informal group though not in the formal structure.

What are norms and how do they impact on the group?

Norms are implicitly agreed upon standards of behavior among group members. They are particularly important in work groups because they can be an important basis for performance.

Informal groups sometimes have more of an influence on setting the work pace or level of quality at which the work is done than do managers. In fact, when group cohesiveness is high, norms can work toward or against the goals of management. Thus, under these circumstances, it is important for managers to be able to exert positive influence.

For example, a well respected manager who can establish cohesive work groups and communicate and influence positive professional values through informal group leaders, can get the informal group to be a positive force toward achieving higher quality work. Less management time is then necessary for external monitoring and control (e.g., close supervision) to achieve this purpose. Conversely, when serious conflict exists between management and the informal group, destructive or resistive group actions can lead to poor control. In these situations, excessive time may be needed to try to get the group to do what management desires, and this must often be accomplished through negative methods (e.g., punishment or discipline).

Do professional groups have a unique structure?

Yes. Professional groups usually have both a formal structure within their professions, and an informal substructure within work groups and among professions. The formal structure includes professional organizations and licensing/certifying authorities outside of the work organization. Such groups have the power to authorize professionals to practice and to impose sanctions when ethics or laws pertaining to practice are violated. Professional groups within an organization operate on the basis of the informal structure by establishing status hierarchies both within professions and between professions. Such hierarchies, particularly between professions, e.g., medicine and rehabilitation counseling, often dictate privileges, priorities and power in treatment or decision making. They may also be responsible for considerable conflict among professions.

Formal substructures or the informal professional structure within professions may also play a significant role in controlling quality of work. For example, in a group of psychologists, a formal quality control committee may be the primary method of providing feedback to management on quality. The informal group may play a significant role in trying to sanction incompetent members.

Does the informal professional group structure have any special impact on management?

Professional groups can be particularly powerful since a basis for internal cohesiveness exists and since they sometimes carry a base of outside support (the profession). For example, if a group of psychologists believes that management is attempting to implement practices that may be unethical, assistance of the American Psychological Association might be sought. Due to negative publicity and potential sanctions by accrediting groups, management might be convinced to rethink their position.

In addition to having a power base, professional groups may be in conflict with management regarding control. Professionals tend to view themselves as functioning autonomously, an expectation developed by virtue of level of training, and socialization into the profession. Thus, resistance often occurs when managers implement routine controls such as standardized procedures, forms, documentation requirements and measures of accountability or performance.

How can managers make effective use of the informal structure?

They can engineer work environments in which the informal structure will support the goals and directions of the formal structure (management). This results in a highly positive culture in which management needs to exert minimum energy on external control.

Managers can also make use of knowledge about informal group roles and status in bringing about change in work units, obtaining resources, and influencing decision making. However, such actions can be or appear to be manipulative and thus special care must be taken to act in an ethical manner.

What can be done to create informal groups and structure that supports management?

Personal experience suggests that creating a management environment with the characteristics of effective helping relationships contributes to positive, integrative informal group responses. Actions that promote employee perceptions of trust, genuineness, caring and concern on the part of management encourage informal groups to want to please managers. In addition, if employees desire participation in decision making, allowing involvement and making use of the products of such involvement add to a sense of trust, joint ownership and commitment. However, managers need to be careful not to use participative methods when they expect to be in total control or only make it look like participation is taking place. Informal groups will usually detect manipulation. Such efforts may destroy trust, create skepticism, and support poor management-staff relationships.

Open and informal communications among staff at all levels, as well as frequent clear and factual communications by management (to dispel rumors) also appears helpful. This seems to support trusting, committed relationships. However, some caution needs to be exercised to assure that informal communications are directed mainly toward business and not social concerns. Encouraging a business emphasis assures that the focus is kept on improved problem solving to the benefit of the organization and its clients. For example, a rehabilitation office manager may encourage staff to discuss case management problems in informal groups, or even put a coffee pot in an area where staff from different professional disciplines may congregate and relate to one another, i.e., as an integrative mechanism.

If the above conditions can be established, the informal group should be more motivated to use all of its resources for the good of the organization. It is also under these circumstances and in this work environment that many of the substructures mentioned earlier, e.g., quality circles, ad hoc task forces and spontaneous problem solving groups, are likely to work most effectively, since they depend upon constructive formal-informal group integration.

How can managers use the informal structure to bring about change?

Change is often dependent upon influencing attitudes and decisions in the formal and informal structures and outside the organization. Thus, by enlisting the assistance of informal leaders, gatekeepers and innovators, managers can widen their scope of influence, and increase their power to effect decisions impacting on their work units.

For example, when implementing a major change in procedures, a supervisor would like to avoid resistance and be assured that employees will follow instructions without excessive supervisory monitoring. Thus, rather than just announcing the change to the work group, it is helpful for the supervisor to first enlist the support of informal leaders, and perhaps innovators. This might be done by discussing the change and its advantages, and airing any potential problems and their solutions. Then, when the change is formally introduced, modifications may have already been made to make it more successful, resistance of the entire group will have been reduced, and some sense of commitment may have already been achieved.

The informal structure may also be used to influence important decisions, particularly those related to resource acquisition or program decisions made by resource providers outside the work unit or agency. As an example, suppose a program manager in a large agency wants to expand staff development in his program. However, it is known that such decisions are made by an administrator two levels above the program manager. The administrator is known to have negative attitudes toward spending funds on external training (e.g., graduate courses) for professionals. She believes that it is their responsibility to pay for training and to attend on their own time.

The program manager is not likely to have much direct influence on the administrator because he does not communicate directly with her. Although he knows that his supervisor will support the proposal, it is clear that significant attitude change on the part of the administrator will be needed to get the proposal approved. Ideally what seems to be needed is an educational effort to help the administrator understand the value of agency support for professional staff development (from someone she perceives as credible and without self interest).

The program manager knows the personnel director who has the ear of the administrator and interacts with her on a day to day basis. The personnel director generally has positive feelings toward staff development. Thus, if the program manager can discuss the merits of his proposal with the personnel director (who may ultimately be consulted by the administrator), and get his support in advance of submitting the proposal, that may have a positive influence on the administrators decision. This is an example of making use of a gatekeepers free access to a formal leader.

Caution must be exercised when using this approach to assure that the program manager is not violating implicit expectations, rules or ethics. For example, if his direct supervisor believed that talking to the personnel director was violating the chain of command or undermining his authority, this approach would be destructive. Such methods work best in an open atmosphere where cross communications are encouraged and where people are not likely to feel manipulated. Important gatekeepers are typically secretaries, administrative assistants, personnel directors and sometimes informal leaders.

SAMPLE POSITION DESCRIPTION
VOCATIONAL REHABILITATION COUNSELOR

Principal Duties and Responsibilities

The job is in the Social Services Department of Metropolitan Rehabilitation Hospital. The principal duties are to provide vocational, educational and personal counseling to clients referred by treatment teams, and to assist clients to prepare for or secure suitable employment and achieve independent living goals.

Collaborates with physicians, psychologists, physical therapists, occupational therapists and social workers at the time clients are admitted and while they are receiving treatment. Provides consultation to treatment team regarding work readiness and readiness for vocational programming. Works directly with client to plan goals, including decisions regarding selection of rehabilitation, training or educational facilities and programs. Also provides counseling and information to clients regarding employment opportunities and the job market. When appropriate, directly provides or procures work readiness, work hardening and supported work services for clients. When necessary or desirable, coordinates provision of services and benefits through State vocational rehabilitation and other agencies.

After client leaves the hospital, provides continuing case management services on an outpatient basis, until suitable employment (or readjustment to prior employment) and independent living are achieved; or until another agency assumes case management services. During this period coordinates and procures medical and mental health services as required to assure that client can continue in training, education job seeking or employment while living as independently as possible.

Provides personal counseling to resolve adjustment problems that impede progress in planning goals, receiving training, obtaining or maintaining employment, and living independently. Makes referrals as needed for more in-depth psychotherapeutic or related assistance.

Prepares required reports with respect to all actions taken, recommendations or decisions made in each client's case.

Supervisory Controls Over the Position

Works under the supervision of the Chief of the Social Services Department, but is regarded as an independent worker responsible for performing all functions outlined in hospital procedural guides while using professional vocational rehabilitation counseling skills. Work is subject to spot check review by the Department Chief and Chief of Staff, as well as formal quality assurance procedures.

Other Significant Facts

Position requires full professional qualifications including national certification as a Rehabilitation Counselor. Incumbent possesses a high degree of professional integrity, sound emotional stability and personal characteristics which inspire the respect and confidence of others, especially clients who are mentally or physically disabled, and members of a wide range of professional specialties.

ORGANIZING EXERCISE 1
ORGANIZATION STRUCTURE

(Group)

New York Family Services is a proposed agency that will provide the following major services:
1. Family counseling
2. Treatment of mental disorders (psychotherapy, medication etc.)
3. Marriage counseling
4. Community education programs (AIDS, alcoholism/drug abuse prevention, teen age pregnancy etc.)
5. Financial planning services

The agency is expected to serve a wide range of clients at all socioeconomic levels throughout the City of New York. New York has five boroughs, each of which is large and geographically separated from one another. Each borough has no less than 1 million residents. The boroughs are Brooklyn, Queens, Staten Island, Manhattan and the Bronx. It is expected that 50% of all services will be provided within a fifteen minute commuting distance of midtown Manhattan. That commuting distance includes all of Manhattan, and the most populated parts of Brooklyn, Queens and the Bronx. The agency will have a maximum staffing of one hundred, consisting of administrators, social workers, psychologists, psychiatrists, finance/accounting, personnel and clerical staff. All treatment staff will be fully trained and licensed at the highest levels in their respective professions. It is expected that most staff will be young and motivated toward career advancement. It is also expected that few standardized treatment approaches will be appropriate due to the diversity of client needs.

TASK

1. Divide the class into groups of three to four members.
2. Each group will develop a proposed organizational structure for New York Family Services to include:
a. A central location. Note its location (borough) and why it was located there.
b. A table of organization (T/O) for the central location. The T/O should include departments, and the numbers and types of staff attached to each department. NOTE: Decide whether a tall or flat structure is appropriate. Then determine what bases for departmentalization would be best.
c. Decide whether you will include geographic departmentalization. If so, how will you do it (where will each location be and what will its T/O look like?) and why will you do it?
3. Each group will present their proposed organization structure and the rationale. The entire group will vote on which is the most functional structure.

ORGANIZING EXERCISE 2
SPECIALIZED AND INFORMAL STRUCTURES

(Group or Individual)

Consider the organization depicted in Figure 2. What type of specialized structures would be most appropriate in the following circumstances **and** what personnel would be included to best achieve the goal in each instance?

1. A limited amount of grant money has become available from the state rehabilitation agency to establish supported work programs. Pro-

posals must be submitted within 30 days. A program must be planned and the proposal written within the next three weeks.

2. The agency, currently located in a suburb of Los Angeles decides to intensify community outreach efforts by establishing a special unit offering comprehensive vocational rehabilitation services in the Watts area.

3. The Director decides that the entire agency needs to establish a long term effort to increase and maintain higher productivity. Creative, new methods will be needed.

4. The Vocational Services Department has had continuing difficulties achieving its goals and achieving positive outcomes. Continuing initiatives are needed over a long period to turn things around.

5. Union interest and pressure is mounting to establish an employee health and wellness program for the facility. The Director is also interested. However, there is concern that very few employees would use the facility. The Director wants to be assured that most employees would use it.

Section IV

CONTROLLING: OVERVIEW AND IMPLEMENTATION
OVERVIEW

As implied in Chapter 2, controlling involves keeping a system in a state of equilibrium and away from entropy. From a practical perspective, managers have the responsibility of doing what is needed to assure that the work gets done in the manner intended and in accordance with what is planned.

The new human services manager with a direct service orientation may sometimes view control of others as inappropriate. However, control of situations and people is an essential function in assuring that an organization achieves its purposes.

Controlling is carried out at both macro and micro levels. **Macro** control includes a philosophy and general mechanisms through which organization members are motivated and encouraged to do their jobs. It exists on a continuum with respect to using centralized vs. decentralized power and authority, as discussed in Chapter 7. Such control is often implicit, based on its development over time in a work unit or the whole organization. Participation by **all** staff in agency decision making is an example of a macro philosophy of decentralized control characterized by management and employee power sharing.

Micro control involves specific functions carried out during the implementation and evaluation phases of the agency/program management cycle. These functions assure that actual results are consistent with organization plans, purposes and expectations.

This Section covers control topics of concern during the **implementation** phase of the agency/program management cycle. Macro control, including its relationship to organization structure is discussed in Chapter 7. Employee motivation, a specific aspect of macro control, is covered in Chapter 8. Understanding how to keep employees committed to what the organization is asking, with a minimum of supervisory effort, is often a major management challenge.

Chapter 9 considers how to do effective, legal and fair employee selection. Selection of well qualified personnel appropriate to organization needs is one of the most powerful control methods, since it can prevent the need to deal with future problems. For example, extensive management energy spent on routine supervision and labor-management issues might be avoided with improved selection.

The supervision process in human services, as considered in Chapter 10, includes training, general administrative supervision, and professional supervision. Training assures higher quality work and increased ability of employees to function with less supervisory direction. Chapter 10 also discusses pertinent administrative supervision functions, and models for helping employees provide the most effective professional services.

From the perspective of implementation, managers must accomplish their goals within policy and other constraints, and at the lowest long term cost. This Section emphasizes the engineering of efficient macro control environments supported by effective micro control strategies (employee selection, training and supervision). This should result in minimum administrative costs over the long run.

Chapter 7

MACRO CONTROL

What is the purpose of macro control?

Macro control insures that employees do what is expected and functional for the organization, rather than simply what they would prefer to do.

What is the nature of macro control?

It refers to the way power and authority are distributed among management and employees along a continuum of centralization to decentralization. At the extremes, centralization has all control centered in the top executive, while decentralization has control completely diffused among all employees. Most organizations can be characterized at some point between these extremes in their overall approach to employee control.

MACRO CONTROL MODELS

What are some macro models of control, and how do they work?

For our purposes, four models, based on the locus of control, are identified. These are management centered, group centered, employee centered and money centered.[1]

What is management centered control?

This is a centralized form of control that focuses on management action. It is consistent with the bureaucratic mechanism described by Ouchi (1979). At its extreme, the bureaucratic mechanism involves the extensive use of formalized (written) rules, policies, and procedures.

---

[1]These models are based in part on the bureaucratic, clan and market mechanisms of control, respectively. Descriptive information in this chapter on those mechanisms is reprinted by permission of W. G. Ouchi, A Conceptual Framework for the Design of Organizational Control Mechanisms, *Management Science*, Volume 25, Number 9, September, 1979, Copyright 1980, The Institute of Management Sciences.

Written performance standards are used by managers to regularly monitor employee performance, with corrective actions taken through formalized instructions, directions or punitive measures. Employee motivation is maintained by distributing tangible rewards (e.g., fringe benefits, promotions, salary increases, awards) in a manner that will be perceived as fair by employees. These rewards are usually extrinsic, i.e., under the direct control of management.

Use of the bureaucratic mechanism assumes that employees accept the legitimate authority of management to control what is done and how it is done. It also assumes that employees will do what is expected as long as they are equitably compensated, i.e., services for salary and benefits.

What are the implications of management centered control for an organization?

In order to be used fairly, the bureaucratic mechanism requires the ability to specify and accurately measure organizational process and output. For example, in a manufacturing process, it may be simple to develop written procedures for how the work should be done and the standards to be used in final quality inspection. Such specification and measurement becomes more difficult as the nature of the work becomes more complex or judgemental.

In human services, some specification is possible, particularly when agencies function under the authorities of laws and regulations. However, specification of the servicing process (e.g., counseling and psychotherapy) and measurement of outcomes is difficult and fraught with uncertainties. Thus, when the bureaucratic mechanism is used by managers in human services, all of its assumptions may not be satisfied. This may be particularly significant for professional employees who may not view management's measures of performance as legitimate or valid. In this situation, particularly when extrinsically based rewards are not valued strongly, the principle of equitable compensation may lose some value as a motivator of performance.

Management centered control is also very costly in terms of energy and salaries. Because of the need to maintain effective external controls, more managers and support staff are needed to develop and maintain rules and procedures, and to monitor compliance.

Does management centered control ever work effectively in human services agencies?

Yes. It may be the control of choice or necessity in tall structures. Also, as noted in Chapter 5, when certain conditions exist, such as the need for many rules and procedures related to legal requirements; or when employees are not well trained to do the work without external controls, management centered control may be most appropriate.

It is important to note that management centered control can be used concurrently with other models. In fact, it is usually necessary to have at least some external control in an organization, or imposed upon an organization (e.g., through regulatory or accrediting authorities).

What is group centered control?

This is a relatively decentralized form of control. It focuses on collective action by general or professional work groups and is consistent with the clan mechanism described by Ouchi (1979). It is characterized by member adherence to implicit rules, values, attitudes and rituals which are internalized through the socialization process. It involves self monitoring and self direction on the part of group members, facilitated through high levels of member commitment to group goals. It is partially an external form of control in that social pressure plays a role in motivating compliance. However, much of the actual control is based on internalization (by individuals) of group values. When external control comes into play, it is through implicit means, not through explicit measurement and evaluation devices like those used in management centered control.

Group centered control is observed within professions and cultures, which develop the necessary behaviors through a long socialization process. In organizations, it is most evident among special interest groups such as managers, professional employees, and labor unions. In some instances it may develop within the informal structure in specific work units, or throughout the whole organization. Highly stable work units which allow a "culture" to develop over a long period of time are prone to the development of group centered control.

What are the implications of group centered control for an organization?

It does not require specification and measurability of processes and outputs, since group monitoring is implicit. Thus, it requires less management time, energy and cost than management centered control. However, without explicit methods, it has less potential to control as specifically or precisely.

Group centered control may also be slower to bring about necessary change. For example, a rehabilitation counselor may resist the efforts of the group to modify his or her ineffective methods of dealing with clients and may not respond immediately to group sanctions. Explicit measurement and actions by management may then be needed to correct the problem or terminate the employee.

How can group centered control be used effectively?

Sometimes, it can be used as an important model for an entire organization. Some Japanese and American companies have been successful in developing organizational cultures that support such control. For example, the Theory Z organization described by Ouchi (1981), represents the American version of a model that has been successful within Japanese culture. Theory Z emphasizes an organizational culture characterized by the values of trust, subtlety and intimacy with the goal of developing an involved, committed work force. Per Feroz & Katz-Garris (1984) and Ouchi (1981), features of Theory Z organizations include:

1. Collective decision making in which all employees have input.
2. Development of a sense of individual responsibility for ones contribution to the team or work group.
3. Commitment by the organization to long term employment for its employees.
4. Slow promotion of employees.
5. Broad career paths with only moderate specialization.
6. Demonstrated and perceived holistic concern by management for individual employees.
7. Values oriented control and direction through an organizational philosophy.
8. Implicit informal control with explicit formalized measures.

Although some American organizations have used aspects of Theory Z with success, including at least one large rehabilitation agency (Solomon, 1984), some managers consider it a fad. It is often pointed out that differences in Japanese and American culture, ideology, labor unions and employee expectations make such factors as decision making by consensus a much more realistic alternative in Japan. At any rate, regardless of the methods, when management can create a work environment characterized by work force involvement and commitment, group centered control will operate to some extent.

Even if group centered control does not operate throughout the entire organization, it can operate among smaller work units. This is evident within the informal structure both in general and professional work groups, as described in Chapter 6. Such control is most effective when managers are able to link the goals of the organization with the clan mechanism of cohesive informal structures.

What is a good example of this?

A supervisor of a small group of rehabilitation counselors in a large agency was able to get his group to control their own levels of productivity and methods of providing rehabilitation services. The supervisor was perceived as highly committed to and supportive of his group. Comments of group members suggested that they believed their needs were being strongly met by the supervisor and they were thus committed to him. Under these conditions, the supervisor was able to stress certain values and priorities consistent with organizational requirements (e.g., high productivity and quality of service) with assurance of compliance by the group.

In dealing with these and other issues, the supervisor was highly dependent upon group decision making. The group was expected to perform at high levels and all feedback on individual performance was shared. Thus, the group was able to monitor whether each individual member was carrying his or her own weight.

Rituals developed within the group acted as rewards or sanctions. For example, some members would make certain comments or use teasing behaviors in group meetings which sent a clear positive or negative implicit message to the receiver.

Results over time usually indicated improved group and individual performance, consistent with expectations of the supervisor. Interestingly, it was rarely necessary for this supervisor to use external methods of control, such as special individual monitoring, disciplinary measures or adverse actions in controlling his employees.

What is employee centered control?

It is a highly decentralized form of control that focuses on intrinsically motivated employee action. **Intrinsic motivation** refers to a desire to do or accomplish something because of internal self reward (i.e., it feels good). Thus, an employee who works toward organizational goals because of intrinsic satisfactions, obtained from the work itself or the work environment, is exerting employee centered control.

Employee centered control differs from management centered control in the types of rewards and who controls their distribution. The former uses intangible, affective rewards chosen directly by the receiver (employee). The latter uses tangible rewards, chosen by the manager, that will presumably generate the affect desired by management. That affect, e.g., satisfaction or fear, would then presumably control future behavior. Thus, management centered control is likely to be perceived as more manipulative than employee centered control. This may be significant, especially to professional employees who have strong expectations for autonomy or freedom from external control. In these situations, systems engineered around the use of employee centered control may help avoid excessive energy wasting consequences, such as high levels of employee resistance, conflict with management and staff turnover.

Employee centered control requires modifying the physical and psychological work environment to produce the conditions for intrinsic motivation of employees toward work unit goals. When this is done, less management energy should be needed for external controls (as in the bureaucratic mechanism). Some process and output specificity and measurability is desirable, however, so that employees may use objective feedback as a basis for future actions. For example, receiving monthly data on the statuses and results of a rehabilitation caseload may help a counselor decide on the actions he or she wishes to take to achieve better results for clients.

How does employee centered control relate to group centered control?

Group centered control involves an employee centered component. Although the clan mechanism depends upon an implicit, subtle form of external control (different from the bureaucratic mechanism), it also allows for individuals to receive intrinsic rewards by choosing behaviors that facilitate success of the group. Thus, individuals may generate feelings of achievement or satisfaction or competence by doing what is viewed as best for the group.

How can management engineer a work environment that supports employee centered control?

This can be done by creating and supporting a social environment and structure of work assignments that meets important employee needs (including autonomy and self control), as well as organization needs. Employee needs and motivational factors must be joined to an appropriate work environment that satisfies the goals of the organization by directing maximum employee energy toward these purposes. For example, projects and tasks could be assigned according to employee interests and special skills. In addition, greater autonomy could be allowed in deciding how to provide services to clients. Such arrangements might best allow professional employees to meet self actualization needs while achieving high agency performance. Job enrichment strategies discussed in Chapter 8 are consistent with this approach.

The above is an ideal concept, since employee needs can usually never be completely integrated with organizational needs. There will usually be differences which can only be resolved through external forms of control.

What is money centered control?

It is a highly decentralized form of control that uses tangible rewards (money) from outside the organization as the motivator of employee behavior. Employees retain the choice to produce work behaviors in direct proportion to the amount of money desired or possible. This differs from management centered control, in which the type and timing of reinforcement is under external (management) control; and from pure employee centered control in which rewards are also self generated, but intangible.

Money centered control uses the market mechanism as described by Ouchi (1979). This mechanism requires the existence of prices and a price mechanism which controls the distribution of rewards. In effect, control becomes implicit because a market determines financial value. Financial value then determines work performance, since that is linked to a reward (money) which is perceived (by the employee) as one of high priority and importance. Private practices in human services operate within the market model context.

The market mechanism requires clear enough specification and measurability of outputs and processes so that they can be valued by consensus in the marketplace. This can be done for many human services activities. For example, a market value can be placed on individual or group psychotherapy sessions and different types and quality of medical services. The market mechanism also requires very little management or other organizational energy, since the market outside of the organization determines the rules and rewards. Thus, when workable, money centered control as expressed through the market mechanism, is very efficient.

When can money centered control be used in a human services agency?

This can be done when a price structure can be established for services, when a market for those services exists and when staff can be compensated on the basis of fees generated. This is often possible in private for profit agencies, but usually not in publicly supported facilities.

CONTROL RESEARCH

What are some relevant research findings on how organizations can use macro control effectively?

On the basis of a review of control research, Tannenbaum (1968) suggested that optimum employee adjustment (satisfaction and performance) occurs under conditions of high total control in organizations. This means that strong centralized control by management **and** strong decentralized control by employees **both** exist. He argues that when organization members perceive a strong sense of personal control, they tend to be satisfied and committed. However, strong centralized control is also needed to provide direction, such as goals and methods; and the leadership required to move uniformly in that direction.

Are there any findings specific to human services agencies?

Some positive relationships have been demonstrated between centralized control, and objective productivity and efficiency measures (Glisson and Martin, 1980; Whetten, 1978). Also, factors associated with centralization such as formalized procedures; clear rules, guidelines and policies; and clear, feasible agency goals and their effective communication, have demonstrated productivity or other performance enhancing effects (Mott, 1972; Olmstead and Christensen, 1973).

The findings relating centralization to quality of services in human services organizations are mixed. Hage (1974), for example, found that high centralization was inconsistent with the high levels of feedback and socialization needed by medical service providers for quality control of complex processes. However, some evidence exists that centralization may be a quality enhancing factor under certain conditions (Friedlander, 1970; Porter, et al, 1975). These conditions exist when tasks are more complex than employee skills, knowledge and experience can handle, and when a stable environment allows for programming of tasks and functions without sacrificing needed spontaneity. Also, in some human services agencies, centralization should enhance quality when rules and procedures must be standardized in order to meet legal requirements fairly and uniformly.

Although centralization appears to have some performance enhancing potential in human services agencies, other evidence suggests it has a negative relationship with employee satisfaction. More decentralized patterns of control or power sharing seem associated with more satisfied, concerned employees (Bachman and Tannenbaum, 1968; Glisson and Martin, 1980; Morse and Reimer, 1956; Shaw, 1955; Whetten, 1978). Thus, human services research also suggests a rationale for both high centralized and decentralized control strategies.

MACRO CONTROL AND ORGANIZATIONAL STRUCTURE: INTEGRATION

What is the relationship between macro control and structure of the organization?

A proposed relationship between control and structure is illustrated in Table IV. Greater centralization and more use of external controls appears consistent with the nature of taller structures. Taller structures are likely to develop in situations where more management control is needed or appropriate.

As the center of control is moved toward the work group and individuals, it becomes possible to establish flatter structures, with fewer layers of management. These are leaner, more cost efficient organizations. Theoretically, the market model, which is the most decentralized can be the flattest organization, since the least amount of internal management control is needed.

In reality, neither structures, nor control models are likely to exist as

TABLE IV
MACRO CONTROL AND ORGANIZATIONAL STRUCTURE

Type of Control

Decentralized————————————————————————————————Centralized

Focus of Control

Outside Organization————————Employee————————Social————————External/Management

Control Model

Money Centered————Employee Centered————Group Centered————Management Centered

Organizational Structure

Flatter————————————————————————————————————Taller

pure types. Organizations are taller or flatter or have mixed structures, with some external, social, employee and sometimes outside organization control.

What kind of control-structure relationships should management strive for?

Group and employee centered controls, and structures that are as flat as possible, are least costly. In human services agencies, such controls and structures also seem consistent with employee satisfaction. However, it is also crucial to have enough centralized control and appropriate structures to insure that adequate direction exists and is communicated, and that agency goals and requirements are met.

How can this be done?

A necessary skill of managers is to understand the work, the work force, and the environment in which the agency functions. This helps to engineer structure and control in an optimal manner. Any changes made may be minor, such as in a large bureaucratic agency where little change is possible, or they could involve slowly restructuring the agency and modifying the entire control philosophy over a period of years. The following chapters examine more specific approaches to achieving optimal control.

Chapter 8

EMPLOYEE MOTIVATION

Why are managers interested in employee motivation?

They are concerned about getting work done in the way intended, at the lowest possible cost. Thus, they must try to maintain a workforce which is motivated to do what is needed, with minimum managerial energy spent on corrective action and problem resolution (direct control). In addition, highly motivated employees help an organization reach its greatest potential for **excellent** performance.

Managing employee motivation sounds manipulative. Is it?

Motivating employees does not imply that managers always know what is needed or that they try to manipulate employees to do what they don't want to do. However, employee interests and needs are not always consistent with organization goals. It is part of the management role to assure that such conflicts are resolved for the good of the organization's purposes.

How can managers resolve such organization-employee motivation conflicts?

This requires consideration of ways in which to satisfy both organizational needs and employee concerns, when possible. Failure to adequately consider employee factors contributes to dissatisfied, less motivated workers. This may lead to higher operating costs due to staff turnover, lower employee interest in high performance, and greater need for direct management control (e.g., closer supervision and responses to complaints, grievances, and increased labor union activity). On the other hand, failure to meet organizational needs leads to inefficiency, ineffectiveness, lack of direction and eventual organization failure. Thus, although managers must be concerned with employee needs and related motivational factors, this is a means to the end of effectively accomplishing the purposes of the organization.

Are there any special problems in this area for human services managers?

Human services managers with a direct service background must be particularly sensitive to the importance of meeting organizational needs, since there may be a tendency to take management action based upon purely humanistic concerns. For example, a manager may avoid taking a disciplinary action because of its potential effect on the feelings of the employee. However, avoidance may be detrimental to the agency or to other employees. Thus, **organizational needs** would dictate taking the disciplinary action.

THE NATURE OF EMPLOYEE MOTIVATION

What is the essence of employee motivation?

According to Gellerman (1963), human behavior in job situations is characterized by people seeking some form of "psychological advantage." In effect, individuals tend to pursue what they perceive to be in their best interests, depending upon what they see as possible and desirable, considering the environment and their ability to affect it. What is perceived in one's best interests could be pay, certain job characteristics, social rewards, a group of factors with different priorities and so forth.

What determines ones best interests?

This depends on factors such as needs, preferences, expectations, culture, personality structure and the work environment.

What is the managers role from an employee motivation perspective?

It is the managers job to help employees seek and find psychological advantage or meet their best interests, while meeting the best interests of the organization. Often, as employees perceive genuine concern about their best interests through the actions of their employer, they become more concerned about complying with the employer's interests. Such **commitment** represents an optimum state of motivation that contributes to the need for less direct management control and lower organization costs.

MAJOR APPROACHES TO EMPLOYEE MOTIVATION

What are the major approaches to employee motivation?

Several theories have been advanced including Maslow's need hierarchy, Herzberg's two factor and related theory, behavioral approaches and expectancy theory. Much of the academic focus has been on needs, preferences, rewards and expectations, suggesting that they are major influencers of employee motivation.

What is Maslow's theory?

Maslow (1954) proposed that human needs are arranged in a five level hierarchy. From the top of the hierarchy to the bottom, these include:

Self Actualization — This is the need to fulfill one's self; to use one's abilities to the maximum and most creative extent. This level is sometimes referred to as **growth needs.**

Esteem — This refers to the need for self esteem; respect, prestige and recognition granted by others; and a sense of competence.

Social — This is the need for a sense of belongingness, love and affection in relationships with others.

Safety — This is the need for a sense of security, protection and stability in the physical and interpersonal aspects of daily life.

Physiological — These are biological maintainance needs, such as for food, water and sex. Physiological needs are the most basic for life existence.

According to the theory, as needs are satisfied at lower levels, higher level needs emerge. For example, needs for esteem and self actualization will not emerge until physiological, safety and social needs are sufficiently satisfied. In the work setting this translates to the requirement to satisfy needs for a reasonable (livable) salary and benefits, and reasonably satisfying relationships with peers and supervisor, before one will be most concerned with gaining special recognition and being highly creative. Thus, if lower level needs are not adequately satisfied by the employer, attempts to motivate employees through other methods, such as through challenging job duties, may have a diminished effect.

Maslow's theory suggests that only unsatisfied needs motivate. However, satisfaction at the self actualization level increases motivation toward reaching higher levels of potential and capacity. Thus, after one has satisfied lower level needs, providing tasks that require creativity and skills consistent with abilities should continue to enhance motivation.

Does research support Maslow's theory?

According to reviews by Korman (1977) little or no support is found for the need hierarchy or for hypotheses dealing with the motivational aspects of unsatisfied needs.

What then is the value of the theory?

It has common sense appeal, and is easy to understand and apply. Generally, it provides a framework for application of common sense principles in work settings. For example, a minimum salary and benefits are needed to satisfy very basic needs (e.g., food, shelter, safety). If those needs are not minimally satisfied, one can hardly expect employees to concentrate mostly on meeting psychological growth needs through their work.

What is Herzberg's theory?

Herzberg's theory (Herzberg, Mausner and Snyderman, 1959) applies specifically to the workplace. The theory proposes that two factors influence worker satisfaction and dissatisfaction:

Motivational Factors (satisfiers)—These are conditions related to the work which lead to **motivation** and **job satisfaction**. If they are **not** present, however, they do not lead to dissatisfaction. The factors identified include **achievement, recognition, advancement, the work itself, personal growth possibilities,** and **responsibility**. Motivational factors are generated through employee-job interactions.

Maintenance or Hygiene Factors (dissatisfiers)—These are job conditions which lead to **dissatisfaction** if they are absent. However, their presence does not build satisfaction or motivation. Maintenance factors include **company policy and administration, technical supervision, relationships with supervisors, peers and subordinates, salary, job security, ones personal life, work conditions,** and **status**. Maintenance or hygiene factors are peripheral to the job itself.

Per this theory, the organization should try to minimize dissatisfiers by assuring the presence of the maintenance factors, while structuring the work to allow for the motivational factors to operate.

Does research support Herzberg's theory?

Studies using Herzberg's methodology tend to find satisfying events associated with job content factors and dissatisfying events associated with job context factors, as predicted by the theory. However, studies using other methodologies find that satisfaction or dissatisfaction can be related to job content, job context or both. Also, some job dimensions such as achievement, responsibility and recognition are more important to both satisfaction and dissatisfaction than other job dimensions, such as working conditions, company policies and practices, and security (Dunnette, Campbell and Hakel, 1967).

What is the value of the theory?

Although there are conflicting research findings and the theory may be method bound (i.e., it's support depends on using Herzberg's research methods), it does provide an easy to understand framework for focusing on intrinsic motivation, which was used as an early basis for job enrichment programs.

What is job enrichment?

Job enrichment involves increasing the number of activities involved in a job (**job enlargement**), and increasing the workers degree of control over the job (to include more autonomy, responsibility and discretion) (Donnelly, Gibson and Ivancevich, 1984; Huse, 1975; Korman, 1977). Huse (1975) refers to this as "providing 'the whole person' with a 'whole job.'" The whole job consists of the elements of planning the job, doing it, and evaluating it, i.e., obtaining feedback and taking corrective actions as needed.

What are some specific approaches to job enrichment?

In accordance with Herzberg's theory, job enrichment involves restructuring jobs to enhance motivational factors. For example, a counselor's job might be expanded to include periodic challenging projects which lead to special recognition when completed effectively.

A second approach involves the theory of core job dimensions (Hackman, Oldham, Janson and Purdy, 1974). This theory suggests that jobs can be restructured by enrichment along five essential dimensions. When this is done for employees who have strong growth needs, the work is perceived as more meaningful, employees experience more responsibility for work outcomes, and they obtain greater knowledge of work results. This leads to increased internal motivation, high quality performance, high satisfaction with the work, and low absenteeism and turnover.

The five core job dimensions are:

Skill Variety — This refers to the variety of skills needed to perform the job.

Task Identity — This dimension refers to performing a complete job (vs. only part of the job). For example, high task identity in a rehabilitation counselor position would involve working with clients through the whole rehabilitation process, from intake to the point of successful adjustment to employment. Positions with less task identity would involve performing only specialized functions with clients, e.g., outreach, vocational assessment, training assistance, or job placement.

Task Significance — This is the impact a job has on others, i.e., how important is it to others? For example, assigning a group of staff psychologists to develop a new employee assistance program for their agency could add task significance to their jobs. This would result because the total job now has a broader and more significant impact on others than before.

Autonomy — This refers to the degree of independence, freedom, and discretion that the employee has in doing the job. Positions with more autonomy allow increased control over what is done, how, and when it is done.

Feedback — This is the amount of information an employee receives regarding the adequacy of his or her work. It is probably most effective when coming directly from the work itself, rather than from another source (Huse, 1975). For example, routine case management feedback regarding caseload composition, case dispositions and productivity, can often be provided through computer printouts.

The core job dimensions model can be used in a systematic manner through use of the **Job Diagnostic Survey** (Hackman and Oldham, 1974). This instrument can help analyze the amount and quality of core dimensions for each job. Further information on formal use of the model is provided by Donnelly, Gibson and Ivancevich (1987) and Huse (1975).

How effective are job enrichment approaches?

Research indicates mixed results. Studies regarding the core job dimensions model suggest that **satisfaction** and **motivation** may be enhanced with job enrichment, for **people with high growth needs.** However, job enrichment efforts may not impact similarly on **job performance**. Generally, there is also some concern about how long job enrichment effects last (Hackman, Oldham, Johnson and Purdy, 1974; Donnelly, Gibson & Ivancevich, 1987).

From a practical perspective, job enrichment may work in some situations and not in others. For example, where a highly trained (or increasingly qualified) professional work force is functioning in a specialized and closely controlled environment, job enrichment according to the core job dimensions model may provide new found and desired freedom to employees. Similarly, in a situation where employees receive poor feedback on work results, improved feedback may have a profound effect on work interest, satisfaction, motivation and performance. On the other hand, where jobs are already fairly enriched or when employees are not overly concerned about such things, job enrichment could be a costly, ineffective attempt at motivation.

Job enrichment need not always be extensive or formalized. Sometimes simple changes that impact on one core dimension may make a significant difference. For example, supervisors who understand their employees' needs and interests can consistently make work assignments or minor changes that increase the challenge of the job, significance of the work, or increase the perception of job autonomy.

Are there other major approaches related to Maslow's and Herzberg's?

The concepts of intrinsic and extrinsic motivation have already been partially considered in Chapter 7 with regard to the control models discussed. **Intrinsic motivation** is based upon self initiated behaviors, related to the work itself, which lead to affectual rewards (such as feelings of achievement, satisfaction or competence). **Extrinsic motivation** is based upon satisfactions derived from external sources, i.e., rewards controlled by someone else and independent of interaction with the work activity itself. As implied in Chapter 7, it is generally desirable to encourage intrinsic motivation of employees toward the goals of the organization.

Research on intrinsic and extrinsic rewards suggests that they are not always additive. For example, when an employee receives intrinsic satisfaction from a work activity, providing an extrinsic reward, such as a monetary bonus, will not necessarily increase motivation. In fact, research suggests that extrinsic incentives **decrease** intrinsic motivation when they are given (without regard for level of performance) for performing an activity over and over again that is already of high interest (Bandura,

1982). However, when such incentives are given for performance achievements, they appear to enhance further interest or motivation. In effect, when external rewards signify increased competence to the receiver, they seem to increase motivation. In these instances, the larger the reward, the greater the increase in interest in the activity (Bandura, 1982).

Intrinsic/extrinsic concepts are also related to the motivational aspects of **goal setting.** As noted in Chapter 3, goal setting tends to promote high performance. Per Bandura (1982), attainable short term goals provide standards against which to judge performance and self efficacy. When self efficacy can be confirmed through this process, then self (intrinsic) motivation is built. These findings support the motivational value of goal setting in planning, as well as the value of enriching jobs along several of the core job dimensions, e.g., task identity, task significance and feedback.

What is the behavior modification approach to employee motivation?

Most behavior modification programs are based upon the original works of Skinner (1953) and Thorndike (1911). These approaches focus on use of environmental reinforcers to shape desired behavior or behavior patterns.

Positive reinforcement involves presentation of a reward stimulus or stimuli, after the occurence of a desirable behavior or response. The reward increases the probability of the response's recurrence. Both extrinsic and intrinsic rewards may be used in work situations. Potential rewards include verbal praise (Huse, 1975), money, status, recognition, friendship, intrinsic rewards related to the work itself, skill acquisition, personal growth (Porter, 1973), freedom to choose work tasks, and opportunities for influence on management (Hamner, 1974).

Negative reinforcement involves removal of a negative or unpleasant stimulus or stimuli as a reward for a desired response. Removal of the negative stimulus increases the probability of the response's recurrence. For example, as one supervisor said (somewhat facetiously), "I reward my employees. When they do what they are supposed to do, I stop threatening to fire them!"

Punishment (not to be confused with negative reinforcement), is direct application of a negative reinforcer (stimulus) to an undesired behavioral response, or removal of a reward, with the purpose of eliminating the behavior. For example, a direct statement of disapproval by the supervisor to an employee who reports late for work, or removal of a privilege, would constitute punishment.

Punishment does not appear to be effective in the long run. It may suppress behavior as long as the threat exists. However, the undesired behavior will tend to return when the threat of punishment is removed. It may also have negative emotional consequences, such as employee resentment or aggression toward the punisher.

An effective alternative to punishment is **extinction**. This involves removing any rewards for undesirable behavior. Eventually, the undesirable behavior should diminish.

Per the behavior modification approach, behavior persists because it is rewarded. Thus, rewards are used as the basis for shaping desired behaviors. Research on how frequently to reward responses (**reinforcement schedules**) suggests that providing a reward every time the desired response occurs results in the fastest initial learning. Once the response is learned, rewarding only on a periodic basis insures strong retention of the response (Donnelly, Gibson & Ivancevich, 1987; Hergenhahn, 1976; Huse, 1975).

How can behavior modification be applied from a practical standpoint?

All managers use behavior modification. However, to be most effective, the principles must be used consistently and systematically.

Generally, **positive reinforcement programs** have been effective in improving organizational performance (Huse, 1975). Such principles are also consistent with encouraging employees to feel good about themselves (or like "winners" per Peters and Waterman [1982]) and to feel positive about and committed to the organization. Positive reinforcement is also a significant component of goal setting and use of feedback in performance enhancement, as discussed earlier.

Punishment and the use of negative reinforcement are very common management practices. From a practical perspective, they are needed to maintain certain behaviors. For example, professional counselors might never do required paperwork or records maintenance without some threat. However, when these techniques become the main approach to employee motivation, undesirable consequences, such as complaints, resentment, and anti-management interactions become more evident.

Blanchard and Johnson (1982) suggest the use of a behavior modification approach using goal setting, positive reinforcement and punishment in their book **The One Minute Manager**. This approach reduces reinforcement principles to easily applicable terms for practicing managers:

encouraging employees to set goals; providing brief, immediate and genuine praise when goals or parts of goals are reached; and providing brief, immediate and genuine reprimands when goals are not achieved. Both praisings and reprimands are directed toward **behavior.** In all cases the employee is provided encouragement, and reprimands are never directed toward the employee as a person.

Other than reinforcement schedules, are there any guidelines on how to use rewards?

Vroom's theory (1964) provides some assistance in this area. It suggests that employees make choices regarding performance behaviors or intensity of work effort based on reward expectancies. Choices are based upon the belief that effort will lead to a particular level of performance and that a particular level of performance will lead to a desired reward.

When using this theory, managers must know their employees well. They must understand each employee's perceptions of performance capabilities and what rewards are valued. They must also be certain to provide the desired rewards when expected performance levels are achieved.

Vroom's theory fits neatly into previously discussed goal setting frameworks. The theory would suggest that realistic goals, jointly developed by manager and supervisor, set the stage for employee perceptions that desired behavior is known and achievable. However, management must then assure that the rewards are consistently provided according to employee expectations or appropriate reinforcement schedules. This is where such programs can easily break down.

If managers cannot provide the right rewards (particularly when pay incentives are implied for high performance), employee trust is lost and behavior modification value is reduced. Such breakdowns may also lead to employee resentment and anger, since employees may believe that management is not acting fairly. For example, some goal setting programs, e.g., management by objectives, imply that monetary rewards will be distributed on the basis of performance. However, if goals or objectives are set at low levels and all employees achieve their goals, **everyone** expects to get rewarded. If management does not have the resources to do that or chooses to compromise the system in order to reward fewer people, employees lose confidence in the system and its full motivational intent is reduced.

DEVELOPMENTAL FACTORS

What role does development play in employee motivation?

Adult and career development literature suggests that people pass through stages of development and periods of transition or reassessment throughout adulthood. Thus, during a career, the nature and intensity of ones work motivation may change.

How can information about development be useful to managers?

Information about typical behaviors, concerns, conflicts and crises in various stages of life can help managers understand how to tap the motivational potential of employees and to anticipate and cope with developmental motivation problems. For example, Table V presents a proposed taxonomy of problems, symptoms, and possible management interventions, along a developmental continuum.

How can the major findings of development research be summarized?

Theory and research has suggested that people go through alternating periods of growth and maintainance, often separated by periods of reassessment and change. To some extent, these periods are related to chronological age. Decline of work capacities often takes place toward the end of ones career due to physiological and psychological factors (Levinson et al, 1976; Vaillant, 1977; Buhler & Massanik, 1968; Super et al, 1963).

Several theorists have also proposed the existence of sequential stages of development. Moving from one stage to another requires successful resolution of or task mastery within the prior stage (Erikson, 1963; Hershenson, 1968).

What are some major areas in which managers can use developmental information?

Dealing with Young Employees — Young employees in the early stage of their careers may be focusing on vocational and other identity issues, as well as intimacy and interpersonal concerns. There may be uncertainty regarding commitment to a specific career or to the goals of the organization. During this period, professionals may be highly committed to their profession, but have low commitment to organizational goals. In some instances, particularly among non professional employees, identity as a "worker" may not be developed enough to assure basic work habits. This

TABLE V
DEVELOPMENTAL PROBLEMS AND INTERVENTIONS

Type of Problem	Symptoms	When Likely to Occur	Possible Management Interventions
Work entry or reentry adjustment	Frequent lateness or absenteeism; Social problems on the job; Dissatisfaction with job; Poor performance, e.g., errors, low productivity; Defiant attitude; Impatience with not being promoted	At entry into first job; At reentry after long periods of not working	Assignment of peer teacher; Intensive initial training and orientation to the system and job; Employee counseling; Upward mobility programs; Active implementation of affirmative action programs
Expansion Needs	Intense desire to advance, obtain training or be rewarded for current job efforts; Job dissatisfaction; Anger toward supervisors or agency for not allowing advancement	During or just after transition periods	Provide job advancement opportunities; Encourage further education and training; Provide more challenging assignments in same job; Provide trial or transitional assignments at higher level; Provide opportunities for creative assignments, e.g., projects; Provide recognition for *genuine* accomplishments; Refer for employee counseling
Stagnation Problems	Loss of motivation or job interest; Negativism; Resentment toward supervisors and the organization; Feelings of job discrimination; Over concerns with self protection; Isolation from other workers;	If expansion needs cannot be satisfied or if life transitions and readjustments are delayed	Job reassignment; Provide more challenging assignments in same job; Refresher training programs; Threat of job termination if improvement does not occur; Job termination action; Refer for employee counseling

TABLE V (Continued)

Type of Problem	Symptoms	When Likely to Occur	Possible Management Interventions
	Resentment of other workers achievements or privileges; Absenteeism and/or poor job performance		
Decline Problems	Increased errors; Judgement problems; Decreased productivity; Absenteeism; Compulsive overwork	During later adulthood; During or after chronic illness	Job reassignments; Alteration of job duties in the same position; Retirement preparation programs; Retirement counseling; Referral for employee counseling

may be seen through problems with tardiness, leave abuse and over-socialization on the job.

Early career adjustment is critical from an organizational standpoint. It may determine the length and extent of the employee's contribution and the amount of future management control that will be needed. Managers can impact on motivation of employees in this phase by establishing clear expectations for behavior and performance, providing strong initial job training and orientation to the organization, and assigning peer teachers or encouraging mentor relationships. Mentors may be particularly important in helping younger employees to constructively pass through developmental stages and to reinforce positive work motivation.

Experiencing psychological success early in ones career may be important in establishing work as a central life interest or main source of satisfaction. Managers can facilitate this process by assuring an ability match and growth oriented supervision in the first job, as well as an opportunity to satisfy higher level needs if they exist.

Managing Transitional Periods — As employees end the early stage of their career (typically in later twenties or early thirties) they may enter a period in which a decision must be made to become more committed to the career or to make major changes (e.g., change to a new career). This may begin a period of psychological turmoil which culminates in a stage of creativity and productivity as one settles into a new career or deepens commitment to the original career. A similar, but perhaps more tumultuous period may occur in the later thirties, forties or even beyond, when ones entire life structure and goals may be questioned. During these transitions, managers can assist by providing direct support, help through employee assistance programs, and possibilities for other career track opportunities. Motivation during these periods may be reinforced through providing experiences that help employees resolve issues of concern. Examples are training and education, rewards for effective job results, more challenging or creative assignments, transitional or trial work assignments at a higher level, greater work autonomy, and sometimes by providing opportunities to be a mentor.

Failure of employees to deal adequately with transitional problems can lead to symptoms of job stagnation, such as negativism, loss of job interest, or resentment toward management. This may sometimes be related to expected job promotions that never materialize. Table V presents some possible interventions in these situations.

Employees in Maintenance Periods — After transitional experiences and in the later stages of a career, employees may settle down to performing the current job with few developmental problems. At this point, there is less concern about promotion or other change, and more interest in genuinely doing an effective job. Motivation during these periods may be facilitated through providing work requiring greater skill and experience, and by providing mentoring opportunities.

Dealing with Older Employees — Toward later ages and the latter stages of the career, symptoms of decline may occur. These include slowed productivity, increased errors, difficulties in adjusting to change and absenteeism due to illness. However, these may be partially balanced by the positive effects of increased job knowledge and experience, and well developed positive work habits. During the later career stages, employees may feel a sense of ego integrity (Erikson, 1963) during which they feel content with their life and its outcome. However, some may feel unfulfilled, depressed, or regretful about the past and feel a desire to have done things differently. Such employees may make attempts to compensate for this through their work using such mechanisms as compulsive overwork; or if they are managers, by making excessive demands on staff. Management interventions at this stage can include job reassignments, alteration of responsibilities in the current job, and retirement preparation programs.

Are there other implications of employee development for managers?

Employee development factors are sometimes important in employee selection. For example, a department consisting of all young professionals may be difficult to manage due to an inability to provide everyone advancement and growth opportunities. This may result in dissatisfaction, excessive competition and dissension. It is often better to have a mix of staff in different stages of development. Those who are in maintenance phases tend to provide stability and seasoned experience while serving as organizational and professional role models. Those in growth phases facilitate high productivity, creativity, and change.

MOTIVATION OF HUMAN SERVICES PROFESSIONALS

Are there any unique factors to consider in the motivation of professional employees?

Yes. Such employees often have expectations originating from the process of choosing a professional career, and from self concept development during the preparation period. Expectations may include good working conditions, status, power and high income. In human services, expectations of status and autonomy are reinforced, as well as a commitment to placing the client's interests first. At higher levels of training and professionalism, low tolerance for outside structure and organizational control may also be internalized.

Gouldner (1958) has identified a cosmopolitan versus a local dimension exhibited by professional employees, that may affect organizational commitment. **Cosmopolitans** are highly committed to their specialized role skills and consider the profession as their main reference group. **Locals** are high on organizational loyalty and low on commitment to specialized role skills. For locals, the organization is the main reference group. Locals tend to make a rapid adjustment to organizations, demonstrate less turnover than cosmopolitans, and are more likely to use rules and regulations to solve problems.

Is there one significant factor that stands out as a problem for organizations in motivating professionals?

Yes. The desire for autonomy among professionals seems almost universal. This clearly contrasts with the desire of organizations to maintain control and to impose constraints, even though the constraints may be legitimate (Etzioni, 1969). For example, rules pertaining to vocational rehabilitation practice in public agencies must be imposed due to legal requirements and need to demonstrate accountability in expending public funds. Also, newer, or emerging professions such as rehabilitation counseling may not generate the confidence to allow levels of autonomy normally granted to more established or highly trained professions. Thus, agencies may impose more constraints on the former through standardized rules and procedures. However, since such professionals have expectations similar to other professionals, considerable dissatisfaction, resistance and non-compliance may result.

Are there any unique factors to consider in the motivation of human services professionals?

Findings of Olmstead and Christensen (1973) suggest that human services professionals seek both intrinsic and extrinsic rewards. However, those with lower levels of formal education rated extrinsic rewards as higher in importance than those with more formal education. Also, results of this study suggested that human services professionals attached higher values to altruism, achievement, self actualization and helping others than to work recognition or advancement.

The interests of human services workers are also of some relevance. Theory and research presented by Holland (1973), for example, suggests that social and conventional interests are not highly consistent. This could indicate a tendency toward **rejection** of activities of a structured, routine, clerical and recordkeeping nature for those who are most dominant in social interests. This may be a significant factor for managers to consider when structuring jobs in human services agencies. For example, assignment of many clerical tasks may be perceived as more tolerable by an auditor, accountant or manager, than by a social worker or counselor.

OTHER FACTORS

Are there other factors that might contribute significantly to employee motivation?

Managers should consider the **expectations** of employees. For example, selection of new employees with expectations that can be met contributes to a more fulfilled, less demanding workforce. Also, comparative importance of expectations of the organization's workforce may be significant, e.g., is job satisfaction a greater expectation than salary increases?

Data from Peters and Waterman's (1982) study suggests that **work cultures** characterized by an atmosphere of extensive positive reinforcement are effective in making people feel and behave like "winners," to the benefit of organizational performance. This differs from behavior modification programs, in that many of the reinforcers develop naturally out of the group culture, rather than from the direct plans and actions of management. The cultural approach can thus be viewed as less manipulative and consuming of management energy, over the long run.

CONCLUSIONS AND APPLICATIONS

What conclusions can be drawn from this diverse information about employee motivation?

The intent of employee motivation is to efficiently achieve desired performance and results. Over the long run, this can be accomplished by maintaining an environment where employees can achieve psychological advantage while meeting organizational needs. Ideally, this means providing reinforcers in the environment that facilitate strong feelings of **commitment** to the organization by employees. Efficiency can probably be increased further when intrinsic motivation can be activated, since this results in greater self control and less need to use management energy for externally based control.

Although providing the conditions for employees to achieve psychological advantage can be beneficial, it can also be costly. Benefits to the organization, in the form of improved long term performance or other significant results, should always be expected to exceed the costs of such actions.

In recent years, much has been written about the value of quality of work life (QWL) programs in which organizations are changed extensively to improve the quality of workplace experiences for employees. Enhancements may range from extensive employee benefits, and a highly democratic workplace, to child care, health care, recreational, and exercise programs and facilities. Emener and Stephens (1982) have, in fact, recommended certain QWL interventions for rehabilitation agencies.

In considering recommendations for QWL improvements, it is suggested that managers carefully consider the long term benefits versus the costs.

Only those changes that are likely to achieve significant results in a cost beneficial manner should be selected.

What are some specific actions that human services managers can take to enhance employee motivation?

First, it is probably important, when possible, to meet needs and expectations related to Maslow's lower level needs (physiological, safety, social) and Herzberg's maintenance factors. This should facilitate employee ability to focus on intrinsic satisfactions from the work itself and the environment. When such needs and expectations are not at least minimally satisfied, employees are likely to spend too much energy on complaining, social commiseration, and looking for other jobs. Managers should try to keep salary and benefits at competitive levels, maintain enough staff to keep caseload sizes reasonable, minimize clerical and paperwork requirements for professional staff, provide an adequate amount and quality of supervision, and maintain a reasonably low conflict social environment.

Second, organization structure, jobs, leadership styles (discussed in Chapter 10), and management strategies should be designed to support intrinsic motivation, as possible and desired by employees. This requires managers to understand the types of reinforcers that will enhance motivation of their employees. Specific methods of increasing intrinsic motivation include providing more autonomy, job enrichment, job rotation (periodically moving employees to different jobs), training and educational opportunities, participation in management decision making, delegation of responsibility, establishing specialized structures (see Chapter 6), developing cohesive, positive work group cultures, and use of realistic goal setting with performance information feedback.

Third, extrinsic rewards, such as monetary bonuses and concrete benefits may help establish desired behaviors and behavior patterns, when used systematically and consistently. Such rewards should be distributed in a manner that enhances rather than decreases intrinsic motivation. Also, in order to maintain employee trust in performance contingent reward systems, rewards must be provided consistently when the expected level of performance is achieved. Individual or group goal/objective setting, with regular feedback, followed by extrinsic rewards for high performance should satisfy all of the above conditions for effective use of extrinsic rewards.

Fourth, the perceived best interests of rehabilitation and human services professionals seem oriented toward autonomous functioning, social tasks related to client servicing, intrinsic rewards as educational level increases, altruism, achievement, self actualization and helping others. These factors should be considered in structuring job tasks for such employees.

Lastly, an awareness of developmental factors by managers may be important in helping employees to find psychological advantage, and in meeting organizational needs. This information should be used in job design, job reassignment, selecting a balanced work force, and in diagnosing and dealing with employee problems.

Chapter 9

EMPLOYEE SELECTION

What is employee selection?

Employee selection involves choosing employees for positions in the organization. This may include selections from the pool of current employees, or from a pool of potential applicants outside the organization. Employee selection involves five phases:

Establishing position qualifications
Recruitment of candidates
Initial screening of candidates
Final screening of candidates
Final Selection

What is the significance of effective employee selection?

Employee selection is one of the single most important management activities. Choice of employees that have the knowledge, skills, abilities, and type of motivation needed, **at the time they enter the organization or job,** reduces future control costs. For example, experienced, well educated, high ability counselors are likely to reduce the need for training and close professional supervision. Similarly, employees who have a track record of strong basic work habits (punctuality, good attendance, submit their work on time and respond appropriately to agency rules and supervision) require little time for close general supervision, disciplinary and adverse actions. Also, potential employees who have a work philosophy and expectations consistent with organization policies are more likely to commit themselves to the goals and objectives of the organization, without special management efforts. In effect, quality of selection decisions significantly influences effectiveness of and amount of resources needed for control.

What are the characteristics of an effective employee selection process?

First, the process should lead to choosing the best qualified candidates. This is the main goal of employee selection.

Second, selection procedures should be consistent with legal requirements and guidelines. This requires that the process be nondiscriminatory (or that affirmative action procedures be followed where specified) per Title VII of the Civil Rights Act of 1964, the Equal Employment Opportunity Act of 1972, and the Rehabilitation Act of 1973. These laws cover employment actions with regard to race, religion, age, creed, sex, national origin, disability and veteran status. Failure to follow legal requirements and guidelines can result in costly discrimination complaints and legal actions by job applicants. When such actions occur, the burden of proof lies with the **employer** to prove nondiscrimination. In some instances, employers may also be subject to loss of government contracts when employment related laws are violated.

Thirdly, the employee selection process should be fair and unbiased. For example, information should be obtained in a way that provides equal opportunity to all candidates to allow relevant information to become known. A potentially incriminating question, or one that assesses special skills, should not be asked of one candidate and not of others. Although this relates to complying with legal requirements, it also assures that all facts needed for the most effective selections are assessed uniformly by selecting officials.

Are there any general guidelines for making effective, legal and fair selection decisions?

Yes. The **Uniform Guidelines on Employee Selection** issued jointly by the Equal Employment Opportunity Commission (EEOC), the Office of Personnel Management (OPM), the Department of Justice (DOJ), and the Department of Labor (DOL), provide a basis for valid, legally defensible (non discriminatory) and fair selection decisions.

What is the legal basis of the Uniform Guidelines?

As noted earlier, when a discrimination complaint is made, the burden of proof lies with the employer to prove non discrimination. If the employer can show that "adverse impact" on the protected group to which the complainant belongs **does not exist** within the organization, then a non-discriminatory selection process has usually been proven.

Adverse impact is a term that can be defined by rule of thumb using the "four fifths rule." Per Elliott (1985), the four fifths rule is explained as follows:

> If the selection rate of a protected group is not at least four-fifths (80 percent) of the rate of the group with the highest rate of selection, then adverse impact is present for that protected group. An example is in order here. If an employer receives applications from 100 whites and hires 60, the selection rate for whites is 60/100 or 60 percent. If, for the same group of jobs, the employer receives applications from 40 blacks and hires 10, the selection rate from blacks is 10/40 or 25 percent. If a total of 30 hispanics apply and 15 are hired, the hispanic selection rate is 15/30 or 50 percent. . . .
>
> Using the definition of adverse impact contained in the guidelines, let us determine if adverse impact present in this example. Keep in mind that the selection rate for any group must be at least 80 percent of the selection rate of the group with the highest rate of selection or adverse impact is present, and the burden of proof will be on the employer. The group with the highest rate of selection is the group of whites (60 percent). The blacks are selected at a rate of 25 percent which is not 80 percent of the rate of the group of whites; therefore, adverse impact is present for blacks. The hispanic group is selected at a rate of 50 percent, which is at least 80 percent of the selection rate of whites (60 percent); therefore, adverse impact is not present for the hispanics in this example.

If the employer cannot demonstrate the absence of adverse impact, then the employer must demonstrate that the selection process is job related. The Uniform Guidelines provide a recognized basis for doing this. In effect, they provide guidelines for selection that assure assessment of candidates according to job related criteria. Although they refer to the term "tests" in the assessment process, that term refers broadly to any information used as a basis for selection, such as interview data, information from application forms, information from references, psychometric test data, and other forms of information.

Specifically, what do the Uniform Guidelines include?

The Uniform Guidelines define standards for assuring **validity** of selection related tests. Test procedures must demonstrate either content validity, criterion related validity or construct validity in order to be considered non discriminatory.

Content validity requires that the test content accurately reflects the content of the job. **Criterion related validity** requires that the selection criteria show a statistical relationship to successful job performance, usually through a correlation coefficient. **Construct validity** requires that constructs presumed as measured are themselves validated and then subjected to criterion related validity procedures (Elliott, 1985). Criterion related and construct validity procedures are most applicable to psychometric tests, while content validity procedures may be applicable to other selection procedures as well as psychometric tests. The employee selection procedures discussed in this chapter are intended to be consistent with the content validity model of the Uniform Guidelines.

ESTABLISHING POSITION QUALIFICATIONS

What is the process of establishing the necessary qualifications for a position?

A job analysis should first be conducted. Based upon this information, a listing of the knowledge, skills, abilities, and other factors (KSAOs) necessary to perform the job tasks is generated. The most important KSAOs may then be isolated for use in the selection process. These become the basis for establishing the basic educational and experience requirements for recruitment and initial screening purposes, and for conducting the final assessment of qualified candidates. Table VI lists examples of complete sets of KSAOs for use in selection of a psychologist and a clerk position.

How is the job analysis conducted?

Several methods are available to conduct job analyses. These include the critical incident technique, functional job analysis, the job element approach, or a combination of these methods (Elliott, 1985). The **critical incident technique** (Flanagan, 1954) obtains information through statements of critical incidents of successful and unsuccessful job behaviors written by those performing the job. These statements are then combined into categories of required job behaviors, such as "ability to effectively interpret test results to clients." The method may be impractical, however, since hundreds or thousands of critical incidents may need to be collected.

Functional job analysis (Fine & Wiley, 1971) involves describing the job in terms of structured, standardized task statements which include "a subject, an action verb, the object of the action, a purpose of the action, tools and equipment used in performing the action and the source of authority for performing the task" (Elliott, 1985). An example is "The

TABLE VI
KSAOS FOR PSYCHOLOGIST AND CLERK POSITIONS

Psychologist

1. Knowledge of physical, mental, and emotional disabilities and their effects on employability.
2. Knowledge of differential diagnostic assessment processes used in vocational, educational, rehabilitation or personal adjustment counseling.
3. Ability to relate to and effectively communicate with clients of differing age, sex, race, ethnicity, and socio-economic background.
4. Ability to apply a large body of rules and regulations, follow rules and procedures, work under time pressure and adjust to changing work situations.
5. Ability to develop (prioritize, plan, schedule, set goals and final objectives) a written plan of vocational or educational rehabilitation.

Clerk

1. Ability to communicate orally with people from a wide variety of backgrounds.
2. Skill in transferring information accurately from one document to another.
3. Ability to complete assignments within established timeframes.
4. Ability to extract specific data from numerous forms, files, manuals and records.

counselor aide contacts clients 6 months after they have obtained employment to determine whether they are still employed and whether they need further services, using the telephone and case records, and following procedural instructions in the operating manual as well as special instructions from the assigned rehabilitation counselor." These task statements are then used as a basis for determining the KSAOs.

The **job element approach** (Primoff, 1974) involves using a group of supervisors or expert workers to determine the job elements required for successful performance. These are then reduced to a small group of major elements. For example, in a psychologist's job, the element "skill in administering individual intelligence tests" might be isolated.

Are there any special methods for collecting job analysis information?

The **Position Analysis Questionnaire** (McCormick, Cunningham & Thornton, 1967) may be used for this purpose. It identifies several job dimensions including information sources required to perform the job, information processing and decision making needed, physical, dexterity, and interpersonal requirements, working conditions and reactions of people to those conditions, and other job characteristics (Donnelly, Gibson & Ivancevich, 1987). Other information sources such as interviews, direct observations and existing position descriptions may also be used.

What can be done to assure validity and legal defensibility of the job analysis and KSAOs?

Insuring objectivity can help. This can be done by using well trained job analysts, obtaining sufficient information about the job, using several subject matter experts (SMEs) (job incumbents) as part of the information gathering process, separating out important from trivial aspects of the job, separating out KSAOs necessary for job entry from those learned on the job (establishing the "true" minimum qualifications), and assuring **documentation** of each step in the job analysis process (for legal and standardization purposes) (Elliott, 1985).

RECRUITMENT OF CANDIDATES

What is involved in recruitment?

Recruiting involves locating qualified applicants to fill positions and encouraging participation in the application process. Recruitment may be conducted within the organization or outside.

What factors influence the recruitment process?

Important factors include availability of candidates, legal concerns, and labor relations agreements. Little formal recruitment may be needed when available jobs are highly desirable, e.g., due to salaries, benefits, or geographical location; or if many candidates are available in the labor market. On the other hand, more extensive efforts are needed when few candidates are available locally, or when adverse organization or geographic conditions exist.

Legal requirements may also dictate the direction of recruitment. For example, if evidence of adverse impact exists, or if an affirmative action plan is in effect, special obligations may exist to conduct extensive recruitment to attract candidates from protected groups.

Labor-management agreements may include provisions affecting recruitment. For example, it may be agreed that recruitment will first be conducted internally, before seeking candidates from outside the organization. This may require considering (or even hiring) any qualified applicant who already works for the organization before recruiting outside candidates, even if more qualified candidates are likely to be located from outside.

What is the process of recruitment?

Usually, a job is announced in writing, through posting (internally), or through newspaper ads, employment agencies, or professional publications. In public agencies, formal posting is usually required when the job is to be announced internally. The posting may include a description of the job, the qualification requirements and an application closing date. Public agency jobs may be announced externally through state employment services and directly through other sources, such as universities, using similar postings, or through newspaper ads or professional publications. Recruitment in private agencies may be less constrained by special rules, but attempts must still be made to avoid discriminatory practices, and to meet legal and existing labor-management agreement provisions.

Are there special recruiting techniques useful in the human services?

Maintaining relationships with universities, and establishing networks with other human services professionals can be helpful. These methods are useful in locating verifiably qualified candidates and candidates from protected groups, such as minority, women and disabled applicants. University relationships may be established through development of practicum and internship sites, teaching, committee work, and joint research ventures. Networks may be established through management participation in professional organizations, on interagency committees, and on advisory councils, at the national and local levels.

INITIAL SCREENING OF CANDIDATES

What is initial screening?

Initial screening involves review of application materials filed during the recruitment period, in order to eliminate unqualified or the least qualified applicants. After initial screening, only the best qualified applicants should remain for final assessment.

What is the initial screening process?

Job interest is usually expressed through submission of application forms, resumes or other requested credentials by applicants. Application materials are screened to eliminate those who do not meet minimum requirements. If a large number of applications remain, they may be subjected to a ranking procedure. This should be based upon amount and quality of required credentials and other factors related to the KSAOs. For example, applications for a counseling position in a hospital chemical dependency unit might be rated on amount and quality of counseling experience directly related to treatment of chemical dependency. Groups of employees (2 or 3 members) familiar with position requirements, should be used for rating and ranking purposes, with use of objective rating systems (such as assigning points for different levels of qualifications).

Upon completion of the list of candidates in rank order, those with the best credentials are then subjected to the next step of the screening process. In public systems, such as the federal government, this may require a final selection from the top three available candidates (when selecting from a listing of external candidates). In other situations, the number of candidates subject to final screening may be more arbitrary or judgemental.

FINAL SCREENING OF CANDIDATES

What is final screening?

This involves all further assessment needed to make a final and permanent selection. It includes more intensive analysis of applicant data with relation to the most specific requirements of the position.

Who does the final screening?

Usually the supervisor, department head or other person who will select the new employee (**selecting official**).

What final screening procedures help to assure valid, legal and fair selections?

Final screening should be based on a logical process of relating applicant qualifications to job requirements. The following procedures appear generally consistent with the Uniform Guidelines:

1. Determine the specific factors that are judged to be needed for an applicant to be successful in the job. These should be related to the selection KSAO's, and should also include essential work context factors. For example, one KSAO for a receptionist position may be "Ability to interact effectively with clients from a wide variety of backgrounds." Specific factors related to this KSAO for assessment during final screening might include nature of attitudes toward minority groups, verbal

communication skills, and attitudes toward the agency (which might be reflected in interactions with clients). The work context might be characterized by a loosely supervised work unit, but with many rules and procedures that need to be closely followed. A specific assessment factor related to work context might be the willingness and capacity to follow rules and procedures with minimal supervision.

2. When assessing applicant qualifications with relation to the specific factors, **measurable, observable** information should be used to the extent possible. Impressions, presumed traits or non job related information lack reliability, will not be supportable from a validity standpoint, and may be discriminatory.

3. The methods used and the types of information solicited should be consistent for all applicants. For example, if references are checked for one applicant, they should be checked for all. This prevents inadvertent loss of information or discrimination, by providing equal opportunity for positive or negative information to be obtained for all candidates.

When assessing applicant qualifications on specific factors, what type of information should be obtained and what are the best methods for obtaining it?

Information on background, historical performance, and skills is usually important. Verifiable information on interests and attitudes may also be helpful. When obtaining and evaluating information, both **assets** and **problem areas** should be addressed.

Reliable, factual background information is needed to assess the applicants specific experience, education and training with respect to the significant job factors identified. Additionally, in many instances historical information on performance (particularly in similar situations) should be a reasonable predictor of future performance. A worker who has been unable to carry out job tasks effectively or who was repeatedly unable to adjust to rules or supervision in prior jobs is at high risk to repeat those behaviors in a new job.

Information on background and past performance can best be obtained through information on the application, information in a personnel file, and from former supervisors. For example, the application may give detailed descriptions of prior job experience, college courses taken and inservice training received. It may also provide hints regarding past performance, such as recognition received in prior jobs, loss of jobs, or reasons for leaving prior jobs. However, background or performance information on an application may not be fully reliable, since job applicants often try to present a positive impression. Objective information from a personnel file (often available if the applicant works within the organization) may provide further information and serve to verify or refute applicant statements.

Information from prior supervisors can also be very useful, if the supervisor is willing to provide facts and give an honest performance assessment. Background facts may be easily obtained or verified. However, some supervisors are hesitant to provide performance information about former employees (particularly negative information) due to potential law suits, or to avoid saying anything that might be harmful to the employee's career. Generally, more useful information will be obtained if the supervisor is willing to discuss the employee by phone or in person, rather than by providing written information.

Sometimes, useful information on performance or skills can be elicited by asking about the person's positive **and** negative points. If the supervisor avoids dealing with the negatives (or says there are no negatives), the selecting official might still pursue that by saying, for example, "It is apparent that Mr. Prince has performed very well. However, we all have some problem areas, even if they are minor. It would be very helpful for me to get some feel for these with regard to Mr. Prince. If we hire him, this would help in working with him."

This writers experience suggests that when negatives are elicited from a supervisor who is very hesitant to provide them, they may **underestimate** the real magnitude of the problem. Caution or further investigation is then suggested in the content area of the problem. Further information should be obtained through other supervisors, references or during an interview with the applicant.

Assessment of specific skills and skill levels is of obvious importance. This may be done through the methods already discussed (applications, personnel file, former supervisors) as well as through references and an interview. However, in some instances, the most reliable and valid methods may be work samples, skill tests, or other psychometric measures. Work samples and skill tests are likely to meet content validity standards of the Uniform Guidelines when they can be shown to representatively sample the actual work to be done. For example, for a job requiring writing skills, a carefully constructed report writing work sample might be used. For a typist position, it would be reasonable to use a typing test that measures typing speed and accuracy. However, if other types of psychometric instruments are used, such as aptitude, intelligence or personality tests, the applicable validity requirements stated in the Uniform Guidelines should be met. This is a complex and costly procedure for human services agencies and thus, use of such tests for selection purposes in these settings should probably be avoided.

Interests and attitudes of potential applicants are important, but questionable areas on which to base a selection (from a legal standpoint). Such information is not easy to relate to job requirements in measurable and observable terms. However, these factors may have an impact on longevity in the job, and how well the potential employee does the job and adjusts to the organization. These areas may be assessed through prior supervisors, references, and during the interview. When effective information is provided during the interview by the selecting official, this may provide a particularly good opportunity for the job candidate to assess his or her own interests and attitudes with regard to the job requirements and expectations.

Table VII summarizes suggested assessment methods for eliciting the various types of selection information as discussed above.

TABLE VII
METHODS FOR BEST ELICITING VARIOUS TYPES
OF SELECTION INFORMATION

	Type of Information			
	Background Information	Historical Performance	Skills	Interests/ Attitudes
Applications	X	X	X	
Personnel File	X	X	X	
Supervisors	X	X	X	X
References			X	X
Interview			X	X
Work Sample			X	
Skill Test			X	

What is the significance of the interview in the selection process?

As a singular basis for employee selection, little support is demonstrated for validity of the interview (Porter, Lawler & Hackman, 1975).

Unless combined effectively with other sources of information and completed within specific parameters, **interviews are unlikely to contribute to effective selections.** Unfortunately, experience suggests that many managers depend on interview judgements as a major basis for their selections.

Validity of interviews can be improved by using interviewers familiar with the job and organization (Mayfield, 1964). Also, interviews should be structured sufficiently, so that a large amount of relevant material is included (Mayfield, 1964) and so that candidates are all given the opportunity to bring out similar relevant material. Also, insuring that the interview questions are consistent with KSAOs, and using multiple interviewers during a single interview, or alternating interviewers in a series of interviews (Mayfield, 1964) should improve validity.

Interviews may be of greatest value in providing information to candidates, giving a positive image of the organization, and helping applicants to understand organizational and job expectations. They may also serve an important public relations function in avoiding complaints regarding selections. For example, when selections are competitive, it is not only important that the process **be** valid, legal and fair, but that it be **perceived** as such. Effective, comprehensive interviews tend to diffuse concerns about bias, and support a perception that final selections will be made on a fair and valid basis. Interviewing all candidates in this manner may insure against complaints and legal actions, and encourage positive feelings toward the organization.

FINAL SELECTIONS

What should be the basis for final selection?

The applicant who best meets the job requirements should be selected.

What are affirmative action programs and what is their impact on final selection?

Affirmative action programs require a commitment on the part of employers to increase the proportion of certain protected groups in the work force, e.g., minorities, women or disabled persons. Such programs may be voluntary, or required through laws, executive orders, court orders, and EEOC mandates. Affirmative action impacts on final selections by encouraging organizations to recruit, and selecting officials to fill jobs with members of the designated protected groups. This does not usually require selecting unqualified people for jobs. However, it does usually require a commitment to more extensive recruitment and to selecting qualified protected group members when those persons are as qualified as other applicants.

What are the consequences of not following the Uniform Guidelines, or ignoring the legality of selection procedures?

Unless an applicant complains of discrimination or unless discriminatory procedures or adverse impact come to the attention of a regulatory authority with jurisdiction over the organization, there would probably be no legal consequences. However, a legally sound decision making process is an ethical responsibility (National Rehabilitation Administration Association, 1979), it provides a good defense against costly legal action and it is also likely to be a more valid employee selection decision making process.

What is the role of the probationary period in final selection?

The probationary period is the ultimate work sample. It provides a trial work period during which the employer may observe how well the employee learns and performs the job. If the employee does not perform satisfactorily, he or she is terminated without recourse. Thus, inclusion of probationary period policies (prior to granting tenure privileges) is a valuable safeguard against the long term consequences of poor selections.

Chapter 10

SUPERVISION

What is supervision?

Supervision is the day to day management of subordinate employees for the purpose of achieving the work unit's plans, and functions.

What is the scope of supervision in human services settings?

It includes management of employee training, administrative supervision and professional supervision. **Management of employee training** includes efforts to provide, support or encourage learning of skills, information or experiences that will enhance job performance or career development in the organization.

Administrative supervision is concerned with maintaining an appropriate atmosphere or climate for employees to carry out their work efficiently and effectively. It also includes specific tasks required to keep the work unit and organization running efficiently from day to day and over the long term. **Professional supervision** includes all performance management and employee interactions directed at improving the quality of professional services to clients.

What are the different levels of supervision?

First line supervisors directly manage employees who do the primary or support work of the organization. In a human services agency, these include direct service, clerical, maintenance, personnel workers and so forth. **Higher level supervisors** generally supervise other supervisors and managers along the chain of command. They may also supervise one or more direct service, or support employees, although that is not their main supervisory focus. For example, an agency director may provide direct supervision to four division heads, an administrative assistant and a secretary. His main job is to get the work of the agency accomplished through the subordinate supervisors, with support of the administrative assistant and secretary.

Does supervisory role, expertise and focus differ at the various levels?

Yes. The first line supervisor is concerned with getting primary and support work done through subordinates, while serving as a spokesperson for management. In human services, the paradox of being responsive to the management role, while identifying with direct service providers interests and needs is often a source of role conflict for the first line supervisor. Without resolution, this can impede identification with the management team and limit effective supervisory behavior.

First line supervisors, particularly those responsible for direct service units, must have a broad range of expertise. This includes knowledge in the professional, technical (legal, regulatory, and procedural), administrative and supervisory areas.

At higher supervisory levels, the focus is on **general** direction of subordinate supervisors and other staff. At these levels, values of management and the organization are usually well accepted and followed by subordinates. This allows the supervisory emphasis to be on evaluating and enhancing subordinate effectiveness. Higher level supervisors need the most expertise in general management functions (e.g., planning, macro control, performance management, organization development and change, communications) and less in professional, technical, supervisory and specific administrative areas. In effect, at higher supervisory levels, the focus is directed more toward **general management** and **leadership** than supervision.

MANAGEMENT OF EMPLOYEE TRAINING

Why is employee training important?

It provides a basis for doing the job more effectively and for meeting the expectations and needs of the organization. Training may also meet higher level needs and expectations of employees, enhancing a sense of commitment to ones work. If training is sponsored by the employer, it may encourage a perception of caring on behalf of management and thus greater employee commitment to organizational goals.

What are the major types of training?

Essential Training — This is training needed to do the job and achieve organizational goals.

Enhancement Training — This includes skill development beyond the minimum needed to do the current job. It also includes training in areas related to future career development.

Training to Maintain Qualifications — This includes training to maintain professional licensing and certification.

Are organizations obligated to provide or support the three types of training?

Essential training is an organizational obligation, since it clearly relates to how well the mission is accomplished. Enhancement training, while not obligatory, can be cost beneficial when it increases employee motivation and commitment; when it provides preparation to meet future organizational needs; or when it supports provision of more effective services to clients. Training to maintain qualifications, while not usually obligatory, can support high quality services and the reputation of the agency as one that maintains high professional standards. Support of such training also encourages staff to maintain and upgrade skills in accordance with up to date professional standards. In addition, it may be perceived as an employee benefit to those who must maintain licensing or certification in order to practice. Thus, providing or supporting such training may have both motivational and performance benefits.

Essential Training

What is the nature of essential training?

Essential training includes orientation to the organization and job, initial training on how to do the job, and continuing training required to keep performing the job effectively.

What is the orientation?

Orientation provides an overview of organization and job characteristics, rules and requirements. It gives employees information about what is expected in performing the job and in working for the organization. It also provides mundane, but essential information to new employees about the work setting, such as who they will be working with and for, policies regarding leave use and important standard operating procedures. The orientation should be done personally by the supervisor, if possible, since some of the expectations discussed may be a basis for later performance evaluations or supervisory actions. Thus, the information provided should have the strength of supervisory authority. The orientation also represents an opportunity to establish a positive supervisory relationship as a foundation for effective employee performance.

When should the orientation be done?

It should begin when the employee begins the job, preferably the same day. The longer the employee works prior to the orientation, the greater the likelihood that misinformation or incorrect assumptions will affect performance or the supervisory relationship. For example, an immediate statement regarding concerns about tardiness may offset the time and potentially negative feelings generated in dealing with such a problem after the fact.

What are some specifics to include in the orientation?

Essential information about the work unit and organization, e.g., structure, purposes of work units and relationships to one another; names, phone numbers and roles of co-workers and other significant personnel.
Discussion of general policies and supervisory expectations, e.g., leave, attendance, timeliness of completion of assignments etc.
Presentation of the job description and performance standards (in writing), and discussion to assure understanding.
Routine information on employee benefits and facilities.

What is initial training?

Initial training includes instruction in laws, regulations, procedures and methods unique to the organization, work unit, and job. This is the essential job related knowledge needed to perform effectively. For example, in a human services agency, a scheduling clerk may need to understand case flow, scheduling procedures, and scheduling documentation requirements. A rehabilitation counselor needs to understand how to apply regulations, case management procedures, dictation rules and documentation requirements.

When and how should initial training be done?

Initial training should begin very early, since it is usually required to do the job correctly. Delays lead to errors which need later correction, or which can cause more serious consequences. In less complex jobs, such as file clerk positions, initial training can be completed quickly with structured instruction by the supervisor or a coworker. It is also helpful if this can be supplemented with a written instruction guide.

In complex positions, initial training may take place over an extended period (as much as a year or more). It may include structured sessions to explain and discuss essential materials, such as meaning, intent and application of laws and regulations, or to clarify agency policy and philosophy. In these situations, close supervisory assistance and assistance from colleagues is also usually needed during the initial training period.

Is there an effective sequence or method for conducting initial training?

Experience suggests that the following components and sequence provide a strong foundation for initial training:

1. Immediately following the orientation, intensive (up to one or two weeks) formal, structured training should be provided by the supervisor or a trainer who is knowledgable and experienced in the work. At a minimum, this should include an overview of all information needed to do the job, and detailed instruction in areas **critical** to getting started. For example, a counselor in a public rehabilitation agency might be given an overview of types of rules and procedures that he or she needs to be familiar with in order to carry out the job. Detailed training would then be provided in the interpretation and application of eligibility determination regulations and procedures, so that work could begin immediately with clients.

2. Reference materials should be provided that include all of the rules, procedures, regulations and guidelines that were noted in the overview. The employee should be able to get most information from these sources to carry out the job after completing the formal structured portion of initial training.

3. With more complex jobs, follow-up training, to cover materials not studied in detail earlier, or to reconsider issues covered earlier after some on job experiences, should also be provided.

What is continuing training?

Continuing training includes any periodic or ongoing instruction related to doing the job effectively, or to maintaining needed skills. It may involve training in agency related matters, such as changes in laws or procedures; or in special skill areas, e.g., a new counseling technique or computer skills. Continuing training may be provided directly through inservice sessions or through training courses outside the agency, e.g., conferences, workshops or university continuing education.

Is continuing training always oriented toward providing new information?

No. It may also be concerned with providing emotional support to staff, changing attitudes or assessing types of needed changes. For example, such training may be used to allow staff to ventilate about system problems (e.g., high workloads) while concurrently brainstorming on better methods to manage the workload. Thus, it may help to counteract negative attitudes and burnout, and lead to improved performance.

Enhancement Training

What is the nature of enhancement training?

Enhancement training includes education and development. **Education** consists of college coursework designed to provide broad theoretical and practical knowledge. Education for enhancement may include single courses or a series of courses leading to a degree. The intent is to develop overall knowledge and skills to higher levels than those minimally required.

Development involves providing training that is likely to prepare employees for other positions in the organization. For example, for a counselor it may include university courses in human services administration, as well as brief management seminars. The intent would be preparation to enter a managerial track in the agency. Development training is important to meeting future organization needs for well qualified staff, and for meeting career development needs of high potential employees. Loss of such staff or reduced motivation due to lack of development and advancement opportunity can be inefficient and costly over the long run.

Training to Maintain Qualifications

What is the nature of training to maintain professional qualifications?

This depends on requirements of the certification body or State licensing authorities. Usually, a specified number of continuing education hours is required during a designated period. Acceptable content areas for training, who can provide the training and methods for course approval are also usually specified.

Can an agency support training required to maintain professional licensing and certification through it's in-service training programs?

Yes. Any essential or enhancement training done within the agency will usually be considered by certification or licensing authorities for continuing education credit. However, requirements vary among these groups. Thus, **advance arrangements** should be made to assure that the training format and content is acceptable. Also, training information should be submitted timely and in the required format. It is often helpful to delegate a knowledgable **training coordinator** to handle such details.

GENERAL ADMINISTRATIVE SUPERVISION

Supervision Climate

What can be done to create an effective atmosphere for supervision?

As implied in earlier chapters, it is incumbent upon managers to create an environment that supports control with the lowest expenditure of management time and energy. As a supervisor, this involves establishing a leadership style consistent with effective human relationships and employee motivation principles. It also involves integration of the supervisor's leadership style with the macro control approach of the organization. While it is desirable to move toward the most efficient model, supervisors are probably most effective when their approach to macro control is consistent with the rest of the organization. For example, supervisors in an agency which stresses management centered control must be concerned that employees comply with rules and procedures. This is important in order to be successful in the eyes of higher level management. Although other forms of macro control may be used by the supervisor (e.g., supporting group centered control), failure to function within the agency context would be dysfunctional over the long term.

What are some human relations essentials for supervisors?

Maintaining an atmosphere of trust, concern, dependability, and responsiveness is usually helpful. When employees believe that their supervisor is trustworthy and that they (the employee) are trusted, that the supervisor is genuinely concerned about theirs and their clients' wellbeing, that the supervisor is dependable, responds in a timely manner to requests, is honest, and is inclined to listen well, then employees are more likely to be responsive to the supervisor.

What styles and personal or environmental factors support effective administrative supervision in human services organizations?

Supervisory styles which use employee centered control strategies, appropriate rewards, and which control environmental variables per the characteristics of high performing organizations (see Chapter 2), encourage a highly committed workforce. Maintaining an enjoyable environment in which employees feel like "winners" and members of a high performing team reinforces such commitment. Under these circumstances, administrative supervision is most effective because of positive, cooperative workforce attitudes.

What does research on supervisory relationships, characteristics and styles suggest with regard to effective supervision in human services agencies?

Research conducted in state rehabilitation agencies suggests that counselors perceived their **relationships** with first line supervisors as the most important feature of their employment (Aiken, Smits and Lollar, 1972). In a study reported by English, Oberle and Byrne (1979), state rehabilitation counselors, administrators and supervisors rated seven personal characteristics as very important to a supervisors success: personal honesty, leadership, efficiency, concern for others, concern for state regulations, flexibility and decisiveness. Other characteristics rated as very important by a moderate proportion of the sample were patience, concern for production, concern for federal regulations, empathy and tolerance of the unknown. A small proportion of the sample considered intellectual ability, political savvy, and autonomy as very important. Differences among groups suggested that **administrators** were more likely to see leadership, efficiency, and decisiveness as very important, while more **supervisors** perceived concern for others, flexibility, patience, concern for federal regulations and tolerance of the unknown/ambiguity as very important.

Several theories have been advanced and tested in the area of leadership. Approaches that seem readily applicable within human services include the autocratic-democratic continuum, employee vs. job centered supervision, and the dimensions of consideration vs. initiating structure.

What is the autocratic-democratic continuum and its relevance to human services supervision?

These dimensions refer to the amount of decision making authority retained by the supervisor or delegated to subordinates. Autocratic supervisors retain a high degree of control while democratic supervisors relegate more control to the work group and individuals. This is analagous to centralized vs. decentralized control as discussed in Chapter 7.

Tannenbaum and Schmidt (1973) suggest that effective leaders do not rigidly follow an autocratic or democratic style, but adapt to their own and their subordinates capabilities and to what must be accomplished. English, Oberle and Byrne (1979) found that in state rehabilitation agencies, counselors, supervisors and administrators perceived the democratic style as the best choice for all levels of agency leadership, although a large majority believed that the leadership level (supervisor, middle manager or administrator) influenced the type of leadership style shown. The highest proportion of respondents believed that a democratic style is most important for first line supervisors, while fewer preferred this style for administrators. There was also a small proportion of counselors who preferred a laissez-faire approach by supervisors, while an equally small proportion of administrators preferred an authoritarian approach by supervisors.

Unfortunately, since the findings in this study were opinion based, results could be influenced by needs and preferences of the respondent groups, rather than style factors which truly enhance supervisory effectiveness. The Tannenbaum and Schmidt position, which considers situational contingencies, seems most applicable in actual practice.

What are the employee centered vs. job centered and consideration vs. initiating structure approaches?

As a result of studies conducted through the University of Michigan Institute for Social Research (Likert, 1979), leaders were classified as employee centered or job centered. **Employee centered leaders** concentrate on building high performing work groups. They focus on the human aspects of employee problems, specify and communicate goals to employees and provide **general supervision.** Thus, employees are given freedom to carry out the job within a structure of expected results.

In contrast, **job centered leaders** are task centered. They provide structure for carrying out the work and **close supervision** to assure that tasks are performed. University of Michigan research suggests that the employee centered method is most associated with high productivity, more positive work attitudes and other positive organizational results.

Consideration vs. initiating structure was investigated through studies at Ohio State University. **Consideration** refers to the extent to which leader-subordinate relationships are characterized by mutual trust, respect for a subordinate's ideas and consideration of his or her feelings. High consideration is representative of good rapport and communication between a leader and subordinate, while low consideration represents a more impersonal relationship. **Initiating structure** refers to a leader's provision of structure to his or her own and subordinates roles. High initiating structure represents active direction of group activities through planning, communicating, scheduling and trying new ideas.

Generally, considerate leadership is consistently associated with job satisfaction. However, findings on the relationship of employee performance to these dimensions are conflicting and mixed (Korman, 1977).

What are the implications of these dimensions for human services agency supervisors?

Human services professionals are likely to prefer the employee centered and consideration approaches, since they are consistent with autonomous functioning and humanistic values. However, these styles may not always be appropriate to organizational needs. Thus, supervisors must be cognizant of the need to provide structure and close supervision in some instances, regardless of employee preferences. For example, when work must be completed in a specified manner by law or procedural requirements, or when distasteful paperwork tasks must be completed by professional staff, a more job centered approach with appropriate rewards, or penalties for non compliance may be needed.

Initiating structure may also be required to enhance efficiency or return a chaotic situation to order. In fact, evidence indicates that when high pressure for production exists, initiating structure tends to be positively correlated and consideration negatively correlated with productivity (Korman, 1977). This suggests that sometimes a supervisor must exert structured control in order to achieve results, with less immediate concern for the preferences of subordinates. In such situations, there may be conflict between management demands and employee needs, which the supervisor is obligated to resolve in favor of enhanced work unit performance.

In her review of supervision theory, Ross (1979) suggests an integrative position with regard to the above dimensions. Drawing upon an analogy between the elements for success in both counseling and supervision, she concludes that both successful (counseling) practitioners and supervisors "must create an atmosphere of warmth, consideration and responsiveness while providing direction and structure for action." Generally, employee centeredness and consideration will enhance employee satisfaction and a positive organization climate. However, it is also clear that elements of job centeredness and initiating structure are also needed on a situation contingent basis to support high performance.

What can a supervisor do to increase his or her influence and power with employees?

French and Raven (1960) identified five bases of power that address this issue:

Referent Power — This refers to power based upon a followers admiration of, liking of or identification with a leader. It is derived from the leader's personal characteristics.

Expert Power — This is power based upon special knowledge, experience, or skills.

Reward Power — This refers to power based upon the leaders ability to provide rewards to the follower, such as a monetary bonus or verbal praise.

Coercive Power — This is derived from the leader's ability to provide punishment to the follower. It is based upon fear that failure to comply will lead to negative consequences. Coercive power provides a basis for the use of negative reinforcement.

Legitimate Power — This is power based upon the follower's position in the organization chain of command and the belief of the follower that the leader has a legitimate right to exert power under such circumstances.

Although the above distinctions are useful, the power types are all variations of reward and coercive power, or the power of the leader to control reinforcers (Shaw, 1976). The more control over reinforcers available to the leader, the more influential he or she is likely to be.

In the National Study of Social Welfare and Rehabilitation Workers, Work and Organizational Contexts, Olmstead and Christensen (1973) found that the greatest influence in these settings (private and public agencies) can be exercised through expert, legitimate and referent power. Reward and coercive power were valued strongly only among para-professional workers.

In summary, the information on power bases implies that supervisors can increase their influence by enhancing their control of reinforcers within the work environment. Developing technical and professional expertise, likability and personal respect, and nurturing strong support of higher level management (legitimate power) should enhance the most important sources of power that support personal control.

Administrative Supervision Tasks—Overview

What are the most common tasks of administrative supervision?

Most supervisors are involved with the following either directly or through subordinate supervisors:

Staff Selection—This includes interviewing and selecting employees. It may also include recruitment. Staff selection is discussed in detail in Chapter 9.

Performance Management—This involves monitoring and evaluating the work of employees with respect to such factors as productivity, quality, timeliness and results achieved. It also involves taking needed actions to maintain or improve performance. Performance management is discussed in Chapter 13.

Absence Control—This involves maintaining a workforce that is on the job for the maximum amount of paid time. It includes control of leave abuse and tardiness.

Disciplinary and Adverse Actions—These include responses to inappropriate employee behavior and inadequate performance, through use of disciplinary measures, such as reprimand or suspension; and through use of adverse actions, such as demotion, or dismissal from a position or the organization.

Conflict Resolution—This includes resolving disputes between employees, among competing or conflicting groups, and between a supervisor and one or more employees supervised. Conflict resolution is discussed in Chapter 15.

Achieving Compliance—This pertains to obtaining employee cooperation in carrying out supervisory instructions, laws, regulations, and procedures.

Achieving Change — This involves getting employees and employee groups to modify work methods and other behaviors to meet changed environmental and organizational demands. Organization change is discussed in detail in Chapter 17.

Approval of Work — This is necessary due to organization requirements or supervisory discretion. For example, in a public rehabilitation agency, approval of rehabilitation plans by a supervisor may be required.

Dealing with Employee Requests — This includes requests for leave, changes in work assignments, attendance at meetings, letters of recommendation, completion of certification/licensing materials and so forth.

Assignment of Work — This involves appropriate assignment and delegation of work to employees, and assuring an efficient work flow.

Absence Control

How can absence control be managed?

Work environment, group and individual factors play a role in absence control. Clearly communicated, modeled (by management), and enforced expectations regarding leave abuse and tardiness is important. Enforcement is enhanced when employees know they are expected to follow the rules both by management and by the work group. This is often learned through observation. If it is the norm for employees to frequently report to work late or to take leave indiscriminately, control of individual employees beyond the norm may be viewed as unfair or discriminatory. Thus, maintaining a desirable group norm for absences is essential.

When individual problems in absence control exist, group centered control may be supportive to management, but the threat of consistently applied disciplinary actions may also be necessary for some employees. For example, chronic tardiness may require **progressive discipline** in the form of a verbal discussion followed by a warning letter and subsequently a reprimand. Each action should be followed by a period of time that allows the employee an opportunity to improve. If no improvement takes place, the next level of action should be taken.

How should a supervisor deal with employee excuses in absence control?

Absence problems are usually accompanied by plausible excuses. However, when the problem becomes chronic, supervisors need to look closely at the validity of excuses as well as whether the chronic level of absence can be tolerated with respect to workload needs, regardless of the reason. When excuses are related to medical problems, a doctor's statement for each absence can usually be required if there is a question regarding the need for chronic absence. This sometimes has the effect of reducing absences to the minimum necessary.

Can absence control be handled in a more positive or preventive manner?

Positive and preventive interventions in absence control include effective employee selection, early clarification of expectations, maintaining a positive organization climate and modifying work schedules.

When selecting new employees, it is usually worthwhile to ask prior supervisors about absences and tardiness. For example, "How many days was this employee absent during the past year?" "How many times was she late for work?" "What were the reasons?" "How did that compare with other employees in your agency?" Excessive leave use in the past may predict the same problem in the future, unless an unusual circumstance was responsible for the prior situation, e.g., maternity leave or medical operation.

During the selection process and orientation training, expectations of the organization with respect to absence should be stated explicitly. This provides a clear message from management to the employee. However, these expectations may be modified by the work group, if management actions are not consistent with what is said. For example, the supervisor may stress the importance of reporting on time and not exceeding the lunch period. However, someone in the work group may communicate the "true" situation "You can take as long as you want for lunch, but don't ever come in late in the morning."

Maintaining a positive organization climate may prevent unnecessary absences, since the choice to be absent often contains an environment related psychological component. If one enjoys the job and coworkers, or feels committed to the work or work unit, there is more liklihood of reporting to work in borderline situations. Even when one is ill, a decision can often be made to go to work rather than stay home. Studies on job satisfaction in relation to absenteeism and turnover support the value of a satisfying work environment (Porter and Steers, 1973). Those who are unsatisfied tend to have more absences and leave the organization.

Modifying work schedules is another preventive approach in absence control. Varieties of flextime or individually modified schedules can provide opportunities to avoid absence or tardiness. For example, a flextime schedule that allows a fifteen minute period before and after a core starting time, may eliminate most brief periods of tardiness. If the core starting time for an 8 hour workday is 8:00, the employee could report as early as 7:45 (and leave at 4:15) or as late as 8:15 (and leave at 4:45). Special schedules can also be used to accomodate for child care, school attendance, medical appointments and so forth. In these situations the schedule is simply modified (where the work permits) to accomodate for reasonable, recurring employee needs.

Disciplinary and Adverse Actions

When are disciplinary and adverse actions necessary?

Disciplinary and adverse actions are usually a last resort, when positive attempts at achieving employee compliance or competent work performance fail. Disciplinary actions are usually used in behavioral or ethical non-compliance or non cooperation situations. Adverse actions, which involve separation action from the job or organization, are used when all efforts have failed to achieve compliance or competent work performance.

What is the process in carrying out disciplinary and adverse actions?

Organizations differ in the specifics based on policies, procedures and labor management agreements. However, these processes usually occur in a progressive manner. An attempt is made to improve the behavior or performance through counseling, suggestions for change, supervisory or other assistance. It is agreed (with the employee) that follow-up will occur at a specified time to determine whether the needed improvement has occured. If at the time of follow-up, improvement has not taken place, formal action (such as a warning letter or written reprimand) is taken. At the same time it is also noted in writing what must be done, by when, and the consequences (next level of discipline, or type of adverse action) if the changes are not accomplished by the employee. Further assistance is also offered to the employee at this time, including the help of an employee assistance program or other counseling related service, if needed. If improvement does not take place by the date noted, then the next level of action is taken. This process continues until the problem is resolved or until termination takes place.

Accurate, factual supervisory **documentation** is extremely important in the disciplinary and adverse action process. Since progressive supervisory actions are often "emotionally loaded," and may be viewed as adversary by employees, information may become distorted. Maintenance of an accurate information trail is important to achieving performance improvement and for use in labor-management or legal contexts. In fact, if accurate, objective information supporting the case cannot be provided in the labor-management or legal situation, the supervisor may be forced to reverse decisions.

Supervisors should keep dated notes as a memory aid. They should also provide written documentation to employees of problems noted, corrective actions requested, suggestions for improvement and assistance provided or recommended.

When disciplinary and adverse actions are bound by labor-management agreements or legal requirements, supervisors must also be certain to follow all procedures. Failure to do so may indicate that employee rights were violated and thus result in inability of the supervisor to take, follow through with, or sustain the necessary action.

Do supervisors usually have difficulty carrying out disciplinary and adverse actions?

Yes. For many supervisors, particularly human services supervisors, this is one of the most difficult tasks. Since negative actions are uncomfortable, time consuming, and cause employee anger and resentments, some supervisors avoid them or apply them inconsistently.

What is the most efficient strategy in coping with control of disciplinary and adverse actions?

Creating a positive work environment with maximum employee commitment. Most supervisory time can then be spent on activities that enhance the organization mission. When disciplinary and adverse actions must occur in such environments, there is often work group acknowledgement, or even tacit concurrence, of the need. In less supportive environments the supervisory task is more difficult, time consuming and anxiety producing, particularly if other employees have negative attitudes toward management. However, in such negative environments, it may become even more important to **consistently** take disciplinary and adverse actions to retain supervisory integrity and control. Unfortunately, in these situations, a pattern of negative control is then perpetuated.

PROFESSIONAL SUPERVISION

What is the nature of professional supervision in human services settings?

Professional supervision can be viewed from the perspective of either clinical supervision or consultation. According to Hart (1982) **clinical supervision** is "an ongoing educational process in which one person in the role of supervisor helps another person in the role of supervisee acquire appropriate professional behavior through an examination of the supervisee's professional activities." He further defines the important elements as an ongoing relationship, clear roles, and focus on knowledge, skills and behaviors of the supervisee.

Feinberg (1981) defines supervision in the public rehabilitation agency as being a more directive, mandatory relationship built into the hierarchical structure of the organization and which is concerned with overall work performance (e.g., professional, technical and administrative). Clinical supervision would be one (perhaps small) component of this role.

The above suggests that clinical supervision relationships are usually hierarchical and sometimes confounded by other than professional components. This contrasts sharply with the **consultation** relationship which is time limited, voluntary, non-authoritative, collaborative on an equal status basis, may involve selection based on special expertise, and is more purely professional in content (Hart, 1982; Feinberg, 1981). Consultants may be selected from within or outside the organization.

What are some clinical supervision approaches?

Based on a literature review, Hart (1982) defines three models of clinical supervision applicable to counseling related personnel:

Skill Development Model — The goal of this model is to increase the supervisee's technical skills and conceptual understanding of clients. The supervisor plays the role of teacher and expert. The focus of supervision is on client problems, background, behavior patterns and motivations, and the methods used by the supervisee in helping the client.

Personal Growth Model — The goal of this model is to increase supervisee insight and awareness of personal emotions, particularly with regard to feelings which are aroused during interaction with clients. The supervisor plays a somewhat therapeutic role (as would a counselor), but the focus is on educating the supervisee, not on problem solving. It is assumed that a more insightful supervisee will be a better helper.

Integration Model — The goal of this model is to help supervisees apply developed technical skills and self awareness to effective relationships with their clients. The supervisory relationship is more of collaborator or colleague than one strongly separated by hierarchical distance. It thus approaches the purer consultation form of professional supervision, although it is likely to be ongoing instead of time limited. The main focus of supervision is on the supervisee-client relationship as an "interactive dyad," i.e., the actions of both persons affect the actions of the other. A second focus is on the supervisor-supervisee interaction "as it affects and is affected by the supervisee-client interaction" (Hart, 1982).

How can clinical supervision and consultation be implemented in an agency?

The skill development and personal growth models are most appropriate for professionals in training, trained professionals with limited experience, and those who are functioning in professional or paraprofessional positions with low levels of formal training. As level of training and experience increases, clinical supervision can become more integrative, and ultimately consultative. As noted by Whittington (1980) with regard to mental health settings, "In the case of fully trained and qualified professional persons, the concept of supervision has no relevance and should be abandoned. In reality, more effective quality control can usually be maintained by making consultation available rather than by imposing supervision."

In agency settings, clinical supervision or consultation is often not provided or is provided inadequately, even when perceived as needed. For example, English, Oberle & Byrne (1979) found that the majority of administrators, supervisors and counselors in state rehabilitation agencies rated the quality of most supervisory case consultation as poor or fair. Sometimes, supervisors are not trained to provide professional supervision. Also, they may be expected by their superiors to focus on procedural compliance by employees rather than on encouraging autonomous professional functioning. In addition, the concrete benefits of time consumed in this area may not seem as evident as completing more pressing and immediate administrative demands.

When integrative supervision (integration model) or consultation is appropriate, the above "reality vs. needs" dilemma can be resolved in several ways. In some instances, senior direct service staff can be used formally in a consultive capacity. Also, in many settings, the informal structure resolves the need for consultation, since staff are likely to consult with those who are most professionally respected or considered experts.

In settings with highly trained and experienced staff, peer groups can become the primary medium for consultation. In these situations, administrative supervisors can then legitimately focus their energy on management and supervisory functions related to work unit growth, development and maintenance.

When skill development or personal growth related supervision is needed, the "reality vs. needs" dilemma is more difficult to resolve. There may be a tendency to opt for limited or no supervision with the long term effect of poorer quality services and results. In these situations, if direct assistance by hierarchical supervisors cannot be provided, experienced staff can be assigned as mentors or ongoing consultants.

A longer term strategy is to select well trained, experienced staff; conduct an effective ongoing staff training and development program; and maintain an organizational climate and policies conducive to low turnover of professional staff. This would presumably resolve the problem, since under these conditions, the need for extensive supervision would no longer exist.

Does supervision really have a significant impact on professional performance?

There are few empirical studies in the area of effectiveness of supervision. However, Hart (1982) did cite one study in his review (Biasco and Redfering, 1976) which showed that supervised clinicians had better results with their clients than non supervised clinicians. Logic also suggests that supervision will have its greatest impact when applied with the least trained and experienced professional personnel. Thus, when these circumstances exist, agency supervisors should find ways to use their own and other staff resources to carry out this function.

CONTROLLING IMPLEMENTATION EXERCISE 1
MACRO CONTROL

(Group or Individual)

Consider the organization diagrammed in Figure 2 (Chapter 5). This is a relatively tall structure consisting of some professionally and some non-professionally staffed work units. Units performing professional functions include staff trained at levels required for licensing and certification (usually masters' and doctoral levels). Staff in support units, such as within the Finance Department, usually have bachelors degrees and/or extensive experience in their specialties and consider themselves professionals also. Units in the Vocational Services Department have bachelors level staffs or employees who have high school educations and have obtained their experience in industry.

The organization is considered private not-for-profit. Clients are charged for services on the basis of a standard schedule of fees. Most clients pay for services directly or have costs covered by insurance companies. Others are supported through payment by other agencies such as the State vocational rehabilitation agency.

TASK

Per Table IV, what might be the most efficient **type** of control, **focus** of control and **control model** for this organization, and, as appropriate, for the various departments and units of the organization?

CONTROLLING IMPLEMENTATION EXERCISE 2
EMPLOYEE MOTIVATION

(Group)

In the organization illustrated in Figure 2 (Chapter 5) and in CONTROLLING IMPLEMENTATION EXERCISE I, the following conditions exist:

1. Salaries are above the national and local average for all employee categories.

2. The facility is located in a very high crime area and some employees have been assaulted outside the facility. One was assaulted inside the facility during the last year and the atmosphere is somewhat fearful. Poor internal security exists.

3. Quality of supervision is considered satisfactory by employees and layoffs are non-existent.

4. Employees who remain with the agency generally stay in the same job for an average of seven years. The most frequent complaints relate to boredom with the same job tasks, too many rules and too much supervision. Advancement to higher level jobs is very slow.

5. Employees feel that most rewards on the job come from feeling good about helping clients. Most feel that management is not willing to provide meaningful monetary or other rewards for good work.

6. The average age of employees is thirty. About 50% are under thirty, 40% are between thirty and forty, about 5% are forty-one to fifty, and 5% are over fifty.

TASK

Management believes that productivity and quality could be higher at this agency. It is their contention that this can be achieved by effecting changes to increase the motivation and satisfaction of employees. This would reduce turnover of newer employees (increasing efficiency) and result in greater employee involvement and commitment to agency goals, including excellence in providing client services. As a consultant, what recommendations would you make based on the material in the text?

CONTROLLING IMPLEMENTATION EXERCISE 3
EMPLOYEE SELECTION

(Group)

In this exercise, a selection panel will review qualifications for and interview three job candidates. They will then make a final selection.

INSTRUCTIONS

1. Choose a selection panel of three members and provide each with the POSITION AND CANDIDATE INFORMATION.
2. Assign the roles of applicants A, B, and C to three other students and provide each with the ROLE DESCRIPTION.

(Note: Instructor may wish to modify POSITION AND CANDIDATE INFORMATION, and ROLE DESCRIPTIONS provided below so that neither the panel nor the candidate role players see each others information).

3. Assign all other students to the role of observers of the process.

TASK

The selection panel establishes items for the interview and interviews each candidate. Each candidate plays the assigned role. At the conclusion of the interviews, the panel makes a selection and states the basis.

After the selection, the observers rate the procedure by answering yes or no to the following:

1. Was the selection based on KSAOs?
2. Was adverse impact appropriately considered?
3. Was adverse impact handled correctly?
4. Was the same information collected and used for each candidate?
5. Was the selection procedure valid, fair and legal? Observer responses to each item are presented to the class and discussed.

POSITION AND CANDIDATE INFORMATION

Position: Rehabilitation Counselor in a general hospital
KSAOs —

1. Ability to apply professional counseling principles to a wide variety of rehabilitation related problems and effectively assist clients with all disabilities. to develop realistic rehabilitation plans.
2. Knowledge of vocational development theories, and information about occupations and the job market.
3. Ability to work cooperatively as a team member with a wide range of health professionals.

Minimum requirements: Bachelors degree plus 2 years of relevant experience; or a Masters degree in a counseling related area and no experience.

Other relevant information — The hospital has not come under the scrutiny of the EEOC or a similar agency. However, it is known that the ⅘ rule is not satisfied with regard to women employed in professional positions. Thus, adverse impact would be found to exist. It is also known that the hospital wishes to hire someone who would be considered highly credible by other hospital health professionals.

Candidate A (female) — BA degree in psychology (1967)

    1982–present — (unemployed)

    1978–1982 — Work adjustment Counselor (Unity House)

    1968–1972 — Employment interviewer (State Employment Service)

    References — reliable worker, average counseling skills, usually relates well with staff, a few very minor complaints from clients about lack of follow through

Candidate B (male) — MA degree in community counseling (1986)

    1986–present — General counselor in mental health center

    References — excellent counseling skills, worked well on mental health team, tends to overwork sometimes which takes toll emotionally

Candidate C (male) — MA degree in rehabilitation counseling (1987)

    1987–present — rehabilitation counselor (State)

    References — new counselor, good rehabilitation knowledge, needs some development of counseling skills, but will probably be a somewhat better than average counselor with a little more experience

APPLICANT A—ROLE DESCRIPTION

Female

BA degree in psychology (1967)

1982–present — (unemployed)

1978–1982 — Work adjustment counselor (Unity House)

1968–1972 — Employment interviewer with State Employment Service

You see yourself as quite knowledgable about the job market, job placement and the problems faced by people with disabilities. You view yourself as an excellent counselor even though you have no academic training in this area. You see **experience** as the most important factor in successful counseling. You also view yourself as a great team worker and highly responsible.

Other: age forty-two, periods of unemployment due to family/child raising responsibilities.

APPLICANT B—ROLE DESCRIPTION

Male

MA degree in community counseling (1986)

1986–present—General counselor in mental health center

You view yourself as being knowledgable in counseling theory and as a highly competent counselor/therapist. You also have knowledge, skill and experience in vocational counseling with emotionally disabled clients, including some minor job placement experience. You particularly like the vocational counseling aspects of your present job. You see yourself as very dilligent and compulsive in your desire to help your clients. You work well with a treatment team, even though you are not too fond of medical doctors.

Other: age twenty-eight; two years in army after high school

APPLICANT C—ROLE DESCRIPTION

Male

MA degree in rehabilitation counseling (1987)

1987–present—rehabilitation counselor (State)

You see yourself as very bright and knowledgable in rehabilitation theory. With some experience you see yourself as becoming a "star." You view yourself as working well with other professionals and clients. You see yourself as advancing quickly and you would like to do this in a setting where you will have great opportunities.

Other: age twenty-five

OBSERVERS RATING SHEET

	Yes	No

1. Was the selection based on the KSAOs?
2. Was adverse impact appropriately considered?
3. Was adverse impact handled correctly?
4. Was the same information collected
   and used for each candidate?
5. Was the selection procedure valid, fair and legal?

CONTROLLING IMPLEMENTATION EXERCISE 4
SUPERVISION

(Individual and Group)

Completing the following scales will help you analyze your approach to administrative supervision. If you are now a supervisor or have had supervisory experience, honestly rate your actual (A) style and bases of power; and the style and bases of power toward which you might ideally (I) strive. In considering the ideal, be sure to consider your own personality traits. If you have never had supervisory experience, consider any leadership roles you have fulfilled and use that knowledge to rate your actual style and bases of power.

Autocratic	(A)	low	1	2	3	4	5	6	7	high
	(I)	low	1	2	3	4	5	6	7	high
Democratic	(A)	low	1	2	3	4	5	6	7	high
	(I)	low	1	2	3	4	5	6	7	high
Consideration	(A)	low	1	2	3	4	5	6	7	high
	(I)	low	1	2	3	4	5	6	7	high
Initiating Structure	(A)	low	1	2	3	4	5	6	7	high
	(I)	low	1	2	3	4	5	6	7	high
Employee Centered	(A)	low	1	2	3	4	5	6	7	high
	(I)	low	1	2	3	4	5	6	7	high
Job Centered	(A)	low	1	2	3	4	5	6	7	high
	(I)	low	1	2	3	4	5	6	7	high

Rank your bases of power from 1-5:

Legitimate Reward Coercive Referent Expert

Actual
Ideal

QUESTIONS FOR SMALL GROUP CLASS DISCUSSION, OR INDIVIDUAL CONSIDERATION

1. Why is your ideal style better than your current style?
2. Is achieving your ideal style and bases of power realistic for you?
3. What can you do to achieve your ideal style?
4. What factors might affect your ability to achieve the ideal with regard to bases of power?

Section V

CONTROLLING: EVALUATION AND ACCOUNTABILITY
INTRODUCTION AND OVERVIEW

Evaluation is the final phase of the agency/program management cycle. It uses after-the-fact feedback information as a basis for taking future actions and for demonstrating accountability. For example, information on agency quality and productivity from prior periods may serve as a basis to adjust staff size, provide more efficient services, and show that professional accreditation standards are met. In effect, evaluation is an ongoing process which impacts on agency planning and implementation with regard to individuals, units, departments, programs and the entire organization. It also impacts on those who retain external control.

As implied in Chapter 2, from a systems perspective, evaluation is a key requirement for maintaining homeostasis and controlling system growth or deterioration. This, of course, requires a feedback process (receiving and monitoring pertinent information), before actual evaluation (deciding what the information means) can take place. Evaluation is then followed by decisions and actions about whether to maintain the status quo or change something. From the perspective of the controlling function of managers, evaluation will be defined broadly to include receiving feedback, evaluating it and making decisions about change.

Evaluation can involve both managers and others. In fact, as we know from prior chapters, direct feedback of information to all involved, provides a basis for self initiated performance corrections and for generating intrinsic motivation. This is particularly the case when staff have clear, measurable goals, objectives or standards. As an employee, it is helpful to have data on ones own performance, as well as information on where the work unit and agency stand with regard to their performance criteria, and other factors. This helps to gain an understanding of ones own contribution to what the work unit and the agency are trying to achieve.

Much routine information can be fed back to employees through computerized management information systems (see Chapter 16 for further discussion on use of computers) for direct comparison with goals, objectives, standards or criteria. For example, case management data such as caseload size, number of rehabilitation plans developed, counselor productivity and results of case quality reviews can be routinely provided to each employee and supervisor. More complex information can be fed back in in-depth analyses or evaluation research reports (see Chapter 12). For example, evaluating the performance of a new program may require analysis and recommendations on the basis of a series of outcome studies.

In this section, Chapter 11 provides an in-depth review of human services performance indicators. The composite of **overall system indicators** — productivity, efficiency and effectiveness — give a simplified snapshot of total performance for a work unit or agency. This can be important to early problem screening and to easily communicating performance to funders or higher level managers for accountability or justification of operating resources. **Process indicators** such as timeliness and quality, and **indicators of results** such as gain scales, goal attainment scales and measures of outcomes, benefits and client satisfaction, allow for more comprehensive analysis of performance. Overall, the human services performance indicators provide a basis for regular monitoring of operations, measuring long and short term goal achievement, conducting some types of program evaluation, and employee appraisal.

Chapter 12 discusses program evaluation. This is a process which uses a variety of data and techniques to improve the effectiveness, efficiency and accountability of organizations and programs. Chapter 13 considers evaluation of employee performance. Employee evaluation is crucial to linking the actions of employees with the organization plan, since the level of an agency's functioning is based upon how well it's employees perform. Employee evaluation, including use of rewards, is an important foundation for motivating staff to contribute to increasing agency excellence.

Chapter 11

HUMAN SERVICES PERFORMANCE INDICATORS

What are the characteristics of effective performance indicators?

They are objectively measurable and easily understood by all who use them. They also reflect factors pertinent to achieving the organization mission within its environmental, political and legal context. When possible, indicators should additionally be constructed for use at all organization levels. For example, a measure of productivity that can be used for the entire agency as well as for individual employee evaluation enhances the linkage between individual and agency performance.

Understandability is particularly important, since performance indicators are used as the medium for communicating and improving performance. This usually requires developing **simple measures** in complex content areas that are difficult to define and even more difficult to validly measure. For example, the "26 closure" in the state-federal vocational rehabilitation program has survived over many years as an indicator of successful rehabilitation results. Although rehabilitation professionals often argue that the measure is inadequate, it is simple, and easily understood by those who need such an indicator. Efforts to better represent the complexity of rehabilitation through weighted and other more complicated indicators have generally failed.

Usually, when measures are too complex, they are rejected or ignored if possible; or when they are imposed by mandate, they may be misused. Thus, even though developing simple but valid human services performance indicators may seem paradoxical, organizations and programs must make every attempt to do so. If indicators are to effectively serve their intent, they must be constructed to consider the needs and tolerance of **all** who will use them.

What are some important types of indicators that can be used in human services organizations?

Overall System Indicators — These include the summary measures of productivity, efficiency and effectiveness. Together, these allow evaluation of **total** work unit (organization or specific work units) performance.

Process Indicators — These include measures of how well agency processes are accomplished. Timeliness of providing services, and the quality of professional and administrative services, decisions and actions are the main indicators of performance.

Indicators of Results — These are measures which reflect outcomes, client gains, and client satisfaction, which result from human services processes.

OVERALL SYSTEM INDICATORS

Productivity

What is productivity?

In a general sense, productivity is the ratio of output to input. In the work setting, **output** is usually represented by the direct results of work processes (such as the number of items produced or the value of goods or services produced). Direct results implies a clear and direct causal relationship between the producer and product (such as factory workers who produce canned goods), in contrast to products or results that may be only partially due to the work unit producer (such as client outcomes in a mental health center).

Input usually refers to some representation of labor costs (such as total hours for which employees are paid), or labor costs plus other costs, such as equipment and real estate expressed in dollar terms. Thus, productivity measures the efficiency with which amounts or values of goods or services are directly produced with respect to costs incurred. When only labor costs are considered (as is often the case), productivity becomes a measure of **labor efficiency.**

How can productivity be defined in human services settings?

Considering the need to assure that outputs measure direct results of staff efforts, the following ratio is appropriate:

Quantity of Staff Outputs

Staff Costs (or Staff Costs Plus Other Costs)

As noted in Chapter 2, **staff outputs,** such as a completed counseling session or a completed case, are units of completed staff efforts on behalf of the agency mission. These differ from client outcomes and benefits in that staff outputs are the only form of productive outputs that clearly and directly result from the action of the work unit or organization. Outcomes and benefits may result from such action, but they may also result from actions independent of the helping organization (Simon, 1982, 1983, 1984, 1987).

What are some practical methods for measuring productivity in human services settings?

The following ratios are suggested for simple application. Note that each is multiplied by 100 to represent a percentage (rather than a decimal value) of costs accounted for by staff output. Also, the ratios are intended for application during specified time periods. For example, output and input data would both be collected for the same three month or six month period.

1.
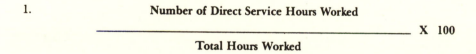

This ratio measures total time spent on direct service work in relation to total time worked by staff. When used with all staff in a work unit or organization, the ratio would always be expected to be less than 100, since time must be spent on non direct service work such as supervision, administration, training, projects and leave. Ratios of less than 60 or 70 would suggest need for analysis of reasons for low productivity.

2.
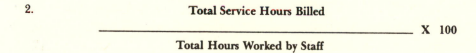

The above ratio is similar to the first method, but is designed to measure productivity of work units that bill for service.

3.

$$\frac{\text{Total Fees Billed}}{\text{Total Agency or Program Expenditures on Services}} \times 100$$

The above ratio also applies to work units that bill for service. However, this measures the percentage of costs that are returned through fees. In this instance, the ratio can exceed 100% (and would be a necessity in profit making organizations) (Simon, 1982, 1983, 1984, 1987).

Efficiency

What is efficiency?

Like productivity, **efficiency** can also be defined generally as a ratio of output to input. However, in human services, it may be differentiated from productivity by defining **output** as the quantity of outcome or benefits achieved by clients, and **input** as the organizational costs or efforts incurred while achieving those gains. Thus, efficiency becomes a measure of client gains achieved with respect to the organization's energy or resources expended. As efficiency increases, less resources are expended per desired outcome or unit of benefits achieved.

Two types of efficiency can be defined in human services: cost efficiency and work efficiency. **Cost efficiency** is defined by the following ratio:

$$\frac{\text{Quantity of Desired Client Outcomes or Benefits}}{\text{Costs Required to Achieve Outcomes or Benefits}}$$

Cost efficiency can be expected to be highest when less cost of inputs results in more desired outcomes or benefits. For example, a psychiatric rehabilitation center that places 25 clients in employment in a year at an inflation adjusted cost of $70,000 has operated more cost efficiently than the prior year when 18 clients were placed at a cost of $75,000.

Work efficiency is defined as:

$$\frac{\text{Quantity of Desired Client Outcomes or Benefits}}{\text{Quantity of Staff Outputs Required to Achieve Outcomes or Benefits}}$$

Work efficiency can be expected to be highest when less staff outputs result in more desired client outcomes or benefits. For example, a job placement service that can achieve 75 suitable job placements with 100 hours of employer contact is more work efficient than one that produces only 20 placements with the same amount of employer contact. Note that in this ratio, **quantity of staff outputs** is considered an **input**. This differs from its use in the productivity definition where it is considered an output (Simon, 1987).

What are some practical ways of measuring cost efficiency and work efficiency in human services organizations?

Below are examples of possible cost and work efficiency indicators. However, the specific nature of the work unit's mission will determine the types of outcomes and benefits which must be used.

As with productivity indicators, efficiency indicators are suggested for use during specified time periods. Note also that these ratios are **not** multiplied by 100 (as are the productivity ratios), since they do not directly represent the percentage of costs or staff outputs (inputs) accounted for by desired outcomes or benefits (outputs).

Cost Efficiency Examples

1.
$$\frac{\text{Change in Earned Income After Services}}{\text{Total Agency or Program Expenditures on Services}}$$

2.
$$\frac{\text{Change in Public Assistance Benefits After Services}}{\text{Total Agency or Program Expenditures on Services}}$$

3. The Council of State Administrators for Vocational Rehabilitation (CSAVR Committee on Program Evaluation, 1984) proposed the following cost efficiency measures for use in program evaluation of state vocational rehabilitation agencies:

a.
$$\frac{\text{Total Vocational Rehabilitation Benefits}}{\text{Total Vocational Rehabilitation Costs}}$$

b.   **Number of "26" (rehabilitated) closures**
     _____
               $100,000 of Expenditure Adjusted for Inflation

Work Efficiency Examples

1.   **Number of Clients Who Attained Employment**
     _____
                     Total Hours Worked by Staff

2.   **Number of Patients Who Successfully Completed Therapy**
     _____
                     Total Hours Worked by Staff

Effectiveness

What is effectiveness?

Effectiveness refers to **how well** the helping mission of an organization or program is accomplished. It represents the proportion of **desirable results achieved** with respect to **all results achieved,** or to the results expected. Effectiveness may be defined for human services by the following ratios:

1.   **Number of Desired Outcomes Achieved**
     _____
                     Total Outcomes Achieved

The above represents the proportion of all clients exiting services who achieve the desired outcome(s). For example, in a mental health center, this might represent the proportion of cases terminating services who demonstrated evidence of improved psychological or social functioning.

This ratio can also be compared against an **expected proportion** of all clients exiting services who achieve the desired outcome(s). The expected proportion then serves as a standard for comparison. This secondary ratio is an indicator of the proportion of the standard that was actually achieved. The standard value may be based on historical data (e.g., average of prior measurement periods) or an assigned value.

2.   **Amount of Benefits Achieved**
     _____
                     Amount of Benefits Expected

The above ratio is also based on a standard, but it measures the proportion of benefits achieved in relation to the standard. For example, it may be expected that on the average clients will earn at least $8000 per year upon job placement after rehabilitation (Amount of Benefits Expected). If the average client earns $9000 per year, effectiveness has exceeded the expectation.

What are some practical ways of measuring effectiveness in human services organizations?

As with efficiency, the nature of the work unit's mission will determine the outcome or benefit indicators used in measuring effectiveness. Also, as with both productivity and efficiency, the measurements should cover specified time periods. However, note that with effectiveness indicators, ratios are multiplied by 100 (as with productivity) to represent the percentage of total outcomes or expected results actually achieved. The following are examples of effectiveness indicators:

1.
$$\frac{\text{Number of Rehabilitated Clients}}{\text{Total Clients Exiting Services}} \times 100$$

2.
$$\frac{\text{Proportion of Clients Terminating an Employment Program with a Suitable Job}}{0.65} \times 100$$

In the latter ratio, 0.65 is the expected proportion (hypothetical) of clients terminating the employment program successfully, based on two year historical data (Simon, 1987).

Evaluating Overall Performance

How should the overall indicators be used in evaluating performance?

For simplicity purposes, a minimum number of representative indicators should be selected to measure productivity, efficiency and effectiveness. For comparability purposes, data should be collected to cover similar periods for each indicator. It should also be assured that the time period for collection (e.g., monthly, quarterly) is sufficiently long to collect reliable information. For example, if an agency generates small numbers of client outcomes that fluctuate widely from month to month, it would be best to use quarterly or bi-yearly data for evaluation of efficiency or effectiveness. Data covering shorter periods would be too unstable for management decision making purposes. If such short term data is used, the manager should wait until enough data is available to reliably discern real trends (e.g., 6 months of monthly ratios) before taking administrative actions based on the information.

What is the process of evaluating work unit or organization performance based on the overall indicators?

Ratios may be evaluated by comparison over time. For example, does the trend of monthly productivity ratios indicate an increase, decrease or general stability?

When the ratio has a built-in standard (see effectiveness) or when a standard value can be established, then ratios for a single period of time can be assigned meaning, as noted in the example regarding effectiveness.

In some instances, the absolute value of a ratio is useful for evaluation purposes. For example, in productivity ratios, estimates can be made regarding acceptable latitude for leave time, supervision and other non direct service activities. Thus, a reasonable expectation can be established for a range of productivity acceptable to management.

Interratio comparisons are most powerful in evaluating overall organization or program performance. Usually, comparing changes over time is most useful for this purpose. As an example, let us consider the following hypothetical substance abuse treatment center information:

Performance Period

	1/87–6/88	7/88–12/88	1/89–6/89
Productivity	72	83	95
Cost Efficiency	0.14	0.16	0.15
Work Efficiency	0.28	0.22	0.15
Effectiveness	65	52	45

The trend over this eighteen month period indicates sharply increasing productivity, stable cost efficiency, decreasing work efficiency and decreasing effectiveness. Knowing that the agency had a large increase in referrals during the period, the data suggests that direct service staff may have excessively high workloads. This appears to be affecting work efficiency and effectiveness. Thus, the performance indicators may suggest the need for more direct service staff (Simon, 1987).

PROCESS INDICATORS

Timeliness

What does timeliness of providing services entail?

Timeliness includes providing services at the time and in the time sequence needed by clients. When services are not provided timely, clients may fail to begin the helping process, drop out before successful completion, or generally fail to make progress. Poor timeliness may also generate complaints that require administrative time and energy, and which may damage the reputation of the organization.

What are some ways of measuring and evaluating timeliness?

Timeliness standards for the most important work unit processes are useful. For example, standards might be established for:

1. Time delay from application for services to initial appointment date.
2. Time delay for scheduling follow-up appointments.
3. Time delay in making benefit payments.

Standards can be established on the basis of **average** time delay—for example, **clients will be seen for intake interviews within an average of ten days from the date they apply for services.** Standards can also be based on a specified percentage of cases that meet a given time delay period—for example, **ninety percent of clients will be seen for intake interviews within ten days of the date they apply for services.**

Quality

What is quality in human services work?

For purposes of this discussion, quality refers to **how well the servicing process is completed** in achieving results (outcomes). In theory, the more effectively services are provided (higher quality), the better the outcomes should be.

As quality increases, so should efficiency and effectiveness, since both are dependent upon outcomes. However, as we know from prior discussion, outcomes in human services are often also dependent on factors other than those related to provision of services. Therefore, the relationship between organization quality; and outcomes, efficiency and effectiveness will usually be less than perfect.

How can quality be measured and evaluated in human services?

Different professions, organizations and fields of practice have developed different methods of quality measurement and evaluation. Usually, these are developed in response to both concerns of the professions and work organizations, as well as external sources such as government, third party payers and accrediting agencies. Most quality review systems involve **peer review** (committees or individuals from inside or outside of the organization), or **supervisory review.**

In professions with highly trained personnel who practice independently, such as medicine and psychology, peer review is the norm. In other specialties and in organizations in which professional and administrative job facets are intertwined, supervisory review or a combination of supervisory and peer review are often used. Generally, the choice of peer or supervisory review is dependent upon who is most knowledgeable in evaluating quality, and the type of review that will best meet the purposes of the review.

In order to effectively measure and evaluate quality, the following is needed:

1. **Criteria** on which to base the evaluation. For example, in counseling, one criterion might be "Was an effective therapeutic relationship established with the client?" Criteria may be selected on the basis of expert opinion or empirically derived information (e.g., studies which show a relationship between a proposed criterion and desired client outcomes).

Criteria should be constructed so that they are reliable (i.e., different raters should agree on ratings and the same raters should rate the same way on different occasions) and valid, (i.e., measure what they are intended to measure).

Both reliability and validity may be problematic in quality review systems. Since criteria must often be general, considerable latitude is left for differences in judgement among reviewers. Validity may be a problem since it is usually most practical to obtain information from case documentation. Under these circumstances, it is often unclear whether the review is a reflection of quality of service or quality of documentation!

2. **A rating system** is needed to evaluate performance on each quality

criterion. For instance, in the above example, was the relationship inadequate, adequate or highly effective?

3. **Standards** should be set for different levels of quality, based on the criteria and how they were rated. For example, the standard for **acceptable quality** might require 85% of all criteria to be rated adequate or better. The standard would be applied to practitioners as well as to the work unit or entire organization.

Quality Evaluation System Examples
What are some examples of quality evaluation systems in human services?

Management Control Project (Chase and Patrick, 1983)—This is a **performance management system** (see Chapter 18) that includes quality evaluation elements. From a quality perspective, it focuses on a few broad, but crucial areas of case management applicable to the StateFederal vocational rehabilitation program. Examples are adequacy of eligibility determinations and individual written rehabilitation plans (see Table VIII).

Service provision is evaluated through several criteria on the basis of case documentation. Each criterion is rated as met (yes) or not met (no) by supervisory personnel. Staff and work units can then be evaluated using standards based on the proportion of reviewed cases that met each criterion. For example, the standard for **comprehensive diagnostic studies** may be set at 35% for a counselor. This system has been adopted (with a variety of modifications) as a basis for providing and evaluating public rehabilitation services by an increasing number of states.

Quality Review System —This is a system currently in development for the Veterans Administration Vocational Rehabilitation and Counseling (VR&C) Program. It consists of a review instrument and total system of quality evaluation and improvement linked to the VR&C Program Evaluation System. The instrument consists of two **segments,** one that measures effectiveness of **professional** decisions and actions and one that measures completion of **administrative and clerical** case actions. Depending upon the types of cases selected for review, one or more **process categories** is reviewed in both segments by a supervisor or peer reviewer. Process categories include **initial evaluation, rehabilitation planning, rehabilitation services, employment services,** and **educational/vocational counseling.** Each process category consists of weighted issues that contain one or more **criteria** to be rated on a five point scale (on the basis of review of case documentation). The scale covers a range from unusually effective

TABLE VIII
PROCESS ANALYSIS CRITERIA AND RATING SYSTEM
FOR MANAGEMENT CONTROL PROJECT
(Abstracted from State of Maryland Sample)

Eligibility Criteria	Rating	
A. Comprehensive Diagnostic Study	Y	N
B. How Functional Limitations & Related Factors Constitute a Vocational Handicap	Y	N
C. Rationale for Reasonable Expectation of Extended Evaluation	Y	N
I.W.R.P. Criteria		
A. Vocational Goal and Rationale	Y	N
B. Objectives & Services Consistent with Functional Limitations	Y	N
C. Established Time Frames for Each Service	Y	N
D. Evaluation Criteria Will Measure Accomplishment of Objectives	Y	N
E. Client Involvement in I.W.R.P. Development	Y	N
Financial Accountability Criteria		
A. Appropriate Severely Handicapped Determination	Y	N
B. Expenditure of Funds Consistent with Agency Policy	Y	N
C. Similar Benefits Considered and Used	Y	N
Case Closure Criteria		
A. Closure Rationale	Y	N
B. Client Participation and Notification of Right of Appeal	Y	N

achievement to not meeting professional or agency standards. Segment scores for each category are then calculated by a computer program and compared against standards. Table IX illustrates issues, and weights for both segments of the **rehabilitation planning** process category. Table X shows criteria for the **plan development** issue of that process category.

Social Work Systems — In the field of social work, Coulton (1979) reported on a comparative analysis of quality assurance systems undertaken by the National Association of Social Workers. Almost all programs reviewed had a peer review component. Such systems tended to contain criteria in the areas of initial contact, assessment, formulation of goals, actual intervention and termination/outcome. Judgements (ratings) on these criteria were qualitative or quantitative, depending on the program reviewed. Examples of general criteria are given for each area in Table XI.

Psychology Example — In the area of psychology, the American Psychological Association (APA)/Civilian Health and Medical Program of

TABLE IX
PROPOSED VA QUALITY REVIEW SYSTEM:
ISSUES AND HYPOTHETICAL WEIGHTS FOR
REHABILITATION PLANNING PROCESS CATEGORY

Segment: *Professional*

Issue	*Weight*
Facilitative Interaction	25
Plan Development	30
Resource Utilization	25
Facilitating Program Completion	20
Total	100

Segment: *Administrative*

Issue	*Weight*
Forms	15
Master Record Maintenance	20
Cost Estimate	20
Case Control	25
Other Administrative Decisions and Actions	20
Total	100

TABLE X
PROPOSED VA QUALITY REVIEW SYSTEM:
CRITERIA FOR PLAN DEVELOPMENT ISSUE OF
REHABILITATION PLANNING PROCESS CATEGORY
(PROFESSIONAL SEGMENT)

1. Was the long range goal logically supported by the medical, social, psychological, and vocational information that was developed during the psychological/vocational evaluation?

2. Did the case manager timely develop with the veteran's participation a plan which was sufficiently comprehensive to meet the specific rehabilitation needs of the veteran, to include: intermediate objectives expressed as expected achievements, individualized evaluation criteria and a frequency of supervision and schedule consistent with the individual veteran's situation?

3. Has the veteran been provided a copy of the rehabilitation plan?

4. Did the file contain a training outline (e.g., course plan from catalog, apprenticeship training outline, etc.) that shows the specific training requirements?

the Uniformed Services (CHAMPUS) Project (Claiborn, Biskin & Friedman, 1982) used claims processors to approve or disapprove claims on

TABLE XI
SAMPLES OF GENERAL CRITERIA FOR SOCIAL WORK PROCESS
(Coulton, 1979)

Area	Sample Criteria
Initial Contact	"Response time to request for social work involvement should be as follows: 1. For emergency situations, less than 30 minutes 2. For priority situations, within same day 3. For all other situations, within second day"
Assessment/Diagnosis	"Are the following areas evaluated: Psychosocial, cultural, psychological, environmental, financial" "Is there a psychosocial diagnosis?"
Treatment Plan/Goals	"Is treatment plan adequate?" "Are appropriate community resources identified?"
Service Delivery	"Are the social work interventions identified?" "Does the intervention indicate adequate involvement with the health care team?" "Are any changes in plan or goal adequately explained?"
Termination/Outcome	"Was there an appropriate disposition of the case?" "Is there a closing note?" "Does the closing note summarize the handling of problems, outcome, reasons for closing, and future planning where relevant?"

the basis of sets of quality criteria. The criteria were based on consensual professional judgement of acceptable practice that could be understood and applied by non-psychologist claims processors. Examples of these criteria are:

1. "Goals must be specifically related to the problems."

2. "Description of problems must include circumstances, frequency, degree of disruption, and point of onset."

3. "Patients in family psychotherapy must receive no more than four individual psychotherapy sessions within a given treatment episode."

4. "Group psychotherapy sessions must have a duration of 60–120 minutes."

Where no consensus could be obtained in certain aspects of psychological practice, peer reviewers were called upon. However, in this situation, only professional opinion regarding the questions under review was used. Explicit criteria, rating levels and standards did not appear to be part of the process.

What is quality assurance?

Quality assurance refers to a variety of methods used to assure that quality service is maintained. It includes credentialing of professionals by universities and other schools, and by licensing and certification boards (including continuing education requirements); setting and enforcing standards for facilities through laws and accreditating agencies; quality evaluation within organizations and through external sources (such as third party payees); and other efforts to bring about quality improvement by organizations and individuals.

INDICATORS OF RESULTS

What are the main types of results relevant to human services organizations?

Results include client outcomes, changes in condition, changes in behavioral or other functioning, changes in financial status, and satisfaction with services. For purposes of this discussion, results may be **intermediate,** i.e., occuring during the servicing process (before completion), or at the conclusion of servicing (**final** results). Generally, sustension of results, i.e., retaining results after long follow-up periods without continuing services, is not considered, since non-servicing related variables tend to intervene and confound the true effects of organization impact. However, this does not suggest that human services organizations should deemphasize focus on long term improvements. It only suggests that such results are often difficult to attribute significantly to past interventions.

What are some relevant results indicators?

These include gain scales, goal attainment scales, measures of final outcomes or benefits, and client satisfaction indicators.

What are gain scales?

These may be used for assessment of intermediate or final results. They include measures which can assess change from the time services are initiated to some later point in time. Such scales may use (client) self report or practitioner report formats. They must show high reliability to effectively serve their purposes and should relate to outcomes desired as a result of services provided. Some representative scales include:

Life Functioning Index (LFI) (Turner, 1982)—This is a functional assessment inventory which uses a self report format. It includes items in the areas of vocation, education, self-care, residence, mobility, and communication.

Rehabilitation Gain Scale (Reagles, Wright & Butler, 1970)—This instrument measures client responses (self report) which reflect vocational success and personal-social adjustment.

Rehabilitation Services Outcome Measure (Westerhide & Lenhart, 1973)—This instrument uses counselor information to measure change in employment prognosis, educational status, economic and vocational status, physical functioning, adjustment to disability, and social competency.

What are goal attainment scales?

These are scales which measure and evaluate services according to the attainment of **individual** client goals (Kiresuk & Lund, 1979). When this can be accomplished reliably, it can provide situation specific information for a variety of evaluation purposes.

The technique of goal attainment scaling involves specifying a range of potential outcome (goal) areas related to an activity and establishing possible attainment levels. In each client situation, the relevant outcome areas are designated. The level of attainment is noted at intake and at completion of services. Total scores can then be calculated at both points and a difference score obtained. This technique and its application in a county mental health setting is described in detail by Kiresuk and Lund (1979). Goal attainment scaling is consistent with management by objectives and other individualized goal oriented management approaches.

What are some measures of final outcome?

In vocational rehabilitation services, a pre-determined suitable employment goal is usually the expected final outcome. In public rehabilitation, this is represented by the **26 closure** (State-Federal program) and the **rehabilitated case status** (Veterans Administration program). In private rehabilitation, employment or re-employment is also usually a primary expected outcome. Suitable employment usually includes competitive or sheltered employment, self-employment, homebound employment, supported employment and in some instances return to homemaker status. Other indicators of final outcome in vocational rehabilitation include achievement of independent living goals, as well as less successful outcomes such as interruptions of services by the client or agency, and unsuitable employment.

As noted earlier, some attempts have been made to devise complex measures of employment related rehabilitation outcomes by using weighted indexes. Such measures have tried to account for case difficulty based on client characteristics or level of outcome achieved. However, the factors involved in weighting are complex, making it difficult to establish an acceptable, easily understandable method. Cooper, Harper, Vest & Pearce (1978) summarize a variety of proposed case weighting systems.

In medically oriented rehabilitation and in other human services, single index final outcome indicators (such as suitable employment) are less applicable or readily available. Thus, multidimensional gain scales or goal attainment scaling type indicators may be more appropriate to assess final outcomes. (Ideally, from a holistic perspective, this is also probably the most appropriate method in vocational rehabilitation. However, the economic framework within which vocational rehabilitation services are usually provided and supported, tends to require dependence mostly on the criterion of suitable employment.)

What are some benefits indicators?

These include:
1. **Increase in earnings** (weekly, monthly etc.) from service initiation to completion.
2. **Reduction in public assistance grants** from service initiation to completion.

How can client satisfaction be measured?

Client satisfaction indicators should measure satisfaction with the services rendered through the organization. Although many scales have been developed for this purpose, the Client Satisfaction Questionnaire (CSQ) (Larsen, Attkisson, Hargreaves & Nguyen, 1979) appears to have particular promise for general application. This scale has an 18 item and an 8 item version. The 8 item version appears most desirable due to its short length and very high reliability (Attkisson & Zwick, 1982). Items on the CSQ are generic and thus it can be used to measure satisfaction with many types of human services. It is noted that this and other measures of satisfaction are likely to tap general life satisfaction and related factors to some degree. However, research with the CSQ suggests that this accounts for 25% or less of the variance of scores (Roberts, Pascoe & Attkisson, 1983; LeVois, Nguyen & Attkisson, 1981).

Does client satisfaction relate to any other performance variables?

Yes. Per a literature review of patient satisfaction in primary health care, Pascoe (1983) found that patient satisfaction reflects quality of health care and is predictive of health related behaviors such as compliance, and switching providers. It was also related to self reports of improved health. Generally, clients who are not satisfied would probably be expected to terminate services and not follow through with recommendations as readily as those who feel satisfied.

Chapter 12

PROGRAM EVALUATION

What is program evaluation?

Program evaluation is a process for developing and using descriptive data, experimental studies and other quantitative information to assess how effectively and efficiently a program is achieving it's intent.

What are the major purposes of program evaluation?

Program improvement and accountability.

How does program evaluation contribute to program improvement?

Program evaluation contributes to **improved decision making** and to **effecting organizational change.** For example, program evaluation information may indicate desirable types of cost efficiency improvements, that different groups should be targeted for services, and that different servicing methods would result in better outcomes. Future planning could then include goals, strategies and resource allocation for serving more appropriate groups. Supervisory and management interventions would focus on effecting change in how services are provided through direct service staff and on the reorganization of work units to improve efficiency and effectiveness.

How does program evaluation impact on accountability?

Program evaluation contributes to accountability inside and outside of the organization by providing data on program performance. Accountability answers the questions:

What are we accomplishing?
How well are we accomplishing it?
How efficiently are we accomplishing it?
Are we accomplishing what is mandated (public agencies)?
What are we doing to improve our efforts and results?

165

Accountability information provides confirmation to sources of funding and resources, to consumers, and the public that the program is (or is not) worth supporting, and to what extent. Thus, it serves a public relations purpose related to resource acquisition. This use of program evaluation may pose ethical dilemmas, since programs may not want to take the risk of looking bad. Thus, comprehensive program evaluation is sometimes avoided or limited to areas that will be known to show positive results.

How does program evaluation fit into the three phases (Planning-Implementation-Evaluation) of the agency/program management cycle?

As part of the **planning** process, a program evaluation component consisting of goals, objectives or standards may be included for each program in the organization. This component differs from long and short term goal setting in that program evaluation is more concerned with establishing effectiveness and efficiency related criteria with **ongoing** performance expectations.

Long and short term goals may include some criteria covered in the program evaluation component. However, they also encompass coverage beyond specific program concerns and focus on areas pertinent during specified time frames. For example, an agency may be responsible for three different programs, each of which has a program evaluation system. The program evaluation systems will be concerned with maintaining the ongoing integrity of each program. However, the agency may have long term (strategic) goals (e.g., new program development and expanded technology) that extend beyond ongoing program performance concerns. Individual work units may also have short term (operational) goals linked to the agency's long term goals, as well as some goals that relate to improving in specific **program** areas over the short term (e.g., increasing number of rehabilitated cases), even though those areas may also have a fixed standard or goal as a component of the program evaluation system.

Program evaluation may impact on the **implementation** phase through inputs, processes or outputs. For example, findings, analysis and change efforts may focus on client or employee selection, or on resource acquisition (**inputs**). Likewise, emphasis could be on the supervision or client servicing **processes**. With regard to **outputs**, concentration might be on productivity, efficiency, effectiveness, and client or employee satisfaction.

Program evaluation impacts on the **evaluation** phase of the cycle by requiring systematic, regular analyses of agency operations and programs through use of the feedback process.

How do research and evaluation research differ from program evaluation?

Research is scientific inquiry with the purpose of studying relationships among variables in order to increase general knowledge. Immediate applicability to specific programs and situations is not a primary function of research.

Evaluation research uses research designs (e.g., experimental or quasi-experimental) to study problems related to making decisions about programs. For example, a study might be done to determine which of several treatment interventions lead to the most cost effective program outcomes. Evaluation research is one technique that can be used in conducting program evaluation.

What are some different types of program evaluation?

Formative evaluation is program evaluation conducted during the development and maintenance phases of a program to improve implementation. It is contrasted with **summative evaluation** which produces a summary statement about program effectiveness (Morris & FitzGibbon, 1978) and which may be done for the purpose of making a value judgement with regard to program continuation. **Goal oriented evaluation** determines how well mission, goals and objectives are being met, while **goal free evaluation** determines how well actual outcomes meet the needs of clients (Spaniol, 1977).

How often should program evaluation be done?

It may be done periodically (on a project basis), or on an ongoing basis. Ongoing evaluation is recommended, since program evaluation then becomes integrated with other continuing management analysis and improvement efforts. Periodic evaluations may have a tendency to be reviewed and "filed," unless controls on implementing results are in place.

What should be the scope of program evaluation?

This depends upon the agency commitment to and resources for program evaluation activities, as well as benefits in relation to cost. It also depends upon external requirements for program evaluation, such as through legislation or accrediting agencies. Table XII summarizes the potential scope of program evaluation. Evaluation may take place with respect to any level or type of coverage in each of the seven areas. It may be as simple as using data derived from routine monitoring, or using subjective information to report on a few aspects of service delivery. However, it may be as complex as conducting experimental and quasi-experimental studies regarding service delivery and program management, which may be used to influence changes in legislation, the agency or a group of agencies.

TABLE XII
POTENTIAL SCOPE OF PROGRAM EVALUATION

Area	Levels or Types of Coverage
Program Responsibility (Bennett & Weisenger, 1974)	Total Program Program Management Service Delivery
Type of Analysis (Bennett & Weisenger, 1974)	Output Process Input
Type of Measures (Bennett & Weisenger, 1974)	Effort (staff time etc.) Impact (on social change) Effectiveness (client outcomes) Efficiency (program economics) Quality (goodness of program)
Data Collected	Evaluation Research Descriptive Studies Simple Monitoring Subjective Data
Variables Impacted (Miller et al., 1977)	Socio/Political Context Total Agency Program
Evaluator Involvement	Total Program Development Process Change Agent Planning Conducting Studies Clerical Data Collection
Information Use	Improve General Knowledge in the Field Organization Development Program Improvement Accountability

PROGRAM EVALUATION EXAMPLES

What are some examples of approaches to program evaluation?

State-Federal Vocational Rehabilitation Program — Based upon requirements in the Rehabilitation Act of 1973, nine program evaluation "standards" were established by the Secretary of Health, Education and Welfare (summarized by Rubin, 1974):

1. "To serve the target population equitably"
2. "To place clients in relevant gainful employment"
3. "To avoid undue delays in the process"
4. "To use resources efficiently"
5. "To ensure manageable caseloads for counselors"
6. "To ensure retention of the benefits achieved through rehabilitation"
7. "To provide needed post-employment benefits"
8. "To identify why clients are not successfully rehabilitated"
9. "To ensure client satisfaction with the written rehabilitation plan"

The mandate for program evaluation standards in this case was an attempt to enhance accountability, establish effectiveness criteria and encourage comprehensive evaluation by state agencies of their programs (Rubin, 1974). However, the nine "standards" were very broad and left room for inconsistency and disagreement regarding measurement and application. Since the initial standards were issued, several proposed revisions have taken place, due to perceived unsuitability of the original standards by state agencies.

Most recently, the Council of State Administrators for Vocational Rehabilitation (CASVR) (1984) suggested the following standards for use across states (summarized from Walls & Tseng, 1987):

1. Ratio of total benefits to total costs.
2. Percentage of accepted cases that are closed rehabilitated (status "26") annually.
3. Percentage of rehabilitated cases that are severely disabled.
4. Annual change in proportion of severely disabled rehabilitated closures.
5. Number of rehabilitated cases per $100,000 spent adjusted for inflation.
6. Percentage of rehabilitated cases that are competitively employed.
7. Average earnings at closure of rehabilitated clients (adjusted for inflation).
8. Annual change in adjusted earnings of rehabilitated closures.

9. Comparison of earnings for rehabilitated closures before and after vocational rehabilitation services.

At this time, these standards have not been implemented by the federal government, nor has any other formalized comprehensive program evaluation system. However, states are required to submit certain statistical data on a regular basis to the Rehabilitation Services Administration. This is followed by feedback and advice based on interstate comparisons. Emphasis on the "26 closure" criterion tends to play a significant role in these evaluations.

VA Vocational Rehabilitation and Counseling (VR&C) Program (VA, 1987)—In 1985, this program began development of a comprehensive goal oriented program evaluation system. The intent was to establish measurable goals and objectives that could be integrated into a total performance management model. This model would be used to regularly evaluate program accomplishments and establish a basis for ongoing program improvement. Development of the system was based on program evaluation models in the rehabilitation field, and on organization development approaches which stress employee involvement as a method of assuring effective, committed implementation. Thus, the strategy was to involve all staff possible at the field and central program management levels as the system was created.

The project was guided by a small committee consisting of field and program management staff. A mission statement was constructed by the committee. Goals were then established by constructing a "goal importance" questionnaire for completion by all field and program personnel, followed by statistical analysis and selection of eight proposed goals by the committee. Volunteer field subcommittees were then established for each goal, to develop objectives, measurement methods and evaluation standards (expectancies), under the guidance of the program evaluation committee. The mission statement and final goals, are as follows:

Mission Statement: To provide comprehensive counseling and rehabilitation service, using the most advanced methods and techniques, for eligible veterans and their families, to ensure their opportunity to attain realistic and satisfying vocational and personal goals.

Goal 1: To ensure that potentially eligible veterans will apply for vocational rehabilitation services as a result of a systematic program of education and intervention

Goal 2: To ensure that client service and cost decisions by VR&C staff will be consistent with legal requirements and the rehabilitation needs of service-disabled veterans

Goal 3: To ensure that clients will compensate for their disability limitations by improving psychosocial, education, and/or vocational skills

Goal 4: Program participants will acquire and retain suitable employment and/or maximum independence in daily living

Goal 5: To ensure that clients will be satisfied that the services they receive are useful in achieving their rehabilitation goals

Goal 6: To ensure that rehabilitation services will be provided in a timely and efficient manner

Goal 7: Program resources will be used efficiently to best meet the rehabilitation needs of eligible clients

Goal 8: To ensure that professional delivery of services will be provided through ongoing staff development, program evaluation and research

The following illustrates several specific objectives and the format for measurement and evaluation:

Goal 6

Objective b:	Employment services will be completed in a timely manner
Data Element:	Elapsed time in employment services status
Who Applied To:	Cases exiting employment services status
When Applied:	At the time employment services case status is closed
Expectancies:	Minimal — 320 days
	Goal — 237 days
	Optimal — 157 days

Goal 4

Objective a:	Program participants will acquire and retain suitable competitive employment
Data Element:	Proportion of veterans exiting employment services case status who acquire and retain suitable employment
Who Applied To:	All veterans exiting employment services case status
When Applied:	At the time the veteran exits the status

Expectancies: Minimal—50%
Goal—60%
Optimal—75%

The VA program evaluation system is planned for initial implementation in fiscal year 1989. To date, objectives for some goals need further development and thus only parts of the system can now be implemented. Further information will be needed to establish whether the system is able to meet its intent and purposes.

Rehabilitation Facility Systems—The Commission on Accreditation of Rehabilitation Facilities (CARF) has published guidelines for installing program evaluation in organizations serving people with disabilities, including standards for such systems (CARF, 1976, 1989). According to CARF (1989), program evaluation is "a systematic procedure for determining the effectiveness and efficiency with which results following rehabilitation services are achieved by persons served. These results are collected on a regular or continuous basis rather than through periodic sampling." CARF further notes the importance of "results" as an underlying principle of this definition. On the basis of identifying results and effects of programs, performance can be improved and community support enhanced.

The basic standards around which the program evaluation system should be developed include (CARF, 1989):

1. "The evaluation system should provide for a statement of purposes [of the organization], program goals, and objectives."

2. "There should be relationships among the statement of purposes, program goals, objectives, population served, and services provided."

3. "Statements of program goals and objectives should meet certain conditions." Goals should be oriented toward specific program levels and objectives should operationalize the results component of goal statements. CARF further emphasizes achievability of goals and objectives, measurability of objectives and the linkage between program goals and objectives.

4. "The evaluation system should provide measures of effectiveness...[i.e.] the degree to which established goals and objectives are achieved."

5. "The evaluation system should provide for measures of the efficiency of the organization."

6. "There should be a system to describe and monitor who is served."

7. "The evaluation system results should be communicated to appropriate parties and should be utilized in organization decision-making."

8. "Appropriate information on results should be made available in an understandable fashion to the governing body and staff, and to the public, including purchasers, contributors, and consumers."

9. "Results data produced by the evaluation system should be made available to decision-makers as soon as possible after the close of a reporting period; also it should be used by management to maintain or improve program performance."

10. "The organization should have a mechanism to review continuously the adequacy of its evaluation system."

The **Standards Manual for Organizations Serving People with Disabilities,** 1989 Edition, expands upon the above guidelines and also includes specific standards for program evaluation systems, including basic elements which should be included. The CARF model is a goal oriented program evaluation approach to the total management of client results.

General Open Systems Model — Baker and Northman (1979) illustrate the use of an open systems model to evaluate input, process, output and their relationships in a school mental health clinic, with the purpose of program improvement. While the earlier examples illustrated systems that evaluate achievement of goals or standards, this open systems model uses a variety of data to examine each system phase and its interactions with other phases within the context of a program's overall intent. The example illustrates a one time evaluation using descriptive and rating data, and statistical analysis of relationships among types of data. Examples of information gathered include:

1. **Input** — Ten categories of problems were noted (e.g. achievement, overactivity, misbehavior at school) with the percent of students presenting each category of problem at the time of referral.

2. **Throughput** — Twelve categories of services were identified (e.g. individual therapy, medication, casework), with the percentage of utilization in clinic cases.

3. **Output** — Based upon review of case records, evaluators rated results of school clinic treatment on a five point scale (outstanding accomplishment, moderate accomplishment, no change, somewhat negative outcome, very poor accomplishment). Of 108 cases reviewed, numbers and percentages of cases in each result category were reported (e.g. 2.78% — outstanding accomplishment).

4. **Throughput-Output Relationships** — Using chi square analysis, it was shown that individual therapy (throughput) was related to improvement (output) when the problem was misbehavior in school.

5. **Input-Output Relationships** — Frequency of improvement (output) was related to each type of presenting problem (input). For example, improvement was shown in 20.83% of overactivity situations.

6. **Input-Throughput Relationships** — Chi square analysis was used to establish relationships between type of problem presented (input) and type of treatment offered (throughput). For example, a significant association was found between the existence of misbehavior problems and the use of medication.

The above illustrates less of a goal oriented approach to program evaluation than prior examples. However, it provides a comprehensive description of what is happening and how various components of service delivery relate to one another. This gives information needed to make corrections so that the overall mission of a program is accomplished more effectively and efficiently.

Evaluation Research Approach — Hogarty, Goldberg & Schooler (1979) illustrate an application of evaluation research in a broad context of community aftercare of psychiatric patients. In this one time study, three community clinics were involved in answering the question "What, if anything, could be done to enhance the notoriously low levels of adjustment that characterize schizophrenic patients while they remain in the community?" This was essentially an experimental study which examined the effects of drugs; the effects of a combination of intensive social casework and vocational rehabilitation counseling called "major role therapy"; and the interactive effects of these two forms of treatment. A major finding from the standpoint of program improvement was that "the achievement of optimum prophylactic and restorative benefits for schizophrenic patients requires both drug and non drug treatment."

It might be questioned whether this study falls in the category of research or evaluation research, independent of a "program evaluation" effort. However, in the broad context of the community aftercare system for treating released hospital patients, the study can be viewed as a **program evaluation** initiative since it is concerned with improving the results of treatment in these settings.

UTILIZATION OF PROGRAM EVALUATION RESULTS

Are program evaluation results always utilized?

No. The extent of utilization depends on such factors as the relevance of program evaluation data to administrators and the degree of involvement of administrators and resource providers in the planning and evaluation process. Also, the involvement of other program participants (e.g., direct service staff) in planning and evaluation, temporary political factors and priorities, and level of threat of the information (to the program) may impact on its use. When program evaluation is generated and controlled by external sources such as government oversight and accrediting groups, utilization may occur because it is mandated. Internally generated evaluation information may be easier to ignore or use minimally, although under the right conditions (e.g., support of top management and staff) there may be motivation for constructive use.

What are some methods to improve utilization?

Program evaluation designed to be an ongoing part of agency management and which is incorporated in organization development efforts should be effective in assuring utilization. This allows the agency/program management cycle to operate according to its intent by encouraging continuous review and adjustment of programs. When program evaluation is clearly part of the total agency management process, including integration into the performance evaluation system (see chapter 13), utilization becomes a priority. Such an approach requires involvement of all staff, **particularly top management,** in development of evaluation components and processes, and in continuous analysis of feedback provided by the system. This should eliminate some threat and place all staff in the best position for effective program decision making and control. Involvement of top management is crucial, since that is where decisions are most often made regarding what is important to the program and organization.

In an article from the The Grantsmanship Center NEWS, Van Maanen notes several techniques for evaluator use in improving results utilization. These are summarized as follows:

1. Using the efforts of highly placed decision makers who strongly support evaluation results utilization and who reward other staff who share that viewpoint.

2. Involving all program participants in the evaluation process from the outset.
3. Interfering as little as possible in the workings of the program during the program evaluation process.
4. Creating mechanisms for continuous, short term feedback to program participants.
5. Candor regarding the limitations and virtues of the evaluation project.
6. Insisting on clear role definitions between the evaluator, program staff and other participants.

Chapter 13

EVALUATING EMPLOYEE PERFORMANCE

What is employee evaluation?

It is a way of determining whether employees meet performance expectations, and of motivating them to maximize achievements related to organization goals.

What is the main purpose of employee evaluation?

To link employee achievement with with how well work units, programs and the organization achieve their goals, objectives, and mission. Since employees are responsible for doing the work, how well they do it is the key factor in determining how much is actually accomplished by the organization.

Are there different approaches to the performance evaluation process?

Great variability exists in human services agencies with regard to how performance evaluation is carried out. In some instances, it is a very formal process that includes written performance standards, a specified evaluation period, scheduled supervisory-employee conferences and rewards or sanctions linked to evaluation results. Less formal approaches may include informal feedback only at the request of the employee or supervisor, non specific or unwritten expectations and vague or non-specific policies for using rewards.

What should formal employee evaluation entail?

It should include a method of **measuring** performance achievements in categories related to important job tasks. Generally, this involves establishing goals, objectives or criteria in each category which can be applied to individual employees. The goals, objectives or criteria should include one or more standards on which to **evaluate** and assign a qualitative level of achievement. For example, if the criteria involves percent of satisfied clients, the standard may be set at one level (e.g., 45% for satisfactory performance), or at more than one level (e.g., 45% for satisfactory performance and 60% for outstanding performance). A method is then needed to summarize category ratings and the overall rating across categories.

Employee evaluation should also include methods for supervisor-supervisee **communication** regarding the basis for and results of evaluation, and to provide periodic feedback of evaluation information. Lastly, mechanisms should be available for **management actions** to improve or maintain performance; to promote exemplary employees; or to transfer, demote or terminate employees who cannot perform competently.

What are the legal implications of formal vs informal employee evaluation approaches?

In the United States, legal precedent favors the use of the formal approach. Since employee evaluation has implications for promotions, terminations and other rewards or sanctions, conflicts related to potential discrimination may arise. As with employee selection, potential grievances and litigation in this area can be costly and time consuming. A formal approach to evaluation is likely to be most defensible in successfully resolving such problems.

What should a formal employee evaluation system include to assure legal defensibility?

Based upon court cases, Klasson, Thompson, and Luben (1980) describe criteria for an appraisal system from the perspective of legal defensibility. They suggest including formal job analysis, performance standards relevant to job dimensions, complete documentation, standardization, high objectivity, and a statement of the purpose of the appraisal and its mandatory use by management. In addition, they suggest an appraisal process that assures well trained appraisers, opportunities for appraisers to observe representative samples of employee performance, standard administration and scoring of appraisals, and use of multiple appraisers when that will improve the quality of assessments.

MEASURING AND EVALUATING PERFORMANCE

What is the role of job analysis in measuring performance?

Job analysis serves as the basis for defining important job functions. Related functions may then be organized into categories for which performance criteria and standards may be defined. For example, one group of related functions for a rehabilitation counselor may include work adjustment counseling, personal adjustment counseling and vocational counseling. These might be organized for performance measurement purposes into the **category** "Provision of Counseling Services." Another group of related functions might be making eligibility determinations, making decisions regarding choice of training programs, and decision making in the area of program costs. These functions could be organized into the category "Program Decision Making." Performance criteria and standards would then be established for measuring performance in these categories.

What are performance criteria?

These represent the **basis used to judge performance** in a specified category of performance. For example, performance in the category "Provision of Counseling Services" may be judged by level of service quality (as measured by a quality control system), timeliness in providing service and number of clients served during a specified period.

What are standards?

Standards represent the **level of performance** required for a specified level of achievement on a performance criterion. For example, using the criterion "timeliness in providing service," the standard for satisfactory performance may be set to allow no more than an average of 90 days to complete counseling services with clients. Performance significantly better than the standard (less than 90 days) would imply better than satisfactory performance, while performance significantly below the standard (greater than 90 days) would imply lower than satisfactory performance.

How do standards differ from goals or objectives?

Standards specify a **minimum required level** of performance (and sometimes other levels) on a performance criterion. Specific goals and objectives define a **desired** or **expected** level of performance with reference to a performance criterion. Sometimes goals or objectives and standards are used similarly; however, standards tend to imply greater absoluteness.

What are the major approaches to measuring performance in human services?

Measurement can be viewed on a continuum from subjective to objective. The most subjective methods use general or global criteria, such as employee personality and appearance, and rely on the rater's subjective judgements as the basis for determining the level of performance (standard) achieved. More objective methods tend to use specific, measurable results oriented criteria, such as "number of rehabilitated cases," and rely on objective data counts to determine the level of performance (standard) achieved.

What are some measurement devices applicable in human services?

Rating scales and **goal oriented systems** are the most commonly used devices.

Rating Scales

What are the major types of rating scales?

These include graphic rating scales and behaviorally anchored rating scales. **Graphic rating scales** usually include a set of standard criteria on which each employee is rated along a numerical scale, or a scale with anchor statements (Donnelly, Gibson & Ivancevich, 1987). **Anchor statements** define standards or levels of performance along the scale, from highest to lowest. Table XIII illustrates several items from graphic rating scales.

Behaviorally anchored rating scales (BARS) use critical incident statements to define various levels of performance along a scale for each relevant job performance category. Knowledgable employees who occupy the position to be rated identify the critical incident statements which serve as minimum requirements necessary to achieve each specified level of performance (standard).

A BARS procedure may encourage greater employee commitment to high achievement because of involvement in system development. It may also allow a more objective rating approach than other rating scales, although a recent study by Murphy and Constans (1987) suggests that

TABLE XIII
EXAMPLES OF GRAPHIC RATING SCALES

1. *Productivity*

   Low   1   2   3   4   5   High

2. *Quality*

   Exceptionally high   _____
   Usually superior   _____
   Average   _____
   Some problems   _____
   Usually poor   _____

3. *Personal Qualities* (appearance, honesty, integrity)

Outstanding	Good	Satisfactory	Fair	Unsatisfactory
_____	_____	_____	_____	_____

4. *Timeliness of Counseling*

1	2	3	4	5
Almost never completes cases timely	Consistently completes cases timely, but usually has a few old cases		Always completes cases timely; never has old cases	

BARS may be no less prone to bias than other rating scales. A sample of a BARS item is presented in Table XIV and is described further with regard to rehabilitation applications by Sample (1984).

What are the advantages and disadvantages of rating scales?

Rating scales are often very simple to use, particularly when they are applied subjectively by raters. However, **unless objective data is used** as the basis for rating, these scales are subject to the following errors (Donnelly, Gibson & Ivancevich, 1984):

Halo Effects — This is the tendency to assign ratings on all criteria based on a general impression. For example, if a rater is very impressed with an employee's work quality, this may carry over to judgements on all other rating criteria. Halo effects may be positive or negative.

Leniency/Harshness Errors — This is a rater bias toward rating all subordinates too easy or harsh with respect to actual performance.

Central Tendency Errors — This refers to the tendency of some raters to rate all employees close to the midpoint, with an unwillingness to assign high or low ratings.

TABLE XIV
SAMPLE OF A BEHAVIORALLY ANCHORED RATING SCALE

Counseling Competence

Most Competent Performance—shows highest level of skill	7—Can be expected to train others, supervise and provide consultation on counseling methods with regard to all types of cases.
	6—Can be expected to provide meaningful assistance with the most difficult clients and client problems.
Average Competence—has skill to handle most routine work	5—Can be expected to provide meaningful assistance to some groups of difficult clients because of specialized knowledge and/or experience (e.g. head injury, psychiatric disabilities).
	4—Can be expected to independently help typical clients resolve vocational, educational and personal concerns.
	3—Can be expected to indicate (on quality assurance review), more than average number of instances where services were omitted or could have been provided more effectively.
Low Competence—has skill to effectively complete a minimum range of counseling work	2—Can be expected to fail to demonstrate, maintain or develop professional skills; receives legitimate complaints from other staff or clients regarding competence.
	1—Can be expected to show lack of skill in assisting clients with simple problems; receives frequent complaints regarding competency and shows high error rate in quality assurance review.

Recency Errors—These are rating errors based on judgement of **recent** employee behaviors rather than behaviors over the entire rating period.

Due to the above, the results of subjectively used rating scales can lead to invalid ratings as well as employee perceptions of bias and unfairness. In addition, such methods are unlikely to meet the criteria for legal defensibility, if that becomes necessary.

Goal Oriented Systems

What are goal oriented systems?

These are methods that establish goals, objectives, or criterion statements with associated standards, for several categories of performance. Such items may be highly specific and measurable, or general and subject to interpretation. They usually focus on **employee behaviors** in completing processes and achieving results. They may be included in a set of performance standards for groups of employees with the same duties (e.g., psychologists or clerks), or they may be constructed for individual employees. The latter approach is used in Management by Objective (MBO) systems. Examples of specific items characteristic of the goal oriented approach are shown in Table XV.

TABLE XV
ITEMS CHARACTERISTIC OF THE GOAL ORIENTED APPROACH

1. *Example of Group Performance Standard Items for a Rehabilitation Counselor position*

Interpersonal Skills

Direct counseling results in no more than three valid complaints (per supervisor judgement) by clients during the review period. Valid complaints may relate to the attitude or treatment directed toward the client by the psychologist, or the service rendered.

Professional Development

Accomplishes at least one substantial staff development experience during the rating period. This should be an activity independent of in-service training, which contributes significantly and meaningfully to increased professional knowledge or skills. Examples include attendance at a series of meetings at a national conference or state professional association conference, taking a university or other course, conducting a research project, or completing library research. The experience should be oriented toward your professional development needs, agreed upon by the supervisor in advance, and incorporated in the annual staff development plan.

2. *Examples of individual objectives for a manager of a work adjustment unit in a rehabilitation center*
   During fiscal year 1989, productivity of work unit staff will increase by 5% over the prior year.
   During fiscal year 1989, at least 60% of clients served in the unit will achieve job placement.

What are some advantages and disadvantages of the goal oriented approach?

This approach can be highly objective. It can thus be applied uniformly and fairly, avoiding some of the pitfalls of subjective rating scales. It is likely to provide clearer performance expectations and information to employees and thus enhance behavior modification in the desired direction. It can therefore provide a clearer linkage to measurable goals and objectives of the organization and its programs. It may also provide defensible information for legal purposes, if necessary.

Disadvantages include difficulties in and employee resistance to establishing specific criteria for measurement. Identifying measurable criteria is of particular concern to some human services personnel who believe that the complexity of the servicing process cannot be measured accurately by objective data and "numerical counts." Other disadvantages include the need for extensive data collection, maintenance, control, and documentation by all levels of staff. In some instances, it may be found at the time of evaluation, that all data is not available, or could not reasonably be collected during the rating period.

Measurement and Evaluation Procedures

What is a general procedure for establishing formal employee evaluation measures?

1. Conduct a job analysis for each position or group of like positions.

2. Group the most important job functions into categories for which performance measures will be developed, and name each category (e.g., counseling skills, job placement effectiveness, administrative efficiency etc.). Usually, two to six categories should suffice.

3. Designate those categories of performance that are **critical** to accomplishing the job (i.e., overall job requirements cannot be met if performance is not satisfactory in these areas). For example, a nurse who does not perform satisfactorily in the category "Patient Care" might not be performing adequately regardless of how well he or she performs in the category "Paperwork Management."

4. Decide on the type of measurement devices to be used.

5. Establish relevant items (criteria and standards) for each category. Generally, items on which employees will be rated should be related to the work unit's and organization's goals and objectives, including program evaluation objectives. For example, if the program or agency has a goal which includes providing services within a specified time period, at least one item in employee performance standards should pertain to that area. This assures the linkage between employee evaluation and organizational achievement. Some potential areas for item development are included in Chapter 11.

6. In goal oriented systems, set goals, objectives or standards at **achievable levels.** They should be difficult, but not impossible to achieve. Standards should include a minimum level for acceptable performance.

7. Decide on a method for scoring each category, including whether some items in a category will be weighted differently than others. The method should be defendable as fair. Some examples of methods for category scoring are as follows:

   a. **When using a goal oriented system** establish a set of items (criteria) for each category, with two levels of standards. For example, for each item, there will be a satisfactory standard and an outstanding standard. To perform at the satisfactory level **on a category**, performance for **all items** must be achieved at least at the level of the satisfactory standard. To perform at the outstanding level, performance for all items must be achieved at the level of the outstanding standard.

b. Follow the procedure in 7,a. However, use only a satisfactory standard for each item. Then use a normative basis to determine the outstanding level of performance for the category. For example, only those employees who rank among the highest two scorers on all items are assigned an outstanding rating on the category. This procedure controls for too many employees achieving the highest standard and thus failing to differentiate the highest from average performers. However, it does not provide clear expectations for employees beyond the satisfactory level of performance.

c. **When using a rating scale**, establish a minimum total score for acceptable performance on each category. For example, if three items consisting of a 1–5 rating scale are used in a category, a total score of 9 might be considered satisfactory performance for that category. Different levels of performance could be assigned different total score cutoff levels.

d. Follow the procedure in 6,c. However, a normative procedure might be used for determining higher levels of performance. For example, only the two highest total scorers (on a category) might be rated outstanding for that category.

e. A weighting procedure can be used in 6, c and d by assigning a percentage weight to each item (totaling 100%), multiplying the weight by the rating on each item, and totalling the weighted scores. For example:

Item	Rating	×	Weight	=	Weighted Score
1	5		40%		2
2	3		30%		0.9
3	4		30%		1.2
		Total	Weighted	Score	4.1

8. Decide on an objective method for assigning a **total rating** (sum of all categories). For example, five overall rating levels could be established: Outstanding, Highly Effective, Satisfactory, Minimally Acceptable, Not Meeting Requirements. For an Outstanding rating, employees might be required to be rated outstanding on all categories. For a Satisfactory rating, employees might be required to be rated at least satisfactory on all categories, while for a Highly Effective rating, ratings of satisfactory

on some categories and outstanding on others might be required. A Minimally Acceptable rating might require at least satisfactory ratings in all **critical** categories.

COMMUNICATIONS IN EMPLOYEE EVALUATION

What types of communications are important in the employee evaluation process?

These include supervisor-supervisee collaboration on what and how performance will be measured, regular feedback of performance information, and appraisal reviews.

Supervisor-Supervisee Collaboration

What is the significance and process of supervisor-supervisee collaboration in developing performance measures?

A collaborative process helps establish employee focus on and commitment to the criteria and standards for measuring and evaluating performance. It also helps to clearly define employee expectations, and may be the most effective alternative with employees who resist being subjected to supervisory evaluation.

The collaboration process can include group development of criteria and standards, when the same items will be applied to more than one employee. It can also include joint development (by supervisor and supervisee) of individual employee goals and objectives. The collaboration process can actually range from eliciting feedback from employees on management developed items to having employees develop the items which are then modified by supervisors, if necessary. Group or individual brainstorming sessions with participation by both supervisors and employees may be particularly effective.

Is collaboration always appropriate?

No. If employees expect or prefer performance standards to be set for them, if they do not value collaborative efforts, and if they are likely to understand their performance expectations and believe they are reasonable, then a highly collaborative process may be unnecessary. With professional employees, however, performance measurement is often complex, and the collaborative experience helps establish consensus on what is important to the agency and why. This can have a positive effect on encouraging employees to be more committed to cooperatively working in the direction of organizational goals, even when these conflict with personal preference or philosophy.

Feedback of Performance Information

What should feedback entail?

Feedback should include all pertinent information about performance: both positive components and areas needing improvement.

How and when should regular feedback be provided?

Feedback on performance should be provided routinely and informally during regular supervisory contacts. It should also be provided by supplying written data to employees on a regular basis, when possible (e.g., monthly or quarterly). If criteria and standards are objective, regular data feedback can provide a basis for self evaluation and correction, and operation of intrinsic reward mechanisms.

Should regular feedback include sharing individual data with the work group and among work groups?

In some work environments, sharing can improve group and individual performance by encouraging competition and group centered control. However, if intense competition is supported by supervisors, dysfunctional results can occur. For example, some employees may be embarassed, discouraged and **demotivated** because they are unable to legitimately keep up with the other group members, even though they can meet their performance standards and provide effective services. Also, when competition is emphasized, greater possibilities exist for reporting inaccurate, inflated data, or for focusing only on what is measured to the detriment of other performance. Thus, while the data may look better, true effectiveness of service can decline. In addition, there may be confidentiality concerns on the part of employees. The best results in using group feedback seem likely when there is full group consensus regarding desirability of this approach in achieving the work unit's goals.

Appraisal Reviews

What is the appraisal interview?

This is a meeting between the supervisor and supervisee to provide and discuss the summary of performance for a specified rating period. It may also include a discussion of how performance improvements will be achieved or how future goals, objectives, criteria and standards will be modified.

What is the summary of performance?

It includes (in writing) the overall rating, ratings on each category and on each criteria. It may also include a narrative summary of special achievements, performance improvements needed and other pertinent information.

How frequently should appraisal interviews be done?

There is no set frequency. However, it may be helpful to link rating periods with the review frequency of work unit achievements and the organization planning cycle. Using that strategy, employee goals, objectives, criteria and standards can be modified as needed to correspond to organization and work unit plans. Generally, an appraisal interview should be conducted at least yearly, with one or two interim, less formal reviews.

What should an interim review include?

At least some indication, in writing, that overall performance is satisfactory, or if not, development of a summary of corrective actions needed and a collaborative plan for improvement.

How should employees be prepared for the appraisal interview?

It is helpful to discuss the evaluation procedure and the process for determining ratings (including any special constraints affecting all employees) with those who will be rated. This helps to avoid any surprises for employees and cushion potential negative responses to the process. Such discussion can usually take place in a group meeting. If self evaluation procedures will be used, employees should be asked to collect supporting data and submit their evaluations in advance of the appraisal interview. This allows the supervisor to review the information and integrate it with other information prior to that meeting, and to prepare the summary of performance.

Should an appraisal interview ever be done prior to preparing the summary of performance?

This is appropriate when the interview is needed to clarify performance achievements before a rating can be assigned. It is also appropriate when self evaluation methods are used and the summary of performance is expected to be based on consensus between the supervisor and supervisee.

How should the appraisal interview be conducted?

As with counseling interviews, rapport building and establishing facilitative conditions such as empathy, warmth, genuineness and positive regard provide an environment for effective communication and potential growth. However, other behaviors are also appropriate for supervisors in conducting appraisal interviews. For example, Wainwright and Minor (1981) suggest the following:

1. State the purpose of the meeting at the outset.
2. Focus on the employee's work rather than personal characteristics.
3. Encourage freedom of the employee to speak.
4. Do not place the employee on the defensive.
5. Be specific, regardless of whether the information is critical or complimentary.
6. Give credit when due, but similarly cover areas needing improvement.

When improvements are needed, it is helpful to discuss and obtain consensus, if possible, on both the employee's and supervisor's responsibilities. For example, the employee may be expected to achieve better performance after being provided training paid for by the agency. However, it should be made clear to the employee that he or she is responsible for the final result. If consensus cannot be achieved, supervisory judgement will usually prevail. Agreements to or assignment of new goals, objectives or standards, plus actions to be taken by the supervisor to assist the employee should be documented. A copy should be maintained by both employee and supervisor for purposes of future followup or reference.

What are the consequences of feeding back negative performance information during the appraisal interview or interim reviews?

While a necessary task, this may result in employee defensiveness. This can lead to further deteriorating performance, particularly with employees who are the poorest performers and thus need the most help (Porter, Lawler & Hackman, 1975).

How can defensiveness be reduced?

The use of highly objective criteria and standards with routine, accurate, automated data feedback can help. This is a somewhat impersonal procedure, but such data is difficult to dispute. Even in these cases, when standards are not met some employees will find it necessary to defend why the standard was impossible. It is then necessary for the supervisor to assess the validity of such claims and deal with this during the interview process.

When highly objective criteria and standards do not exist, the **self evaluation** procedure with an appraisal interview to resolve supervisor-supervisee differences (prior to issuing the summary of performance) may be helpful. An alternative is the use of **peer evaluations.** These may be particularly helpful when evaluation criteria are vague, in situations in which trust levels are high among peers, and when peers are as knowledgable about the work as supervisors (e.g., peer review of service quality). When trust levels are low among peers, however, defensiveness may be increased.

MANAGEMENT ACTIONS

What types of management actions result from evaluation of employee performance?

These can include special rewards, implementing performance improvement plans, actions to transfer employees to other jobs, and actions to terminate employees.

Special Rewards

What are special rewards?

These include extrinsic and/or intrinsic rewards for exemplary performance. Extrinsic rewards can include bonuses or merit pay, special privileges or status symbols such as a larger office, promotions and fringe benefits. They may also include interpersonal reinforcements that make employees feel good about themselves and their work. For example, paying special attention to employees through individual and group praise, or simply encouraging group "celebrations" (parties, doughnuts etc.) for good performance can be effective applications of extrinsic rewards. (Note that such recognition can have the characteristics of both intrinsic and extrinsic rewards.)

Using intrinsic rewards requires creating the conditions which lead to self, affectual reinforcement. For example this could involve providing more challenging assignments to an employee.

What is the purpose of special rewards?

To motivate continuing exemplary performance and serve as an example for others to follow.

Which are more effective, intrinsic or extrinsic rewards?

Both can be effective. Intrinsic rewards are most efficient, because they support employee centered control and require less organizational energy for management control. However, they are not always readily available for use by supervisors. Extrinsic rewards are also effective, particularly when they are viewed as important by employees. While human services professionals tend to view intrinsic rewards as important, many employees also respond positively to extrinsic rewards, such as salary increases. With extrinsic rewards, effective distribution is essential in order to avoid negating any positive benefits.

What is required for effective distribution of extrinsic rewards?

At a minimum, employees must perceive that rewards are related to performance. This requires that the performance evaluation system be viewed as measuring and evaluating accurately **and** that the type and amount of rewards are distributed **fairly** on the basis of performance. In addition, as discussed in Chapter 8, care must be exercised to avoid use of extrinsic rewards in a manner that is likely to **decrease intrinsic**

motivation. Generally, extrinsic rewards tend to enhance motivation (when intrinsic motivation already exists) only when the rewards signify increased competence to the employee. As implied in Chapter 8, in these instances larger extrinsic rewards appear to produce increasing levels of intrinsic motivation. Providing extrinsic rewards without regard to perceived level of performance may decrease intrinsic motivation (Bandura, 1982). Porter, Lawler, and Hackman (1975) also summarize several conditions which they suggest must be present for extrinsic rewards to motivate performance:

1. **Important** rewards can be provided.
2. Rewards can be widely varied, dependent upon current performance.
3. Meaningful supervisor-supervisee appraisal sessions can take place.
4. Performance can be measured inclusively and objectively.
5. Public information is made available on how rewards are given.
6. High trust exists.
7. Superiors are willing and can explain and support the reward system to employees.
8. The system will not cause negative outcomes to be tied to performance.

What types of employee evaluation systems best support the effective use of extrinsic rewards?

Goal oriented systems with specific, measurable criteria and standards on which supervisor-employee consensus has been obtained. As noted in Chapter 8, goal oriented approaches of this nature **also** support intrinsic motivation. More subjective systems, particularly when used in an atmosphere of low supervisor-employee trust, tend to support perceptions by employees of supervisor favoritism, and belief that rewards are linked to factors other than relevant, competent performance.

What is the significance of the relationship among rewards, employee satisfaction, performance and turnover?

Over the long run, the reward system should promote satisfaction among the highest performers and dissatisfaction among the lowest performers. Since dissatisfaction is associated with turnover, it is important that the most satisfied employees are also the best employees. In this regard, Porter, Lawler and Hackman (1975) note

> An organization may be most effective if it contains some employees
> who are very much satisfied with their extrinsic rewards, a large group

who are above average in their satisfaction, and a third group who are dissatisfied. This kind of variation in satisfaction will contribute to organizational effectiveness, however, only if careful control is maintained over who is dissatisfied and who is satisfied. Stated most simply the best performers must be the most satisfied and the worst performers the least satisfied.

Performance Improvement and Other Management Actions

What are performance improvement plans?

These are plans developed to improve deficient performance. They may also include plans to improve satisfactory performance to higher levels when agreed upon by the supervisor and employee.

What is required in developing and implementing a performance improvement plan?

The supervisor and/or employee should determine what is needed to improve performance (e.g. resources, employee action or supervisory action) and agree to take the necessary steps. A schedule for performance changes should then be established with specific dates for supervisory follow-up. Generally, the plan should be committed to writing, particularly when deficient performance is involved. The written plan, plus follow-up notes should serve as a defensible basis for taking later adverse actions (e.g., transfer, demotion or termination), if needed.

How does employee evaluation relate to promotion, transfer, demotion and termination actions?

Promotion is often a special reward for sustained effective performance. As part of the employee selection process, selecting officials may review evaluation information from current and past jobs. Thus, evaluations often contribute significantly to being chosen or passed over for a higher level job.

Evaluation information is essential for transfer and demotion decisions. Transfer may be a corrective action when all efforts have been made, without success, to deal with performance deficiencies, **and** there is another organization position in which the employee could perform. Although employees may be forced into such situations contrary to their preferences (if they choose to remain with the organization), consideration of such alternatives may satisfy other organization needs and be helpful in demonstrating attempts at employee accomodation. Efforts to accomodate rather than terminate immediately may be helpful if subsequent termination is necessary and legal action results. Unfortunately, both transfer and demotion actions can be demotivating and result in management problems because of employee dissatisfaction.

Performance related termination actions are taken when all efforts at improvement (as demonstrated through the employee evaluation process) have failed, and transfer or demotion is not a viable option. When termination is a possibility, full documentation should be maintained of all evaluation related information, including efforts at and results of improvement efforts.

EFFECTIVENESS OF EMPLOYEE EVALUATION SYSTEMS

Are employee evaluation systems usually effective in human service agencies?

Sometimes. However, in some instances they do not meet their intent due to weak implementation. For example, all necessary components may not be included (e.g., feedback), some elements may be ineffective (e.g., criteria or standards), or managers may not be trained or able to carry out the process uniformly or fairly. Human services workers often complain about not being rated on the most important factors, subjective or meaningless ratings and biased distribution of rewards (if any). It is suggested that improvements are needed in this area of human services management practice in order to effectively strengthen organization results.

What are some limitations on effective employee evaluation in human services?

Such systems can never achieve perfection. Since much of the effectiveness of employee evaluation depends on employee perceptions, and since defensiveness will always exist in dealing with supervisor perceived poor performance and reward distribution, some employees will always be dissatisfied or at least mildly annoyed with being evaluated. In addition, legitimate difficulties with measuring complex human services will continue to exist.

How can supervisors best cope with the limitations?

Through attention to effective measurement devices, appropriate collaboration with employees, regular feedback mechanisms and implementation of effective reward mechanisms.

EVALUATION/ACCOUNTABILITY EXERCISE 1
PERFORMANCE INDICATORS

(Individual and Group)

The following represents 1988 performance data for the Counseling Services Department of a large rehabilitation center:

Total Hours Worked (all staff)—30,000
Hours Direct Service—20,000
Supervision Hours—2000
Clerical Overhead (non direct service) Hours—2000
Hours of Leave (sick, vacation)—5000
Special Project Hours—1000
Number of Cases with Successful Outcomes—100
Total Department Expenditures—$300,000
Total Cases Exiting Counseling (all outcomes)—300

Notes: Two of the most experienced counselors had extended periods of absence due to hospitalizations in 1988.

TASK

The first item below should be done individually. Students should then be divided into groups of four to eight to compare results and any reasons for differences. The second item should be done as a group exercise. Groups can then report and compare their results.

1. Calculate 1988 figures for the following indicators (note that 1986 and 1987 figures are shown for comparison):

Indicator	1988	1987	1986
Productivity		80	82
Cost Efficiency		0.0006	0.0007
Work Efficiency		0.007	0.009
Effectiveness		0.4	0.4

2. Describe what the total data signifies and possible reasons for any trends.

EVALUATION/ACCOUNTABILITY EXERCISE 2
PROGRAM EVALUATION

(Group)

Consider the Unity House description in Introduction Exercise 1 (at the end of the INTRODUCTION SECTION).

1. What **types** of program evaluation might have been appropriate for Unity House? Why?

2. Establish three key ongoing goals to be used for goal oriented evaluation. The goals should be useful for program improvement and accountability purposes.

3. Suggest one evaluation research study that might have been conducted within the first three years of program operation (that could have helped improve the program in future years).

EVALUATION/ACCOUNTABILITY EXERCISE 3
EVALUATING EMPLOYEE PERFORMANCE

(Individual or Small Group)

The following is a partial listing of job functions for a group of rehabilitation counselors in a public agency.

1. Interpret and use psychological test reports for helping clients establish rehabilitation plans.
2. Make eligibility and entitlement determinations.
3. Interpret and use client background data to help clients with vocational planning.
4. Analyze the effects of disabling conditions on vocational potential.

TASK

Assume that the above functions will constitute a single category for which performance measures will be developed.

1. Name the category.

2. Using the **goal oriented system** approach, establish at least three items which will measure performance for the category.
3. Establish an objective scoring method to rate the category as achieved at the satisfactory or outstanding level.

After individuals or small groups (three to five) complete the above, the results can be presented to the larger group for critique. The following should be considered:

1. Is the category title representative of the functions?
2. Do the items contain specific criteria and standards that can be easily measured?
3. Are standards or goals set at achievable levels?
4. Is the category scoring method objective and easily understandable?

Section VI

COORDINATING

Chapter 14

COORDINATION OF SERVICES

What is the coordinating function of managers?

It assures that services needed for clients are obtained and synchronized effectively. For example, a patient undergoing medical treatment for a traumatic head injury should receive rehabilitation and social services that are timely and relevant to his or her situation. Delays or the wrong services could undermine adjustment and rehabilitation progress. Managers from most human services organizations, agencies or departments have some responsibility to assure that their own clients and clients they serve from other sources receive such coordinated services.

What does coordinating services entail?

It requires **procedures** to insure that the tasks and roles of the coordinating work units mesh effectively. This is accomplished through specified referral mechanisms, clarification of responsibilities for providing services and mechanisms for inter-unit communications.

To be most effective, coordination procedures require **integration** among work units. As described in earlier chapters, integration is a social process that supports effective coordination through the sharing of norms and values. It is particularly important in achieving coordination among professional workers and work units that are highly differentiated from one another, i.e., have very different priorities, interests and orientations. In these situations, integration is the cornerstone of assuring that coordinative procedures are effectively put into practice.

What are some important factors in determining the degree of integration needed to achieve good coordination of services?

These include the level of differentiation, physical or geographical distance, inter-work unit attitudes, and climate of interpersonal relationships between or among work units.

How does differentiation manifest itself?

Highly differentiated work units view the nature and importance of their roles differently. For example, staff in a treatment program may see symptom reduction as the overriding area of importance in working with clients. Vocational rehabilitation may be viewed as desirable in some cases, but of minor significance to the main needs of clients seeking services. Thus, coordination of services with rehabilitation programs may be seen as valuable, but of low priority and of little worth in terms of expending resources. On the other hand, a vocational rehabilitation program staff may see treatment as one **essential** part of the rehabilitation process. Thus, treatment services must be effectively coordinated in order to achieve the end result (suitable employment). The differences in orientations of these units would probably require integrative mechanisms to achieve needed coordination, particularly since only one of the groups perceives a strong need for the others services.

Differentiation in human services relates partially to professional or personal orientation and identification. Different professional specialties, and groups within specialties, sometimes operate from conflicting helping perspectives. Status differences among professions may also impact on attitudes regarding coordination of services. Thus, units differentiated on the basis of various professions (e.g., psychologists, physicians, social workers, rehabilitation counselors etc.) may benefit from special methods to enhance integration.

How does physical or geographical distance between work units impact on need for integration?

Generally, work units in the same location or contiguous to one another have more opportunities for staff interaction than those separated by geographical distance. Thus, integration is more likely to occur through natural social processes. For example, if a treatment and rehabilitation unit are housed on the same floor of a hospital, chances are greater that staff will interact socially and work together, than if the treatment unit is housed in a building three miles away from the rehabilitation unit. In the latter instance, staff may never even meet!

How do inter-work unit attitudes affect the need for integration?

Generally, coordination is enhanced (and need for integration lessened) when work units have favorable attitudes toward one another (Roessler &

Mack, 1975), when work units share a common perspective regarding their need for interdependence (Dellario, 1985), when professionals between work units respect one another (Dellario, 1985) and when there are pressing needs for coordination by the agencies (such as money shortages) (Cubelli, 1965).

What is the climate of interpersonal relationships and how does that impact on the need for integration?

This refers to the tone of interaction between staff in different units. The tone may be one of cooperation, conflict, or neutrality. Integrative interventions may be necessary when conflict exists, or when neutrality exists due to indifference or apathy.

COORDINATION PROCEDURES

How can coordination procedures be established?

When coordination is needed between or among work units **in the same organization,** procedures can be formalized in writing to clarify types of referrals, referral procedures, types of services and service priorities to be provided by each unit. Such documentation serves as a basis to carry out the process efficiently, to encourage uniform application of procedures by staff in the involved units, and to resolve misunderstandings. In large organizations, such procedures are often covered in operating manuals.

Written agreements are particularly important in **interagency coordination.** They establish a formal basis for relationships between two or more agencies and serve a purpose similar to internal written procedures. However, interagency agreements are often more detailed than internal procedures, since they serve to describe a whole range of services and procedures which may be unfamiliar to the staffs of coordinating agencies.

Written agreements should be written to enhance application by direct service users (user friendliness). For example, a simple chart comparing each agency's benefits rather than detailed narrative descriptions would be valuable for quick reference. A sample format for a written interagency agreement is shown in Table XVI.

TABLE XVI
SAMPLE FORMAT FOR A WRITTEN INTERAGENCY AGREEMENT

1. *Statement of Purpose*
    Note reason for the agreement and the legal basis, if any.
2. *Objectives*
3. *Parties to the Agreement*
    Note each agency involved, with a general description of services, benefits, processes and special features.
4. *Responsibilities*
    Include such items as:
    a. Special services to be provided by agencies to each other.
    b. Specific coordinative arrangements and procedures, or special areas of cooperation.
    c. Referral procedures.
    d. Provisions for information exchange.
    e. Provisions for staff training.
    f. Provision to have periodic staff meetings to resolve difficulties in implementation of the agreement.
5. *Provision for periodic review and updating of the agreement.*
6. *Listing of key personnel, addresses and phone numbers.*
7. *Optional Appendixes.*
    a. Comparison of services and benefits chart.
    b. Detailed descriptions of programs and services.
8. *Signatures of top level administrators and department heads as applicable.*

Are written interagency agreements usually sufficient to achieve coordination?

No. Since management and staff at different agencies usually have different priorities, continuing integrative efforts are almost always needed to make the agreement work effectively.

Aside from integrative methods, what can be done to enhance the effectiveness of written interagency agreements?

Before writing the agreement, it is sometimes helpful to do a pilot test of the coordination process to determine what works and what does not. Also, regular updating of the agreement (e.g., yearly) to incorporate changes based on experience is a recommended practice.

INTEGRATIVE METHODS

What are some integrative methods?

Direct Management Action — This method involves integrative action by one manager. It is appropriate for intra-agency integration, when a single manager is responsible for the work units that need to coordinate. For example, in a hospital, the assistant administrator may need to play an integrative role between the Department of Medicine and the Department of Social Services. This may require conducting periodic meetings between department managers or liaison staff to assure that procedures for meeting total patient needs are followed and that interdepartmental problems are resolved quickly.

Managerial Relationship Building — This involves establishment of formal or informal relationships between or among coordinating work unit managers. Better cooperation and coordination then results from actions taken by the managers with their staffs. For example, directors of agencies may see each other socially or as active members of professional organizations. As a result of these continuing contacts, informal or formal commitments may be made regarding cooperating with one another. Subsequent direction from the agency head to staff regarding interagency cooperation will often help produce the desired results.

Liaison Personnel — This method involves the appointment of liaisons by one or both work units trying to achieve coordination. The liaison serves as coordinator for all dealings with the other unit. For example, a State vocational rehabilitation agency may appoint a liaison to a county welfare agency. Similarly, the welfare agency may appoint a liaison to the county rehabilitation office. These liaisons would periodically visit the agencies to which they are assigned; train staff in their own agency's functions and procedures; and accept, follow through with and follow-up on referrals.

Maintaining such personal contact at the direct service level can help encourage continuing cooperation. This may be particularly effective with physically or geographically distant work units or those with a history of low motivation among staff for finding areas for cooperation. Generally, liaison personnel who are highly motivated to make the relationship work are most effective. Possible configurations for using liaison personnel are illustrated in Figure 5.

Integrated Units — This involves the permanent location of a portion of one work unit into another work unit. For example, a state employment service may physically locate job placement specialists to a Veterans Administration vocational rehabilitation office. The integrated units configuration is illustrated in Figure 6.

Integrative Committees — As noted in Chapter 6, these are permanent committees of members from each agency or department who meet to

1. Both Units Appoint Liaison

a. Liaison (L) from Unit A communicates with Liaison (L) from Unit B

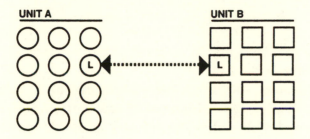

b. Liaison (L) from Unit A communicates directly with all staff from Unit B.
Liaison (L) from Unit B communicates directly with all staff from Unit A.

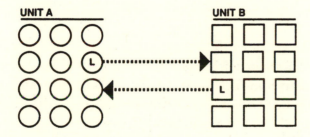

2. One Unit Appoints Liaison (L)

(who communicates with all staff from other unit.)

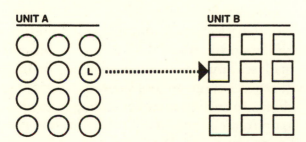

Figure 5—Configurations for Using Liaison Personnel.

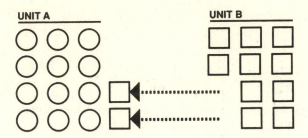

Figure 6—Integrated Units Configuration.

solve continuing problems and to facilitate improved services to clients by the participating work units.

Multi Service Centers—This involves co-locating multiple services in a single center (Wright, 1980). Interaction can then more easily occur between and among highly differentiated work units that were previously geographically dispersed.

COORDINATING EXERCISE 1

(Group Discussion)

The Vocational Rehabilitation and Counseling (VR&C) Division at a Veterans Administration Regional Office (downtown) and the Stress Recovery Unit (SRU) at a Veterans Administration Medical Center (in a suburb fifteen miles from the Regional Office) need to improve coordination of services. The need is felt most acutely by VR&C staff who often have clients needing treatment quickly for Post Traumatic Stress Disorder, but who cannot get immediate services. This sometimes results in a client dropping out of a vocational rehabilitation program or progressing poorly. The SRU serves a broad veteran population, and only incidentally provides services to VR&C clients.

The orientations of the VR&C staff and SRU staff are quite different. VR&C staff see training and a job as the key to rehabilitation and life satisfaction. SRU staff see multimodal treatment as being of primary concern. Vocational aspects of life are not viewed as central to treatment success, although clients in treatment are encouraged to seek vocational endeavors if they so desire. The priority of the SRU is treating the client who meets Post Traumatic Stress Disorder diagnostic criteria and is experiencing severe community and family maladjustment. Generally, management relationships between VR&C and the SRU are neutral, with a verbal agreement to jointly cooperate in working with clients.

TASK

Since VR&C staff see a need for better services through the SRU (yet SRU staff do not see as strong a need for better coordination with VR&C), how would you as the Chief of the VR&C Division try to improve coordination?

Section VII

COMMUNICATING
INTRODUCTION AND OVERVIEW

Managers have the responsibility for transmitting and receiving information and for influencing information exchange. Communication is the basis for carrying out all of the other management functions and for insuring the organization's continuing existence. It is also the medium through which most purposes of human services organizations are achieved.

Chapter 15 discusses seven areas in which communications play an especially important role for managers: information dissemination, conflict resolution, labor-management relations, marketing and outreach, negotiating, resource acquisition, and client (customer) satisfaction. Effectiveness in managing these areas should result in a growth oriented facility, with a higher performing, more satisfied workforce, and adequate operating resources.

Chapter 16 considers the specific channels through which communications take place: spoken, written, computers and the public media. Developing good skills in each of these areas helps maximize the potential benefits of communication for the manager, work unit and facility.

Chapter 15

CRITICAL AREAS OF COMMUNICATION

What types of communications are most important to human services managers?

M anagers must be able to communicate well with and through their staff. Important areas include two-way information dissemination, helping to resolve conflicts, negotiation, and promoting effective labor-management relationships.

Managers must also be effective communicators with those outside the work unit. This includes being able to market services, negotiating for and acquiring needed resources, and satisfying customers and clients. It also includes providing leadership in the human services community and otherwise influencing others for the benefit of the organization and its constituents.

INFORMATION DISSEMINATION

What is the significance of information dissemination?

Based on their study of welfare and rehabilitation agencies, Olmstead and Christensen (1973) noted that "People need information in order to perform their jobs properly. Equally important, the lack of information breeds frustration which can affect every aspect of agency operations." They concluded that communication (defined in terms of information dissemination) "is probably the most critical aspect in any organization because everything else depends upon it."

What are some effects of ineffective information dissemination?

When timely, accurate information is not available, employees may be unaware of work unit or organization goals, objectives and policies. Routine information needed for client or personal decision making may also be unavailable. Also, dissemination and discussion of client information is particularly important in human services settings to enhance the quality of services provided.

Lack of information may support feelings of alienation between management and employees. As implied by LaPlace (1983), poor or closed communications by management may signify lack of positive regard and respect for employees. This may encourage employees to depend upon informal communication networks fueled by hearsay or speculation. Although informal networks ("grapevines") will always exist, a strong formal network is important to provide accurate information and clear direction, and to avoid confusion and paranoia.

What type of climate supports effective information dissemination and constructive use of formal vs informal communication networks?

Frequent, clear, factual communications by management and encouragement of open and informal interaction among all staff is helpful. This supports an atmosphere of honesty, trust and concern on the part of management for employees, and for serious concern about effectively achieving the agency's mission.

What methods can be used for routine information dissemination?

Staff meetings conducted on a regular basis are effective for disseminating information that applies to most staff. **Individual** or **limited group meetings** can be used to save time when information pertains only to some staff.

Written summaries of information or **newsletters** may be useful. However, exclusive use of written materials does not assure dissemination since staff do not usually read everything, nor does it allow for two way communication. **Written memoranda** are appropriate when **formal** documentation is needed for directives and other items requiring compliance or future follow-up.

CONFLICT RESOLUTION

What is the significance of conflict resolution to managers?

Disagreements and conflicts frequently occur in work units. When they are resolved, work can proceed unimpeded or even more constructively . When they are not resolved, frustrations build and dysfunctional consequences often result. For example, staff may avoid communicating with one another or with managers about important matters. In addition, retaliatory actions may occur which impede agency operations. Depending upon the nature of the staff and work unit climate, conflict resolution efforts can constitute a large portion of management time.

What are some important general principles in resolving conflicts?

1. Managers should avoid results in which any parties to the conflict perceive themselves as losing a battle. When people believe they have lost to someone else, future dysfunctional consequences may result. Conflict resolution should result in the perception that a problem has been solved for the benefit of everyone, i.e., everyone wins.

2. Research in the area of third party dispute resolution suggests the importance of leaving as much control for solutions as possible with the involved parties. Thus, a resolution most consistent with the needs of those in dispute is likely (Brett, 1984).

What are some simple conflict resolution techniques?

Techniques useful for managers in working with staff include:

Problem Solving (Roark, 1978)—This method focuses on identifying the best solutions to a specific problem. Cooperation among parties rather than competition is stressed. Relevant factors are confronted honestly and directly until an agreeable solution is found.

Bargaining (Roark, 1978)—This approach depends upon compromise to achieve resolution of a conflict. However, since this process involves settling for less than a participants original position, discontent may surface later (Roark, 1978).

Power (Roark, 1978)—This method involves imposition of a solution and requires compliance by the involved parties. The emotional components of the disagreement are not resolved. When minor disagreements occur among staff, or management and staff, the use of power, i.e., a management decision, may lead to the most practical, least time consuming solution. For example, in a conflict between two employees regarding roles in completing a task, a management decision may be sufficient. However, when ego involvement of one or more of the parties to a disagreement is high, use of power may aggravate the situation.

Smoothing (Roark, 1978)—This method involves "overlooking, hiding, or discounting the issues involved in order to maintain apparent harmony by catering to the parties involved rather than facing the issues" (Roark, 1978). For example, a supervisor might try to convince disagreeing parties of the insignificance of the issue causing conflict.

Avoidance (Roark, 1978)—This method does not address the needs of the individuals involved or the issues. The situation is simply ignored. **Which conflict resolution methods are likely to be most effective?**

Problem solving is most effective, when possible, since everyone wins and since those in dispute play a major role in finding a solution. Unfortunately, the method does not always work, particularly when strong emotions cannot be put aside enough to approach problems objectively.

Bargaining can be effective when participation of the disputing parties is high and a "loser" does not emerge. **Power** can and should probably be used when dysfunctional consequences are not likely. Since it is least time consuming, it is the method of choice when there are no advantages to using more time consuming methods.

Smoothing and **avoidance** have few advantages, unless confronting issues and emotions are better circumscribed. This can be the case when the issues are unresolvable, or confronting them would lead to worse consequences. For example, attempting to resolve a strong conflict between two managers, one of whom will be retiring in three months, would be fruitless if the only reasonable alternative is siding with the retiring employee. It might be least dysfunctional to use smoothing or avoidance as a temporary measure.

LABOR-MANAGEMENT RELATIONS

What is the manager's role in communicating with labor organizations (unions)?

The managers responsibility is to represent the interests of the organization's governing body in communicating with labor organizations. Unions represent the special interests of organized groups of non-management personnel. Such interests usually include salaries, benefits, working conditions, implementation of organization policies and so forth.

Labor unions provide a special voice for the needs of employees as a counterbalance to the need for management to run the organization as it sees fit. The natural conflict in goals that often emerges can lead to strained relationships, open hostility, and destructive actions. For example, when unions are strong, and serious unresolved conflict exists, agency operations can deteriorate as a result of strikes, grievances and retaliatory actions against management. In some instances, this can result in the destruction of an agency.

Thus, where labor organizations exist, it is beneficial if labor management communications can remain honest, open and directed toward achieving the greatest good for employee needs, organization efficiency, and benefits to clients. This is a responsibility of both management and the union. Management, must recognize the need in these situations, for some power sharing through negotiation, bargaining and compromise. Without such recognition, a strictly adversary relationship may exist.

How can managers facilitate effective communications with labor organizations?

They can negotiate in good faith, and follow the provisions of bargaining agreements. They can also encourage, support and work closely with unions on projects that benefit both the organization and employees, e.g., employee assistance programs and quality of worklife improvements. Such cooperation supports a joint sense of involvement in achieving a better organization, in enhancing resolution of conflicting issues and in avoiding destructive actions. Maintaining informal relationships with union leaders may also be of mutual value in avoiding conflicts, and more amicably resolving them when they do arise.

How important is a managers identity in communicating with labor organizations?

It is very important for managers to maintain their identification with organization management. Although a cooperative relationship with the union is desirable, the manager should not confuse the differences in interests represented. This becomes most important in substantive negotiation of agreements and in individual employee issues (e.g., disciplinary actions, adverse actions, grievances) in which management cannot afford to compromise its position.

Is management identity a significant problem?

This is a problem for some managers who strongly identify with their employees and/or who do not feel fully a part of the management team. First line managers may be most susceptible since they work most closely with labor organization employees. They may also be the newest managers (who often come from the ranks of unions), or disenchanted experienced managers.

How can management identity problems be avoided or resolved?

Taking actions to facilitate a cohesive management team can be helpful. Managers who feel that their needs are being met by the management team are more likely to identify with the interests of management. Particular attention needs to be paid to integrating new first line managers into this structure.

MARKETING AND OUTREACH

What is marketing in human services?

Per Cronin (1987), "marketing is the ongoing process of identifying and satisfying the needs and wants of individuals and organizations." In human services, the process is applied to services and benefits provided and goods produced by the organization. For example, a mental health center must identify the services needed in the community, assure that they are publicized to appropriate groups and that their value is communicated. A rehabilitation center may manufacture items or provide job placement services which may require similar marketing processes.

Why is marketing of services and benefits necessary in human services organizations?

Marketing is needed to assure that the most relevant services are offered and that they are used by those who can benefit from them. From a practical perspective, a competitive service providers environment requires active marketing strategies to assure that facility services are maximally reaching target groups and that new services and target groups are being created. This is particularly pertinent in the private profit and private not-for-profit sector. In the public sector, marketing often consists of **outreach** efforts to assure that those entitled to services and benefits are aware of and use them.

Is there a practical method for establishing a marketing strategy?

Cronin's (1987) Rehabilitation Marketing Analysis and Planning Process (REMAP) is designed to help rehabilitation managers answer the questions "What have we accomplished" and "What needs to be done now," with regard to marketing. The method is highly systematic and appears applicable to most human service organizations. The steps include:

1. **Situational Analysis** —This step evaluates marketing efforts com-

pleted to date. It includes analysis of usage rates before and after specific marketing efforts, evaluation of the public's awareness and perception of the facility, and determination of the resources available to assist in marketing efforts (e.g., personnel, financial, facilities).

2. **Identification of Competitors** — This includes identifying the types of services available, where (through what organizations) they are available, and direct and indirect competitors. This step allows a facility to differentiate itself from other service providers, establish reasons for using it rather than another facility, identifying new services that might be provided, and where the most comprehensive marketing efforts must be concentrated to deal with competitive threats.

3. **The Market Assessment** — This step involves analysis of the markets served by the facility and delineates in what geographical areas marketing efforts are most needed. A number of methods are identified by Cronin to assess the **primary market** (geographic territory encompassing 2/3 of facility users), **market penetration** (level of use of the facility's services in existing markets), the **target market** (the group most likely to be the heaviest users of services offered), current market opportunities such as unserved or underserved markets and new markets, and current market threats such as changes in funding priorities, new competition and technological advancements.

4. **Identifying Decision Making Roles** — Cronin notes five roles identified by Kotler (1984) that can be played by those making decisions to use a service. It is important for those who market services to identify who plays each role, since this determines "how marketing efforts should be constructed and to whom they should be directed." The roles are:

a. **Initiator** — This person initially suggests use of the service. Initiators are gatekeepers who must be sold on the service before the decision process regarding use can begin. Examples of initiators are family members, or professional staff persons at a facility.

b. **Influencer** — This is any person who provides input into the decision making process (i.e., whether to seek and where to receive the service).

c. **Decider** — This is the person who determines whether the service will be received and where. It could be the client or patient, a physician, rehabilitation counselor, family member, etc.

d. **Buyer** — This is the payment source such as a government agency, insurance company or the client. Marketing activities may be necessary to convince buyers of the value of the service.

e. **User** — This is the client. Marketing in this instance extends to providing treatment that results in client satisfaction. If clients are unsatisfied, this can lead to negative publicity and reduction of future clients.

5. **Identifying the Marketing Plan** — This step involves establishing measurable, performance oriented market objectives. Objectives should be results oriented and focus on facility utilization. A marketing plan should be identified to include the services to be offered, prices for services, promotional plans for each service and market, new facilities or equipment needed, personnel needed for the marketing effort, and the marketing budget needed.

6. **Planning for Control** — This step is a feedback mechanism to monitor marketing performance. It includes assessing actual performance compared to planned performance, assignment of each marketing function to a specific position and annual review of the entire marketing plan.

In his article, Cronin offers specific details for carrying out each step of the process.

What does the outreach process in public agencies entail?

It includes all efforts directed at identifying potentially eligible clients who need and can benefit from agency services and benefits, educating them regarding the services and benefits, and motivating them to apply when appropriate.

What communication related management functions facilitate the outreach process?

Public relations activities support outreach. For example, maintaining relationships with other agencies and keeping other agency administrators up to date on services encourages referrals. Also, use of public service announcements and success stories in public media educates potential users about services, and encourages self and other referrals. In addition, direct contacts with groups that include potential clients, or relatives, friends and associates of potential clients can serve an effective outreach role. For example, some administrators do presentations regarding agency services at community service organization or special interest group meetings, or belong to such groups. Open forums designed to educate and allow consumers to air concerns also supports the outreach function.

Outreach may also be done by direct contact with potential clients. When such persons can be identified in advance, contact can be made by mail, phone or in person to provide information, and to encourage participation.

NEGOTIATING

Why is negotiation important?

Managers must use negotiation in circumstances such as conflict resolution, labor management relations, contracting, and resource acquisition. In these situations, positions of the involved parties often differ. This requires managers to find ways to maximize **their** gains while maintaining constructive continuing relationships. Negotiation is a general technique for achieving such purposes.

What are some principles for maximizing gains in negotiations?

In her review of research in this area, Brett (1984) discusses positional approaches and principled bargaining. **Positional approaches** refer to those in which parties take positions and negotiate to a settlement or impasse. **Principled bargaining** involves using a set of bargaining principles which focuses on maintaining the long term relationship between the negotiators.

With regard to the positional approach, Brett found consistent support only for the strategy of starting negotiations at the highest (strongest) position and conceding as little as possible (but enough to avoid impasse). With regard to specific tactics, her findings suggest only that threats should not be made that the negotiator is not willing to act upon.

In principled bargaining, Brett refers to Fisher and Ury's (1981) principles which include:

1. **A focus on interests (vs positions).** A position is what a bargainer requests. An interest refers to why the bargainer has taken the position. For example, a union may take the position of requesting across the board salary increases of 10%. The interest might be the concern that similar staff in other agencies are paid higher.

2. **Problem(s) should be separated from people.** This implies that focus should be on the bargaining task with efforts to control emotions, and to allow emotional venting (without reciprocal venting or retaliation).

3. **Options should be invented for mutual gain.** This is essentially a **problem solving** strategy to resolving conflict.

4. **Objective criteria or standards should be invented.** For example, a standard on which to base decision making, such as precedent or market value, may be agreed upon. Per Brett, this shifts the focus of negotiations to alternate standards rather than positions. Once a standard is established, the settlement is based on that. For instance, in the salary negotiations example above, agreement that salaries should be based on national or local averages would solve the issue.

5. **The negotiator should know his or her best alternative to a negotiated agreement** (if a settlement cannot be reached with the other party). This protects the negotiator from a poor settlement.

Brett notes that no research is available on the efficacy of the Fisher and Ury (principled bargaining) vs positional approaches.

What are some practical negotiating strategies?

Fuller (1981) suggests the following basic negotiating techniques:
1. Have the meeting at a location that you choose.
2. Keep the number of participants on negotiating teams small.
3. Learn as much as possible about the opponent (e.g., negotiating style, areas of expertise, expectations and goals, and facts related to the negotiation issue).
4. Have a meeting with your own team prior to any negotiating sessions, to establish your position and to specify member roles.
5. Establish negotiation goals and expectations, including potential trade-off items and alternative results that would be acceptable.
6. Maintain flexibility with regard to strategy during the meeting.

Per Fuller, the basic ingredients for successful negotiation are "preparation, the establishment of your objective, control of your emotions, and hard bargaining."

RESOURCE ACQUISITION

What is resource acquisition?

Resource acquisition is the process of obtaining needed funds for human resources, materials and physical facilities.

Are all managers involved in resource acquisition?

Yes. Within organizations, managers at every level depend upon their superiors to provide resources. At the top management level, administrators depend upon governing boards (e.g., board of directors), legislators and political leaders, government and foundation grants, and other external funding sources. In some instances, managers are also involved in direct fund raising ventures such as soliciting donations, sales, rentals, and special events. (Note that Rigger and Matkin [1986] suggest that a tremendous number of funding sources can be located by simply reading income analyses of human services facilities).

What is the role of managers in resource acquisition?

All managers play some **public relations** role in this area. Within the organization chain of command, managers account for the value, effectiveness and efficiency of their work unit activities through communication to their supervisors and other key decision makers, or influencers of decision makers. They also communicate through goals, objectives, strategies and procedures what they are doing or propose to do to best achieve the organization mission through their work unit. Such communications influence decision makers to distribute varying amounts of resources to different areas.

The value of influential communications becomes more significant as total resources become scarcer. In many human services settings, resources are very limited. Thus, resource acquisition by managers of work units is often a very competitive communication process with other work units.

Top level administrators are also often engaged in a competitive communication process when attempting to acquire resources. This is particularly the case in obtaining funds through legislation and government budget allocations, from grants, foundations, business sources, private individuals, and when competing for direct paying clients or those supported by third party payments. Long term communication efforts aimed at building power and influence are often required for such individuals.

What affects a managers power and influence in competing for resources?

Personal, political, factual and contextual factors have impact. **Personal power** is discussed in Chapter 10 with respect to influence and power with supervisees. Within the management structure, **legitimate and expert** power may be most effective in achieving influence. **Referent power,** particularly when it is based on a leaders charisma and communications skills, may be extremely influential both inside and outside an organization. This can be especially true outside the organization, since highly charismatic, effective communicators may not be subject (in that context) to the scrutiny and accountability that occurs on a day to day basis inside an organization. High level administrators who exhibit such power may be extremely effective in acquiring resources for their organization.

Personal relationships also affect power and influence. Inside the organization, positive relationships with ones supervisor, higher level managers and gatekeepers enhance personal power. Positive relationships are those that are non-adversary, and which support the needs of others in power and the mission of the organization.

Political relationships involve use of informal influences in the decision making process to modify normal power relationships. For example, the manager of Unit A has previously helped the manager of Unit B solve a significant problem. The manager of Unit A now needs support in convincing the agency administrator to fund a new project. The manager of Unit B has a close relationship with the administrator. Manager A thus calls upon manager B to assist him in getting a positive decision from the administrator. Without the informal influence of manager B, the project would not get approval because of it's low priority to the administrator and manager A's low influence.

Factual bases of influence include objective information related to accountability and servicing needs. For example, a data based needs assessment showing a market for a new program is an objective reason for requesting increased funding. Information of this nature, communicated effectively, is essential for most human services managers in acquiring resources. Such information should be easily understandable and transmitted in the decision maker's or decision influencer's preferred style of communication (e.g. by word of mouth or in writing.).

Contextual factors include the priority structure within organizations and the political climate within and outside the organization. When priorities of the organization and its decision makers favor the work of a particular unit, then power and influence of managers from that unit are increased. For example, if agency priorities are to exploit new sources of revenue producing projects in the community, managers of work units that conduct effective projects are likely to have the most influence in obtaining resources.

Political climate refers to the tendency of decision makers or legislators to support or not support programs, services or causes at a point in time. This climate may depend upon the interaction of power dynamics within and between organizations, legislatures, political figures, consumer groups and other special interest bodies and individuals.

When competing from a weak power position, how can influence of human services managers be increased?

The development and use of referent and expert personal power can help. Also, managers can understand and make use of the formal and informal group structure inside or outside the organization. For example, keeping up effective relationships with gatekeepers, getting support of informal leaders within the power structure, and maintaining good relationships with external power sources (such as consumers and politicians) helps make the political process work to the benefit of those with less direct power.

CLIENT (CUSTOMER) SATISFACTION

Who is the "customer" in human services and how does that differ from the "customer" in private business?

In private business, the customer is usually the person or group to whom a product or service is sold. In human services, those who pay for services may be the person to whom a direct service is provided (client or patient), public funders (e.g., government agencies through 3rd party payment, contracts or direct grants), or private sources of funding (e.g., insurance companies, foundation grants, donations). Thus, the concept of "customer" for human services extends beyond the usual business definition, to include all parties who provide resources for the organization to function and exist.

What is the significance of customer satisfaction in human services?

As noted in Chapter 2, Peters and Waterman (1982) found that close nurchuring of customers is an important characteristic of the best performing companies. This also makes sense for human services organizations.

In business, customer satisfaction leads to repeat and expanded sales, and increased revenue. In human services it leads to more referrals, and to potential expansion of services or the base of clients served. This results in maintained or increased resources.

How can customer satisfaction be maintained and increased?

Managers should keep in close contact with customers to assess needs and satisfaction levels. This can include conducting open forums, client interviews, or having client satisfaction surveys completed as a part of program evaluation. It should also include keeping open relationships with funding sources which allow for feedback of problems and concerns.

Immediate responses to customer complaints is important. As is evident, when a consumer senses concern and gets an immediate reaction to a problem, the likelihood of a continuing or enhanced relationship with a business or service organization is increased. When concerns are ignored or receive slow responses, the probability of doing business elsewhere or supporting another organization is increased.

Chapter 16

COMMUNICATIONS MEDIA

What communications media are most important to human services managers?

S poken, written, computer, and public media communications are important. **Spoken communications** are used as a basis for maintaining everyday relationships and for dealing with most routine interactions. **Written communications** are used for formalized matters such as rules, regulations, procedures, instructions, reports, requests and for providing certain information. Effective writing skills or the ability to generate effective written material through others is **crucial** to successful management.

Communication through computers is important for processing and transmitting large amounts of data. Computerized data processing can improve the quality and amount of information available for accountability purposes, management, and improvement of services. It may also facilitate efficient staff utilization. Finally, **public media** (e.g., television, radio, newspapers) **communication** involves using speaking or writing to directly or indirectly communicate with the general public. This is a highly potent form of communication that can have major positive or negative impact.

SPOKEN COMMUNICATIONS

What is the significance of relationship building through spoken communications?

This is very important for human services managers. Managers should spend a high proportion of their total effort developing and maintaining relationships. This means spending a great deal of time **out of the office** interacting with employees, formal and informal leaders, funders and consumers. Such interactions help a manager maintain visability; communicate interest, caring and concern; and facilitate conflict resolution, marketing and resource acquisition.

What are some guidelines for effective relationship building through spoken communications?

Communications should usually be open, honest and at the level of one adult to another. Encouraging such relationships (by managers) facilitates mutual trust, respect and commitment. Practical suggestions for relationship building by managers include:

1. Respond **immediately** (with action) to requests by employees or "customers."
2. Return phone calls **immediately.**
3. Give **concrete answers** to problems whenever you can.
4. **Listen** non-defensively to complaints.
5. **Focus on facts** rather than emotions in dealing with complaints, concerns or requests.
6. Maintain awareness that spoken communications is not the preferred mode of everyone. For example, a higher level manager may prefer written communications for certain or most requests. Assessment of communication preferences is valuable in deciding how to achieve the best relationships and results with individuals.

WRITTEN COMMUNICATIONS

What is the significance of written communications?

Much organization communication is in written form. Such documents often formalize spoken communications, since the written word can be verified, reviewed for meaning, reproduced and used uniformly by others. When reducing communications to writing, it is essential to get the point across accurately, clearly and with appropriate affect.

Oftentimes, minute differences in how meaning is communicated can mean the difference between success and failure for a manager. For example, in a request to one's supervisor or to the agency director, a tone of defiance vs one of appreciation and cooperation can influence the result. Similarly, when recommending an employee for a monetary reward, the supervisor's ability to clearly describe what will be perceived as pertinent by decision maker(s) may determine whether the reward is approved.

Written communications also contain an **image factor.** For example, poor grammar, spelling, format or neatness may have as much or more impact on the receiver than the communication itself.

When are writing skills most important to managers?

Writing skills are significant when personally seeking jobs, accelerating ones promotion opportunities, assisting others in getting hired or promoted (Just How Important Are Writing Skills, 1983), helping others get rewarded, acquiring resources, and communicating with staff and customers. With regard to personal advancement of managers, writing skills may be a key factor in competing for promotions (Be Patient in Developing Writing Skills, 1982).

What are some writing essentials for managers?

Brevity — Reports, letters, memoranda and so forth should be short and to the point. When such documents exceed one or two pages, the communication may not be read or attention of the reader may be lost.

Correct Spelling and Grammar — It is not uncommon to see communications with poor spelling and grammar. Such materials often miscommunicate the intent of the message. They also reduce the credibility of the writer.

Organization — Written communications should be well organized. In reports and requests; conclusions, recommendations or suggestions should follow directly from findings, facts or logic stated earlier. In order to be credible, the linkage between the recommendation, suggestion, or request and its basis, must come across clearly and logically to the reader.

What can a manager do to avoid a poor written communication in an important situation?

It is helpful to have one or more knowledgable colleagues or employees review the material. This can validate whether the intended meaning and tone are being communicated and whether any errors exist.

What should be done if a manager cannot develop good writing skills or prefers not to write?

It is then **essential** to have an employee on staff to whom such duties can be delegated. Since external written communications can have a profound effect on resource acquisition and credibility, someone must be available to effectively manage this task.

COMPUTERS AND DATA COMMUNICATIONS

How can computers help a human services organization?

Computers can be used for administrative, direct service and research applications. Major **administrative applications** include word processing, data base management, computational functions and desktop publishing. **Direct service applications** include client training and education (Gottleib, 1986), client assessment, testing and evaluation, occupational information dissemination, client decision making assistance, client characteristic-job requirement matching systems for counselor and adjudicative decision making (e.g., insurance and workmans compensation claims) and report writing. Research applications include model building and statistical analysis for program evaluation, and evaluation research.

What is the major administrative value of computerization for an organization?

It can provide better information for work unit management and provide higher quality services for clients. It can also improve organization productivity, efficiency and effectiveness, and reduce staffing needs.

What are some disadvantages of computerization for an organization?

1. At the outset, it may be met with resistance and require extensive efforts to acclimate staff to change (e.g., using equipment, cooperating in supplying administrative data, or using computerized materials with clients).

2. It may produce **more** administrative information than is needed to run the organization at the optimal level. Management of **information overload** may therefore be needed to avoid wasted time spent on reviewing computer generated data.

3. Computerization may **not** increase productivity, efficiency and effectiveness to the extent expected. Computerization requires time for data input and retrieval, it requires consistent maintenance of data bases (input of new data, removal of old data) to maintain accuracy and it requires consistent cooperation of those who must supply data to the computer. For example, if data bases of client characteristics are maintained for accountability reporting, the data retrieved on group characteristics of clients will only be accurate if data input into the system on individual clients is accurate.

4. It may generate **too much** employee interest. In some instances

employees may spend more time than is needed working with the computer or assisting others because of a personal interest in computers. Such employees may become "experts" at the expense of other job functions. This may be helpful to the organization if no other expertise is available, or in initially motivating staff participation. However, it can also result in poor manpower utilization.

What is the most important factor in successful implementation of computerization in human services organizations?

Preparing the organization for technological change appears to be most important (Eighth Institute on Rehabilitation Issues, 1981). Human services workers tend to be people oriented. By nature, they may be less ready than those who are oriented toward data and things to adjust to computerization. In addition, there may be some threat of computers replacing human interaction as the medium for assisting clients. Sampson, (1984) suggests enhancing the acceptance process through active involvement of staff during the planning stages, support by top level administrators, clear roles and responsibilities and regular communication during implementation of changes.

What are some examples of administrative applications of computers?

Wordprocessing — This is a major timesaver for organizations that type and process written documents. It allows corrections and changes to be made to documents without complete retypes (as is necessary with a typewriter). Spelling can also be checked automatically. In addition, documents can be saved for later use, they can be automatically merged with other information (such as client names and addresses) and they can be automatically generated in whatever quantity needed. Thus, for routine office typing, and document storage, wordprocessing is a revolutionary change from past practice. It can be highly cost effective and sometimes reduce the need for clerical staff.

Wordprocessing can also be used by managers and staff to directly produce reports, case documentation and so forth. Such use avoids duplication of effort, e.g., handwriting a report, then having it typed; and excessive physical movement of documents among staff. Also, direct use of wordprocessing **while writing a document** saves time in organizing, composing and correcting.

Database Management — This function allows stored data to be sorted and accessed in virtually any manner. For example, caseload data might be accessed monthly (or on command) for a specific counselor. As illustrated in Table XVII, this could include each client's name, date of initial appointment, presenting problem and age of case in elapsed days. Average elapsed days might also be automatically calculated. Database management programs can often merge information with other types of programs (such as wordprocessing) and perform timed functions, such as automatic generation of follow-up letters or reminders at specified times.

TABLE XVII
EXAMPLE OF FORMAT FOR COMPUTER GENERATED CASELOAD DATA

Client Name	Initial Appointment Date	Presenting Problem	Elapsed Time (days)
R. Apple	12/18/88	Adjustment	103
S. Caleb	11/ 4/88	Vocational	147
J. Dolan	1/ 4/89	Vocational	86
J. Daugherty	9/ 5/88	Emotional	208
L. Elliott	3/10/89	Educational	21
V. Haltenor	12/21/88	Emotional	100
C. Kearney	2/14/89	Vocational	45
R. Likens	8/31/88	Adjustment	213
J. Mosely	3/29/89	Adjustment	3
C. Murtin	11/ 8/88	Emotional	151
K. Rosen	12/ 4/88	Emotional	117
Z. Smith	1/18/89	Vocational	72
O. Snavely	3/ 1/89	Educational	30
S. Vorseth	10/30/88	Adjustment	152
	Caseload Average Elapsed Time		*103*

Computational Functions — These include complex arithmetic and mathematical manipulations usually done by **spreadsheet** type programs. Simple arithmetic instructions or complex formulas can be used to forecast, monitor and calculate. This function can be used for budget preparation and control, payroll calculations and check generation, performance indicator calculations and report generation etc. The ability to test the effect of varying inputs on results in complex situations is an important advantage of using computer computational functions. For example, in planning a budget, items and projected costs can be changed or moved to test the effect on the total budget.

Desktop Publishing — This allows materials such as brochures, pamphlets and books to be produced in a professional manner through use of a computer program. Such applications can save costs and in some instances produce revenue for human services facilities.

It is noted that the above describes some of the simpler administrative functions that computers can serve. As technology has improved, programs have been developed to allow some of these functions to interact and be applied simultaneously to all phases of the organization.

Are there computer packages that can be of specific administrative use to human services organizations?

Yes. However, due to rapid developments in this field, it is not appropriate to attempt to describe specific systems in this text. Several systems have been developed and are in the process of development for rehabilitation and human services applications. Information on such systems is best obtained through establishing networking contacts with private or public agencies that have implemented computerized packages.

Prior to purchasing a package, it is helpful to observe and discuss the system with an organization that has already implemented it. Advertising claims may not adequately represent both the advantages and shortcomings of a particular system and the level of support that its manufacturer may provide.

How is computerized data typically communicated?

Computer communications are done "on-line" or by using "hard copy" information. **On-line** use involves direct interaction with a terminal by the user. For example, if a manager wishes to access monthly productivity data on each staff person, he or she directly calls up the data on the computer and views the information on a video display terminal (VDT). A copy of the data may also be obtained through a printer attached to the system. The printed copy is referred to as **hard copy**. Each user of computer information may have access to a terminal for on-line interaction, or hard copy data may be supplied regularly or upon request.

Is on-line access to a computer always necessary?

No. In some instances it is sufficient to supply hard copy information or feedback from a centralized source. For example, monthly feedback to staff of performance information (e.g., productivity, quality and timeliness) can be done through distributing printed reports to each employee. This provides a continuing record for the supervisor and employee which can be generated from a single source. In other instances, such as when frequent access to case information is needed or when the wordprocessing function is used, on-line availability through individual terminals is needed. When determining how many individual terminals are needed, managers should analyze usage requirements, including time losses in waiting to use terminals and lack of use due to unavailability of terminals.

What is "user friendliness" and how does this impact on communication of computerized data?

User friendliness refers to the ease with which computer programs and related data can be understood and used by their consumers. Computer programs which are not user friendly may make communications too complex and difficult to understand. Thus, the impact of their use on desired results may be poor. For example, providing hard copy management reports that are difficult to read and interpret will discourage managers from using them. Similarly, a computer program for administering a psychological test that does not clearly state instructions will be frustrating for clients and will result in invalid scores. Thus, user friendly programs and data formats facilitate acceptance and effectiveness of computer communications.

What role should managers play in computerization?

Managers are probably most effective when they have experience in interacting directly with computers. Understanding established through direct use helps develop a perspective that improves decision making and avoidance of management information system excesses (Schwartz, 1987). Also, such involvement supports the priority of computer implementation initiatives and thus may help counteract employee resistance.

Are managers typically resistant to using computers?

This occurs frequently. For example, according to studies cited in Newsweek (Schwartz, 1987), most top executives never use computers. In addition, older managers are much less likely than younger managers to use computers (e.g., 14% of 50–59 year olds vs 35% of 30–39 year olds). Lack of use could be related to disinterest in learning a new body of knowledge or fear that one will not be able to learn the new information. Human services managers could be particularly prone to such resistance if there is also an aversion to data/things activities.

PUBLIC MEDIA COMMUNICATIONS

What is public media communications?

This involves communications through news media such as newspapers, radio and television.

Why is public media communications important?

From a positive perspective, public media can help human services managers reach a large segment of the public for marketing and public relations purposes. However, managers may also need to explain problems or defend their programs when facility related information becomes newsworthy. For example, alleged sexual abuse of clients, serious employee complaints or fraudulent activities might attact investigative reporters and potential negative publicity. Thus, managers should be prepared to use and deal effectively with the media under both positive and negative circumstances.

What is the role of the news reporter with relation to the organization?

When the proposed story is positive and informational, both the organization and reporter have something to gain. Information can be given freely and both parties are happy. The reporter gets the story and the organization gets some positive publicity.

When "bad news" is involved, reporters may be pressured to work quickly, prolifically and as accurately as they can. However, events may be intensified in the name of journalism (Morris, 1982).

What are some guidelines for managers in dealing with the news media?

1. Decide whether you (or someone else) is the person with whom reporters should speak. In some organizations, all press contacts are handled through a public relations office or person.
2. Know your reporter, and the format and theme of the program.

The reporter's credibility and style (e.g., expose, or information gathering) may be of particular significance.

3. Be as prepared as possible, both in general and specialty areas.
4. Establish professional rapport with the reporter.
5. Give yourself time to think. Do not be pressured into quick, but possibly inaccurate responses.
6. Tell the truth. If you do not know an answer to a question, say you do not know and offer to find out the answer. If you cannot divulge the answer, say "no comment."
7. If you do not wish to have a statement quoted, do not make it. Statements made "off the record" may be published.
8. State the most important facts or conclusions at the beginning of an answer, then expand on that.
9. Do not argue with the reporter or repeat negative words.
10. Do not accept a reporter's misinformation. Correct this for the record.

(Cutlip and Center, 1978; Morris, 1982)

COMMUNICATIONS EXERCISE 1
CONFLICT RESOLUTION/NEGOTIATION

(Group)

Setting: Vocational Rehabilitation Department of a rehabilitation hospital

Department Structure: This department consists of a work evaluation unit, a training and adjustment (T&A) unit, and a job placement (JP) unit. Supervisors of each of the units report to the department chief.

Situation: The supervisors of the T&A and JP units are in conflict regarding a referral from T&A for job placement. The client is a 19 year old male who is recovering from a closed head injury. He has been evaluated and spent seven weeks in a work adjustment and job readiness program in the T&A unit. His behavior is somewhat erratic and most staff agree that he is a questionable candidate for employment at this time. The supervisor of the JP unit refuses to accept the case. However, the supervisor of the T&A unit believes the client should be given a chance to prove himself. Both are adamant regarding their positions on this issue. In fact they have had frequent disagreements on such issues before although they usually are able to resolve differences among themselves. The supervisor of the T&A unit generally believes in letting people try, even if they may fail. He perceives that kind of learning experience as important to career development. The supervisor of the JP unit is a pragmatist. He believes that client failures turn off employers to hiring people with disabilities in the future.

TASK AND PROCEDURE

This exercise is done with groups of six to eight. One volunteer will serve as the department chief, two others as the supervisors of the T&A and JP units and the rest as observers. In a role playing scenario the supervisor will meet with the two supervisors. An attempt will be made to resolve the conflict using the methods of conflict resolution and/or negotiation discussed in Chapter 15. Upon completion, the observers will discuss the following:

1. What was the dominant approach to conflict resolution?
2. Was more than one approach used?
3. If bargaining was involved, was a positional or principled approach used?
4. What special strategies were used by the involved parties? How effective were they?
5. Was the conflict resolved effectively? Why?

COMMUNICATIONS EXERCISE 2
PUBLIC MEDIA COMMUNICATIONS

(Group)

Situation: Information has been reported to the local TV station that attendants in a private nursing home have been beating and otherwise abusing patients. The information was reported by family members of two patients. One of the family members claimed her father had been slapped repeatedly when he refused to follow instructions about bathing. The other family member said he had "heard about such incidents" from his mother, but could not substantiate them with facts. The recently hired nursing home administrator was not aware of any problems until he received a request for an interview from the TV station. Prior to the interview he found out that one minor incident did occur in which a patient kicked an attendant. The attendant then pushed and restrained the patient. No further information was immediately available. No one admitted to the slapping incident, but staff complained that patients often become unruly and must be "handled."

TASK

The class will be divided into groups of four to six. One volunteer in each group will role play an investigative reporter, the other the nursing home administrator. Others in the group will be observers.

Both role players will be given time to prepare, then to develop rapport with one another. The interview will then begin. At the conclusion of the interview, the group will discuss how the situation might have been perceived by the public and how well the administrator followed the guidelines in Chapter 16 for dealing with the media.

Section VIII

ORGANIZATION DEVELOPMENT AND CHANGE
INTRODUCTION AND OVERVIEW

According to Huse and Cummings (1985), organization development is "a systemwide application of behavioral science knowledge to the planned development and reinforcement of organizational strategies, structures, and processes for improving an organization's effectiveness."

For practical purposes, organization development focuses on improving the competence of entire organizations or work units. In human services, emphasis may be on both benefits to employees, and benefits to the work unit in the form of better productivity, efficiency and services generation.

Formal organization development is most likely to be initiated when serious problems or a need for major change is perceived. **Formal,** in this context, refers to a structured process in which an internal organization development specialist or outside consultant enters into a relationship with a work unit or organization for the purpose of conducting this process.

Organization development requires **change** in order to improve work unit conditions. Thus, effecting change is an integral and continuing part of the process. **Organization development related changes** are usually broad efforts related to employee and organization well being and improvement.

Other types of major changes are also needed in organizations. These include innovations, such as attempts to introduce new ideas and techniques; attempts to change specific methods of providing services, or administrative processes (e.g., computerization); and implementation of new requirements, such as legislative changes.

Formal Organization Development Models

The **planning** and **action research** models offer contrasting approaches to carrying out organization development. Both involve:

237

1. A series of steps in which a consultant and client system (organization) work closely together including:
    a. Exploration of a situation needing a change effort,
    b. Diagnosis,
    c. Planning for action,
    d. Implementation of change
    e. Evaluation of the effort.
2. Active involvement of the client system with a consultant.

The **action research model** places greater emphasis on data gathering and diagnosis (of the type of changes needed) before action is taken, and on evaluation of results. It is also oriented toward a cyclical process of rediagnosis, to see whether new action is needed, after initial changes have taken place.

In the **planned change model**, the diagnostic phase is directed toward identifying improvement goals to achieve while using a pre-determined approach to bringing about change. The T-group, i.e., a group experience designed to improve personal insight, development and sometimes to explore group dynamics and relationships, is an example of a pre-determined approach.

The Organization Development and Change Function of Managers

From the perspective of this book, it is the manager's role to **informally** conduct organization development (and change) on a **continuing** basis. When operating from this perspective, the manager is **always** assessing the health of his or her work unit and its change needs. When it is determined that changes should take place, they are made (at the time they are needed) so that the work unit can (in theory) always function at the most optimum level.

Managers who use the organization development and change function effectively are able to regularly anticipate the need for changes, make the changes and take other necessary actions to support the current and long term effectiveness and survival of their organizations. This retards system movement toward entropy and helps prevent the need for **formal** organization development projects designed to rescue an unhealthy organization.

Change

Human services managers often operate in environments which require the need to implement complex changes rapidly. For example, in vocational rehabilitation, changes in services provided (e.g., independent living, supported work), administrative and servicing methods (e.g., computerization) can require extensive training and reorientation of staff. Often, change efforts (e.g., new legislation) may take years before implementation is complete. Needs for organization development related changes often accompany other rapid changes, since organizational structures, processes and relationships with the environment must often also be modified in these situations.

Considering the above, the ability to proactively and reactively **cope with change** may be the single most important skill that a "surviving" manager must have. Human services managers must recognize that change is the **normal** state of affairs, not the exception. Thus, it is most constructive to approach management from the perspective of "What is the most functional way for us to bring about change" vs. "How can we avoid change and maintain the status quo"?

Organization Development and Change As An Integrating Function

The organization development and change function provides a basis for the manager to integrate information from all other functional areas to determine the methods and strategies that will most effectively maintain negative entropy and homeostasis. For example, if it is known that employee morale is declining with an effect on productivity (due to employee turnover), then the manager should be looking at organizational factors that are contributing. These factors could include communication related areas, such as the approach to labor-management relations; or control related factors, such as whether jobs are structured to generate intrinsic motivation. As problem areas are identified, change efforts may be instituted through the associated management functions.

An Organization Development and Change Frame of Reference

In approaching the organization development and change function, viewing organization operations from a systems perspective is usually helpful. As noted in Chapter 2, this requires considering the interdependency of system components and the dynamics of system functioning. For example, it is clear that modifying one aspect of a system will impact on other components and dynamics. Because of the complexity of system functioning, effective organizational diagnosis is particularly important before implementing major changes.

Managers should consider a contingency approach to organization development and change. In some instances, organization development specialists have a specific approach which may be applied in most instances (e.g., teambuilding, management by objectives or T-groups). However, a manager who is knowledgable in the broad range of available techniques within each management function and is able to apply practical diagnostic skills, is in a position to potentially choose the most efficient direction. In some instances, however, consultant services may be needed to assist with this task.

Finally, when implementing change, managers should consider the complexity and degree of permanence needed. Major long term changes often require more extensive efforts than temporary or minor changes. For example, resolving the problems of a major structural change or implementing extensive changes in legislation require long term controls and follow-up actions. Without such safeguards, any progress made at first is likely to be lost.

Practical Management Applications

In this section, Chapter 17 describes a model and methods for change that can serve as a practical guide to managers in carrying out the organization development and change function. Chapter 18 describes two systems, management by objectives and the management control project, that can be implemented as planned change initiatives in human services facilities. Both offer the possibility for agencies to move toward more efficient control strategies and better client services.

Chapter 17

OPTIMIZING PERFORMANCE:
A MODEL AND METHODS FOR CHANGE

Is there a practical model that can be applied by managers in carrying out the organization development and change function?

An integrative **action research** model which can be applied by managers is presented by Donnelly, Gibson and Ivancevich (1987). The sequential steps below summarize a modified version which may be used totally or partially by human services managers. It may be used for both continuing organization development and for other change initiatives. The steps are:
1. **Recognizing the need for change**
2. **Diagnosis**
3. **Selecting the change strategy**
4. **Implementing change**
5. **Evaluating change**

RECOGNIZING THE NEED FOR CHANGE

What is the process in recognizing the need for change?

This involves responding to the forces for change reflected in information from outside and inside the organization (Donnelly, Gibson & Ivancevich, 1987). In human services, external forces are likely to include changes in client needs for services, legislative changes, changes in competing services within the community, technological advances, resource constraints, demands of consumer groups and changes in professional standards. Forces from within the organization may include problems related to performance, employee needs or demands, and management concerns or priorities.

Managerial sources for recognizing the forces for change include direct interaction with the environment and control data collected inside the organization. With regard to environmental interaction, participation by managers in regular contacts with other agency personnel, professional groups, consumers, political leaders and funding sources helps to maintain a proactive stance on changes needed to keep services beneficial, competitive and worthy of support. For example, if a rehabilitation center director finds out through his contacts that the state mental health agency will be providing grants for job placement services, this may become an expansion opportunity for the facility.

Data collected through feedback processes (e.g., program evaluation), supervision, and through regular interactions with employees helps to detect internal problem areas. It may also help managers to determine when innovative changes are appropriate even when problems do not exist.

DIAGNOSIS

What is the process of diagnosis?

Diagnosis involves identifying symptoms, contributing problems, underlying sources and appropriate change interventions related to internal dysfunction or desired organization improvement. **Symptoms** refer to observed deficiencies in performance or system output indicators, goal achievement, program evaluation standards etc. Examples of potential symptom areas include productivity, efficiency, effectiveness, client satisfaction, quality, and employee satisfaction. Symptoms may be evident from routine data fed back in reports, observation or evidence of recurring problem incidents (e.g., excessive employee grievances).

Contributing problems refer to specific organization factors that contribute to or cause symptoms. For example, jobs that permit little autonomy for professional staff may contribute to dissatisfaction. This may be aggravated by imposing new employee attendance rules and perhaps taking disciplinary actions when they were not believed by staff to be warranted. This may in turn generate labor-management problems and grievances. In this instance, there are a series of problems contributing to the symptom. However, during the diagnostic process, it might be noted that the **underlying source** is lack of effective communication between staff and management. If communication was improved, most of the other problems would not exist or could be corrected.

During diagnosis, the underlying sources of symptoms must be sifted out from surface problems. Change interventions or what aspects of the organization to modify in order to remove or ameliorate the underlying problem source, must then be identified.

Diagnosis also involves identifying **environmental information** that requires internal or inter-organization change, and the interventions needed to achieve the change. For instance, evidence of changes in population demographics and service needs may require long term change efforts among many agencies to provide coordinated service to new clientele. Long term community planning to serve homeless persons and those contracting AIDS are examples. As a part of this process, interventions may be both reactive and proactive. **Reactive** interventions might change existing facilities to accomodate the environmental factors. However, **proactive** interventions would involve exerting leadership to change the factors that require accomodation. For instance, using the above example, administrators could actively propose and lobby for new legislation that would establish specialized treatment facilities for homeless persons or AIDS sufferers. Strategies for enhancing power, influence and using relationship building for the purpose of positive proactive environment change are discussed in earlier chapters.

How important is diagnosis?

Diagnosis is a crucial step for managers in the ongoing process of organization development and change. Timely, accurate identification of symptoms, and contributing problems/sources, prevents wasted efforts and facilitates continuing high level performance.

What practical tools are available to the manager for diagnosis?

Practical diagnostic tools include analyses and feedback data collected on a regular basis, program evaluation information, attitude surveys that can be administered to employees, data and personal input from external sources, and meetings with and among employees. The latter is of particular value in organizations and work units where employee involvement in decision making is stressed and open communications are maintained. When involvement with employees in decision making is part of the management frame of reference, data and other objective information can often be used to stimulate discussion that leads to problem solving, strategies for change and less resistance to change. Several of the specialized structures and the informal structure discussed in chapter 6 can be helpful in this regard.

How objective must diagnostic data be?

Valid, accurate data is important. However, although objective methodology (statistically validated questionnaires, statistical data analysis etc.) is most scientific, managers often have little time or resources for such activities. When organization development and change is done on a continuing basis, managers must use the most practical, least time consuming approach to collecting valid information and making decisions. This usually involves quickly collecting the best available data and using individual and group intuitive analytical processes.

Is there a low time consuming diagnostic procedure that can be used by managers on a continuing basis?

The following general framework and perspective is suggested:

1. **Know the total organization and specific work unit outputs and performance factors that are important.**

As a manager it is important to identify what the work unit or total organization considers to be important. From a systems perspective, this usually includes high levels of productive oriented outputs (productivity, efficiency, effectiveness and quality), client satisfaction (including all "customers" as discussed in chapter 15), and a positive organization climate. A balance among these outputs would also be expected, so that none is excessively emphasized at the expense of the others. Other important factors include expectations stated in long and short term goals, objectives and strategies, as well as program evaluation criteria.

2. **Understand what is important from an environmental perspective.**

This includes perceptions of resource providers; professional, community and political leaders; other agency and work unit leaders and consumers. It also includes important new developments in such areas as laws, professional concerns and management methods that may impact on need for reactive response or proactive leadership. Understanding what is important from an environmental perspective (before it impacts observably on the organization) is largely intuitive and judgemental.

3. **Monitor the important outputs, performance factors and environmental sources on a regular basis.**

It is important that the manager have continuing awareness of how the work unit or total organization is functioning, and the status of potential environmental factors. Thus, avenues for data feedback and new information from internal and external sources must always be in use. When symptoms or other pertinent information suggesting need for change become evident, that should be a signal for further diagnosis and consideration of corrective action. (Note that this does not suggest a "kneejerk" reaction at the first sign of aberrant data or threatening information, only **continuing** sources of awareness to the existence of developing problems or desirability for change).

4. **When continuing symptoms are observed, identify the contributing problems and underlying sources.**

This is often an intuitive process and may provide opportunities for participative problem solving at all work unit levels. Ideally, it is helpful to have empirical data showing relationships between symptoms and potential problems or sources. The most productive areas for intervention can then be selected on a more objective basis.

Some empirical data on symptom-problem/source relationships can be found in the literature and may be useful to managers. For example, data from the extensive study on rehabilitation and welfare agencies by Olmstead and Christensen (1973) (cited in Chapter 2) showed relationships between organizational factors (problems/sources) and important measures of agency and individual performance and satisfaction (symptom areas). Other factors, research, suggestions and methods discussed in the various functional areas of this text may be associated empirically or analytically with symptoms during the continuing diagnostic process by managers.

5. **Identify change interventions most appropriate to the underlying sources or externally identified need for change.**

Major categories of interventions include:

Structural — This includes formalized task and authority relationships (Donnelly, Gibson & Ivancevich, 1987) and how an organization divides labor or differentiates its parts (Huse & Cummings, 1985). It also includes integrative and coordinative mechanisms (Huse & Cummings, 1985), control systems and methods, work flow and procedures, and physical space configurations (French & Bell, 1984). Examples of structural interventions include creating a new department, reducing the number of departments by combining functions, assigning a liaison from one department or agency to another to improve coordination, implementing a job enrichment program, installing a new performance evaluation system and combining community agencies or consolidating functions to reduce overlap.

Process — In this context, process refers to human interaction and communication within or among organizations. It includes management-employee communications, informal communication networks, leadership styles, inter and intragroup processes and relationships, dynamics of organization culture, nature of employee participation in decisions and social involvement in the organization and so forth. Examples of process focused interventions include conducting team building exercises (helping work groups become more proficient in accomplishing tasks), providing a management training program, providing feedback on an employee attitude survey, and conducting intergroup or interagency conflict resolution.

Individual — This area includes non-technological changes that impact directly on individual employees (beyond the effects of structural and process interventions). Examples include environment enhancements such as health and physical fitness programs, day care services for working parents and flexible work hours. Direct services to employees such as employee assistance programs and career planning interventions are also included.

Technological — These changes include introducing new techniques through which the work is accomplished. Both machine technology (such as computerization and automated interagency information sharing), and new conceptual methods, such as a new approach to client treatment or work unit management (e.g., management by objectives or the Management Control Project) are included.

Should managers select a single change area to use?

Generally, major changes will require interventions in more than one area. For example, if an important underlying source established during diagnosis is low intrinsic motivation among employees, management might consider changes in the following areas:

Structural — modify jobs to include more variety

Process — make extensive quality of work life (QWL) changes to increase employee participation in decisions; establish greater employee cohesiveness and morale (e.g., through team building); and initiate a long term management effort to establish a strong, positive organization culture.

Individual — provide career counseling to employees followed by attempts to assign work most consistent with employee needs and interests; establish a continuing program to provide employee development experiences according to individual needs; and redirect employee recruitment efforts to hire employees whose skills, interests and needs are more consistent with organization goals.

Technological — implement a management by objectives system, including computerization to assure effective information feedback and data control.

One management strategy might be to implement the technological and some of the individual changes. Some structural and process change would also be needed as part of the management by objectives system (e.g., changes in the performance evaluation system and methods, and in the nature of the employee participation process).

How does one decide on which change areas to focus?

In deciding upon major change areas, managers must weigh the costs, potential benefits and side effects. If a minor change in a single area can accomplish the job, that should be done. Effective continuing diagnosis through a good understanding of ones work unit, or organization and its environment, should help sift out the extensiveness and type of change needed. For example, assignment of effective integrators (liaisons) to reduce conflict among work units (structural change) may be much less costly and have a higher chance of being effective than initiating an extensive team building program (process change). However, the team building approach may have the side effect of also strengthening employee involvement in working toward organization goals. The manager must ask, "is the potential side effect desirable or necessary enough to justify the extra costs?"

What are some organizational conditions that determine whether changes will be effective?

Donnelly, Gibson and Ivancevich (1987) suggest that the leadership climate, formal organization and organizational culture impact as potential limiting conditions. With regard to leadership climate, they suggest that any changes that do not have support and commitment from management have a low chance of success. In addition, attempts to change styles of managers to those inconsistent with higher level management are likely to be unsuccessful. For example, change within a single work unit to a participative management style may be contrary to the directive style expected by an agency director.

Changes must also be consistent with the formal organization with respect to top management philosophy, policies, legal precedent and structure. For instance, a local office of a public rehabilitation agency could not decide to modify formal agency staff evaluation or client servicing procedures without agency agreement.

The nature of cultural (including professional) norms and values also conditions the potential effectiveness of change. For instance, in human services agencies, attempts to reduce employee autonomy or implement servicing practices perceived (by the group) as unethical will result in overt and covert resistance.

SELECTING THE CHANGE STRATEGY

What internal change strategies are available to managers?

As illustrated in Table XVIII, strategies can occur along a continuum from administrative directives (after the change has been decided upon by management), to establishing high levels of employee involvement in decision making and commitment to the change prior to implementation. At the extreme right of the continuum (see Table XVIII), management relinquishes all authority for deciding upon and implementing the change(s) to the work group. A more moderate strategy involves sharing authority between management and the work group. The most conservative strategy only provides employees written directives on implementing the change. This continuum is similar to that described by Greiner (1967) with regard to unilateral, shared and delegated change strategies.

How should one select a change strategy?

Generally, the least costly strategy that will accomplish the change should be used. This should include consideration of long term implications. For example, a legislative change requiring modification of staff values (in order to be successful over the long term) would clearly justify more costly interventions than a temporary change. Unfortunately, using short term low cost strategies on extensive, long term changes is a common and costly management error.

TABLE XVIII
CONTINUUM OF CHANGE STRATEGIES RELATED TO COMPLEXITY AND STAFF RESISTANCE

Strategy

Written Directive by Management	Written Directive Plus Training by Management	Staff Participation (with Management) in Planning Change and Decisions Regarding Implementation	Delegation of Planning and Implementing Change to Staff

Complexity

Simple————————————————————————————————————Complex

Staff Resistance

Low—————————————————————————————————————High

What are the most important factors that should influence the choice of change strategy?

Complexity of the change and actual or potential resistance to carrying it out are important. When the change is simple and resistance is very low, directing the change verbally or in writing may be effective enough. For example, when changing to a schedule of flexible working hours requested by employees, a simple memo and explanation in a staff meeting may be sufficient. However, proposed changes in the way clients are scheduled (in order to improve staff productivity) may be strongly resisted. This might require shared management-staff planning or even relinquishing the problem to the staff for resolution and implementation.

What factors influence resistance to change?

Tannenbaum and Hanna (1985) describe the process of change for individuals in terms of three phases: "holding on," "letting go" and "moving on." Holding on is most consistent with the resistance to change phenomena. Its dynamics are described by Tannenbaum and Hanna as follows:

> In sum, whenever a new situation or our own evolving growth prompts us to make a change in our construction of reality (identity, world view, philosophy of life), there is a need to hold on. Accepting this need and moving beyond it are dependent on the centrality of our current

construction of reality, the strength of the negative emotional charge it is grounded in, and our ability to experience the feelings and emotions that surface in attempting to let go of it.

The above framework suggests that as changes more directly impact on individual (and group) core values and identity, the holding on phenomenon is most evident and letting go becomes more difficult to achieve.

Dreyfack and Bower (1982) describe concrete factors that also appear to impact on resistance to change in work settings. These include:

1. The purpose of changes has not been explained clearly or convincingly.
2. People are afraid the changes will result in more work being assigned.
3. There is a fear of failure with new and unfamiliar responsibilities. (An example in human services is the implementation of machine technological changes, such as computerization.)
4. People cannot see any gain (for themselves) from the change.
5. They blindly follow someone else who is resisting the change (for political reasons). (Followers may also go along with the group or a strong informal leader.)
6. Individuals may be worried that the changes will reduce their authority and status.
7. There is resentment because management did not consult with those who the change will affect, before implementing it.
8. There is fear that new procedures or systems will add restraints.

Is resistance to change ever constructive?

Yes. It prevents change from occuring **too** rapidly (and contributing to chaos). It also provides a perspective as to why change should not take place. For example, sweeping changes may be proposed in social welfare legislation. However, strong resistance of recipients and the human services community may provide reasons why the legislation should be modified.

What is the process of overcoming resistance to change?

This involves helping employees move through the holding on phase to the point of readiness to let go and move on. As changes become more personally significant and complex, more time must be spent **prior to the change** in working through the need to maintain the status quo.

Lewin (1951) described the change process as proceding through three steps: "unfreezing," "moving" and "refreezing." **Unfreezing** involves reducing the forces maintaining status quo behavior in the organization. This step is most pertinent to overcoming resistance to change and from a practical perspective could include the following:

Providing Information — As noted by Dreyfack and Bauer (1982), employees should be told why the changes are needed, how they will gain as a result and how the organization will benefit. Supporting data and other objective information may be particularly important. Appealing to a sense of community or "why this is important to all of us" can be significant when the communicator is trusted and viewed as having high concern for group values (e.g., service, professionalism and quality).

As part of the information process, potential myths that can increase fear and anxiety should be dispelled as early as possible (Dreyfack and Bauer, 1982). For example, changes sometimes signify loss of jobs or income. These concerns should be addressed before they get entrenched in the "rumor mill."

Employee Involvement — As implied earlier, this can take place at several levels. With minor, less significant or complex changes, involvement may need only include opportunities to ask questions, make suggestions or contribute ideas. More significant changes suggest the advisability of shared or delegated planning. With regard to sharing or delegating decision making, Donnelly, Gibson and Ivancevich (1987) suggest that the following basic preconditions must exist for meaningful employee participation:

1. Employees must want involvement.

2. They must be willing to voice their ideas, and have some degree of expertise in the area of analysis. Technical expertise is not needed, but knowledge of the impact of changes on their jobs is important.

3. Managers must be secure enough to allow genuine participation without feeling a threat to authority. Employees will usually sense shammed participation attempts or when authority and decision making is not really being shared.

Avoiding Surprises — Surprises regarding change may be upsetting personally and also upset a work unit's equilibrium. They may also cause unconscious resistance (Dreyfack and Bauer, 1982). Dreyfack and Bauer suggest "spoonfeeding" major changes on a piece by piece basis and assuring steps prior to the change that reduce its shock impact.

Enlisting the Aid of Influential Persons — Both formal and informal leaders are helpful in this regard.

What is a "champion" and how can he or she help in the unfreezing process?

Per Peters and Waterman (1982), these are zealous (volunteer) innovators who are obsessed with getting something accomplished. They are often viewed as organization "renegades" who "bullheadedly" push innovation forward in a pragmatic manner.

Because of their obsession, champion types may be helpful in reducing resistance by spreading their enthusiasm and drive. Observation suggests that influential champions (informal leaders) can be particularly effective in the unfreezing phase and throughout the change process.

Do managers usually deal effectively with resistance to change?

In some organizations, resistance to change is ignored. In such places an underlying assumption is that employees are being paid to do what they are directed. Therefore, "that is what they will do." In reality, what often happens is that directives are issued with little or no compliance. Controls are then initiated to check for compliance and to serve as a basis for action if directions are not followed. The effect is usually a slow process of change based initially on coercive activities. Although changes may eventually take place, they often require extensive energy for external management control over long periods of time.

What is the impact of not dealing with resistance to change?

When resistance is high, changes take longer to implement. In addition, when the changes occur, they may be incomplete. For example, when an agency must implement far reaching legislative changes which include a new service philosophy, failure of staff to adequately commit to and integrate the new philosophy will lead to inconsistent applications with clients. Some procedures may be followed, but they may seem "nonsensical" if one continues to follow the old assumptions.

In environments characterized by rapid change, failure to adequately address resistance can create an unbearable burden on organizations and managers. The more external control that must be exerted, the higher the cost of administrative overhead. Since resources are usually scarce in human services, this signifies the need to reduce services. Such a "snowballing" control effect was one stimulus for developing the Management Control Project (Chase and Patrick, 1983) for State rehabilitation agencies. That system is helping to counteract a trend that found agencies responding to oversight deficiencies (employees not following rules and procedures) by adding on layers of ineffective controls.

Failure to deal with resistance to change may also impact negatively on employee commitment. When employees change for the sake of compliance only, they are less likely to act with a sense of ownership. Then, later decisions and actions (related to the change) that could have been employee initiated and resolved, require further management assistance. As implied throughout this book, high employee commitment, involvement and self control are associated with more efficient, effective organization functioning. This occurs because less costs are needed for management overhead and because competent, committed direct labor personnel are in the best position to know how to do their jobs effectively.

IMPLEMENTING CHANGE

What is the process of change implementation?

This process is consistent with Tannenbaum and Hanna's moving on phase and Lewin's moving and refreezing phases. Moving refers to the shifting of work unit or organization behavior through changes in structure, process, environment and technology. Refreezing produces stability at a new level of homeostasis. This is done through supporting mechanisms that reinforce the new behavior (Huse & Cummings, 1985). Refreezing provides the mechanism to assure that the change remains permanent and complete.

What are some methods to use in implementing change?

1. Generally, the nature and details of changes should be written and distributed to those affected. This formalizes the change and provides a document for reference.

2. When changes are extensive and complex, phased implementation (one phase at a time) with time for adjustment and equilibrium reestablishment during interim periods is helpful.

3. Complex or extensive changes require maintaining open communications among all involved. This allows for necessary feedback to make timely adjustments. For example, in adjusting to new treatment programs in a mental health center, staff meetings and good intra/inter-unit

communications are needed to assure the effectiveness of treatment and coordination of services.

4. Those involved in the change should maintain the attitude and understanding that complete change takes time. Impatience can lead to dysfunctional consequences. For example, major changes in legislation often take years to fully implement at the agency level.

5. Timing of change implementation is important. Since major change causes disruption to normal operations, implementation during slack periods is desirable (Donnelly, Gibson & Ivancevich, 1987).

6. "Champions" and other supporters should be encouraged to take charge and assist during the change period.

7. Managers should engineer an environment of positive reinforcement as the change takes place. This includes many of the factors described by Peters and Waterman (1982) in the "excellent" companies and noted in Chapter 2.

EVALUATING CHANGE

What is the purpose of evaluating change?

To determine whether changes are being implemented as intended and whether desired results are being achieved (Huse & Cummings, 1985). Evaluation information is used as a basis for modification of the change effort, as needed.

How does change evaluation relate to the evaluation phase of the program/ agency management cycle?

As in other applications of the program/agency management cycle, **evaluation of change** is concerned with measuring whether planned actions lead to intended results. In fact, change efforts should be an integral part of the cycle. For example, as evaluative information becomes available to management from observation, performance indicators and so forth, it may become evident that a change effort is needed (e.g., starting a new program or improving efficiency of an existing program). The change effort can then be incorporated into short and long term planning. As the changes are initiated, evaluation of their implementation and results (e.g., as measured by observation and performance indicators) takes place. Corrective actions are taken as needed in planning and implementation, and the cycle continues. Any major changes, including organization development, innovations, new legislation, facility expansion etc. can fit this model.

What major aspects of change should be evaluated?

It is important to evaluate both how well the change itself is being carried out (during the moving and refreezing phases) and whether the expected results are being achieved. The first aspect is important, because failure to completely implement changes could be a reason for poor results.

What tools should managers use in evaluating change?

Sophisticated tools including measurement scales and research designs are available. These are generally used by organization development specialists and researchers. However, when managers are carrying out organization development and change as a continuing management function, practical constraints usually do not permit time consuming scientific evaluation. Managers need to depend upon the tools which with they are most familiar: verbal feedback, observation and routine performance indicators. These tools are also the basis for evaluating the routine health and functioning of their work units. They are thus also highly appropriate for measuring the effects of change.

APPLYING THE MODEL

What is needed for managers to apply the model suggested in this chapter?

Applying the model requires a perspective of awareness and a readiness to conduct **proactive** management. One must always be looking for both problems and opportunities for improvement. There must also be a readiness to take both leadership and management action at any time in order to keep a work unit or organization at its optimum functioning level. The model should be most effective when actions through the steps are predicated on this perspective of continuous "fine tuning."

What can be expected if this is done?

The work unit or organization should more consistently perform near its maximum level.

Chapter 18

PLANNED CHANGE IN HUMAN SERVICES: TWO SYSTEMS APPLICATIONS

This chapter discusses two management systems which can be implemented using the "planned change" approach to organization development. Both systems, Management by Objectives and the Management Control Project, are control systems that have potential for improving long term performance in human services. Both have had major impacts on management in organizations, the latter specifically in public rehabilitation systems.

MANAGEMENT BY OBJECTIVES (MBO)

What is management by objectives?

MBO is a system of associating performance objectives with positions and linking these objectives together according to an organization plan. In effect, it is a method of establishing a performance linkage between the plan of the organization and the people who implement it.

From a process perspective, Odiorne (1965) defined MBO as "a process whereby the superior and subordinate managers of an organization jointly identify its common goals, define each individuals major areas of responsibility in terms of the results expected of him and use these measures as guides for operating the unit and assessing the contribution of each of its members." Huse and Cummings (1985) define MBO as "systematic and periodic manager-subordinate meetings designed to accomplish organizational goals by mutual planning of the work, periodic review of accomplishments, and mutual solving of problems that arise in the course of getting the job done." This latter definition expands upon Odiorne's to include non-managers and to stress involvement in problem solving at all organization levels.

What is the basic purpose of MBO?

To improve the performance and overall contribution of organization members in achieving the organization mission. From this perspective, it is a motivational system.

What factors contribute to the motivational value of MBO?

1. MBO requires communication and clarification regarding organization, work unit and individual goals/objectives at all levels. Thus, expectations are clarified. This also helps reduce role ambiguity and role conflict, and their associated psychological stresses.

2. Performance is evaluated on the basis of measurable results with respect to pre-set goals and objectives. Objective indicators and behavior are stressed rather than personality factors. This provides a basis for employees to obtain and use valid, reliable feedback information to self-evaluate and self-correct performance. It thus supports intrinsic motivation mechanisms and employee centered control.

3. When MBO is used in a participative manner, it supports employee involvement in planning and problem solving. This may enhance commitment to organization goals and reduce the need for external management control.

What is required to successfully implement an MBO program?

MBO programs are total management systems that require special efforts to avoid failure. Empirical studies suggest the following (Hollmann, 1976):

1. The program should be introduced and implemented by **top management** (rather than, for example, a personnel department). This provides the priority necessary to help overcome resistance and fully carry out the requirements.

2. Introduction of the program should include a clear statement of its purpose.

3. Charts and forms should be minimized.

4. There should be a detailed orientation, and training for managers at all levels.

5. Whether or not to include participative goal setting should be based on a thorough diagnosis of internal climate and leadership patterns.

6. Objectives should be clear and prioritized. The MBO training program should have a phase devoted to the formulation of objectives.

7. Regular feedback sessions should be held with each subordinate (generally more than once yearly). Factors involved in determining frequency of feedback include subordinates experience with MBO, length of time covered in objectives, complexity of subordinates jobs, subordinates previous success in achieving objectives, subordinates need for independence and desire for feedback.

8. Caution should be used when giving criticism during feedback sessions. Any criticism should be constructive and related clearly to a problem solving approach. It should concentrate on what the subordinate can do to improve performance.

9. Supervisory support of the program is very important. This involves support for an increase in time spent on the program, and actions that support subordinates as they use MBO.

10. Organization support should exist for:

a. Linkage of MBO to a reward system.

b. Continual monitoring, to include attitudes, supervisor-subordinate relationships and performance checks.

c. Regular assessment of the program.

What are some problems cited by managers who have participated in MBO programs?

Research (Stein, 1975) involving 428 lower and middle managers in 10 companies indicates the most frequently cited problem areas (in rank order) as:

Measurability problems
Inadequate reviews
Lack of management commitment
Inflexible policy
Lack of downward communication
Lack of supervisory training
MBO was not part of the total management system

What are the steps in implementing an MBO system?

Huse (1975) suggests the following steps for goal setting and performance review procedures in an MBO program (adapted from work by Huse and Kay [1964] at General Electric):

Work Group Involvement — This step is essential and requires members of the primary work unit to define **overall** group and individual goals and tasks. Action plans are then established for achieving both organization and individual goals.

Joint Manager-Subordinate Goal Setting — This step includes a close examination and clarification of roles and responsibilities of each job incumbent.

Establishment of Action Plans for Goals — Each subordinate should develop action plans for achieving goals. This can be done individually or in group meetings. Huse (1975) notes that plans should reflect the individual style of the subordinate, not the supervisor.

Establishment of Success Criteria — This involves a process of jointly agreeing on the criteria for determining whether the goals have been met or not. In this step, the intent is to establish a true common understanding between supervisor and subordinate of the task and what is really expected. It is considered the most important step in the entire MBO process, since miscommunication on expectations is a common occurence. In this step, Huse stresses that "criteria and standards of success should not be limited to easily measurable or quantifiable data." Although MBO tends to stress objectivity and measurability, the point of this step is **mutual agreement regarding expectations.** Objectivity and measurability can facilitate that process. However, when measurability is difficult or impossible (as sometimes occurs with complex tasks in human services), the interpersonal process is essential to assuring that expectations are clear. This is a major source of breakdown in performance management systems.

Review and Recycle — This involves review (by the manager) of work progress. It may be done directly with the subordinate or in a group situation. Three stages of this process are described by Huse:

1. The subordinate reviews progress, discusses achievements and obstacles faced.
2. The manager discusses work plans and objectives for the future, and action plans are developed.
3. General discussion about the subordinate's future plans, ambitions and concerns. This final phase includes considerable coaching and counseling.

Maintenance of Records — Due to variability in jobs, tasks and styles, data recording methods should be left to supervisor-subordinate pairs or work groups. A suggested form for those wishing to use it can be provided, but it should not be mandatory. The intent is to emphasize process and results, not discourage effective participation or facilitate resistance due to administrative barriers. (It should be noted, however, that some standardization may be needed to assure adequate documentation to support personnel actions taken, in the event of legal actions, per discussion in earlier chapters.)

More detailed references on practical implementation of MBO programs include Huse and Kay (1964) (from which the above steps are adapted by Huse), and Meyer, Kay and French (1965).

MANAGEMENT CONTROL PROJECT

What is the Management Control Project?

It is a management system designed to improve the measurement and accomplishment of case service processes and results, as well as attitudes of counselors toward their work and agencies. It was developed specifically to overcome management problems experienced in State vocational rehabilitation agencies. Such problems included dysfunctional agency responses to program audits and reviews which showed that legally mandated services were not being provided effectively. For example, the General Accounting Office (GAO) and other oversight groups had repeatedly cited problems with poor case documentation, services provided to ineligible clients, high numbers of clients not gainfully employed, insubstantial services to clients, etc. The usual agency response was to implement additional management controls, such as more supervisory reviews (e.g., each eligibility determination would be reviewed by a supervisor), and additional regulations, policies and procedures. These attempts at greater accountability were not effective or efficient. In addition, research suggested that well trained staff were discouraged by a system that did not support professional and autonomous functioning, and offered few promotional opportunities. (Ledbetter, 1980; Chase & Patrick, 1983)

What does the management control project attempt to do?

It is designed to reduce the number of agency controls and to increase the autonomy and responsibility of direct service personnel.

How is this done?

The focus of control is shifted from managers to those providing services by:

1. Establishing an objective method for measuring performance. As described in chapter 12 and illustrated in Table VIII, process analysis criteria have been established which define expected areas of performance.

2. Providing extensive training at all agency levels in what is expected for acceptable performance in each area. This training attempts to insure that there is a common understanding among and between administrators, supervisors and employees regarding performance expectations.

3. Maintaining regular communications up and down the agency chain of command regarding achievement of the criteria and associated needs.

4. Establishing performance standards based upon performance achievements on the criteria.

5. Providing regular feedback to employees regarding their performance.

6. Reducing procedural requirements for direct service staff. This is a most dramatic change that stresses the attempt to shift to counselor autonomy. In effect, providing clear expectations for results, and encouraging clear spoken communications at all organization levels theoretically precludes the need for extensive procedures, and external controls to insure that the procedures are carried out. The dramatic effect is illustrated by the fact that some state rehabilitation agencies have reduced procedural manuals from hundreds of pages to almost nothing.

Can the management control project approach be integrated with management by objectives?

Yes. Management by objectives principles are and can be further incorporated into the management control project to enhance communication and effectively link servicing results to organization and work unit goals/objectives.

Is the management control project approach transferable to other human services settings?

It should be transferable to any setting in which movement toward greater employee centered control is desirable. The servicing criteria would change, but the basic philosophy and approach would remain the same.

How can this approach improve the overall efficiency and effectiveness of human services agencies?

It provides a basis to focus on "bottom line" servicing **results** rather than procedures and processes that do not contribute to servicing goals. In addition, the emphasis on employee centered control and mechanisms that support intrinsic rewards precludes the need for spending excessive energy on external management control. The role of managers becomes one of communication and support in **helping** (rather than forcing) employees to more effectively and productively meet organization and work unit goals and objectives. Theoretically, this should allow maximum resources to be expended on client services, since less resources should be needed for agency/program management and control. In effect, more cost effective flatter structures, which are most consistent with the employee and work characteristics of professionally functioning human service agencies, are then feasible.

What are the research findings on the management control project?

In a study of three state rehabilitation agencies after management control project installation, Chase and Patrick (1983) found:

1. Increased accuracy of eligibility decisions.
2. Improved evaluation and understanding of client rehabilitation needs.
3. Improved assessment of client rehabilitation potential.
4. Better client understanding of the process.
5. Reduced numbers of client appeals.
6. Improved rehabilitation planning based on client needs.
7. Increased client involvement in the planning and rehabilitation process.
8. Increased perceptions of autonomy and control by counselors in accomplishing their work.

Other research by Patrick and Patterson (1986) comparing counselors who did and did not function under the management control system approach found:

1. Increased case documentation accuracy among management control project counselors.
2. No effect of the management control project on job attitudes (job satisfaction and work alienation).

Obviously, research on the management control project is still sparse. Although the theoretical basis for the approach appears sound, existing results raise questions about the actual impact on job attitudes. Also, while case documentation suggests many improvements in the delivery of rehabilitation services, the data is unclear in differentiating effective documentation from effective counselor actions.

Many factors may effect results, such as completeness of implementation, time since implementation, and the state of the agency prior to implementation. For example, if counselor attitudes were previously positive, **dissatisfaction** could result after a new system is implemented. This underlines the importance of diagnosis as part of the organization development process. Whether the action research model is used, or planned change is being contemplated, it is necessary to understand the likely effect of a change effort.

What additional suggestions can be made for managers who wish to implement the management control project approach?

Chase and Patrick (1983) suggest the following:

Adopting a Philosophy — an organizational philosophy which internalizes and communicates:

1. Beliefs about the organization and its delivery of services.
2. How the organization will manage itself as a system.

The philosophy cannot simply be a statement. It must be expressed through behaviorally demonstrated commitment.

Reinforcing Performance Standards — For those who do not respond positively through communication of expectations alone, behavior must be externally reinforced. Good behavior should be rewarded positively and there should be consequences for poor behavior.

Maintaining and Reinforcing the System — Even after positive initial experiences with the management control approach, there is a tendency to slip back into traditional management behaviors. Initial demonstration project experience suggested that many agency staff are more comfortable with **adding controls** to solve problems than with persisting with the new approach. Continuing reinforcement of new techniques is needed to overcome this barrier.

ORGANIZATION DEVELOPMENT/CHANGE EXERCISE 1
AGENCY DIAGNOSIS

(Group)

You are the Director of a large mental health clinic. You tend to maintain the organization development and change perspective discussed in this section of the book and have noticed the following symptoms:

1. Written client complaints have increased slightly in the last two months.

2. A client satisfaction questionnaire that you use with all terminating clients has shown a slight change in the direction of dissatisfaction for the past six months. Clients are still expressing satisfaction, but not as strongly as in the past five years.

3. Staff productivity has been very high during the past year. In fact, it has never been higher since the agency has existed.

4. Effectiveness has dropped off slightly during the past six months.

5. Timeliness of services is declining. The waiting list for services after the intake interview is six weeks (non emergency situations).

6. Number of employee grievances has increased 20% over the past year. Many of the grievances are related to what are believed to be unreasonable demands placed on treatment staff by supervisors. Employee turnover has also begun to show a slight increase, but it is difficult to observe a clear trend.

The macro control strategy of this agency has generally been group and employee centered. However, in recent years, budget cuts have gradually forced a more management centered approach. Treatment staff have gradually spent more time with clients and less time with each other. There is a lot of complaining among staff and "talk" about finding other jobs. However, staff are also paid high salaries compared to other facilities.

TASK

On the basis of the above information, discuss the following:
1. What problems does the Director face and what might be the underlying source(s)?

2. Does it appear that a serious (entropic) situation could be developing?
3. Depending upon the answer to #2, is action by the Director at this time appropriate? Should he have detected and acted upon the situation sooner? Should he wait a little longer to see whether things take care of themselves?
4. What types of change interventions might be appropriate in this situation?

BIBLIOGRAPHY

1. Aiken, W. J., Smits, S. J., and Lollar, D. J.: Leadership behavior and job satisfaction in state rehabilitation agencies. *Personnel Psychology, 25:*65–73, 1972.
2. Attkisson, C. C. and Zwick, R.: The client satisfaction questionnaire: psychometric properties and correlations with service utilization and psychotherapy outcome. *Evaluation and Program Planning, 5:*233–237, 1982.
3. Auvenshine, C. D. and Mason, E. J.: Needs assessment in planning rehabilitation services. *Journal of Rehabilitation Administration, 6:*56–62, 1982.
4. Bachman, J. G. and Tannenbaum, A. S.: The control-satisfaction relationship across varied areas of experience. In Tannenbaum, A. S. (Ed.): *Control in Organizations.* New York, McGraw-Hill, 1968.
5. Baker, F. and Northman, J.: Input-throughput-output evaluation of a school mental health clinic. In Schulberg, H. C. and Baker, F. (Eds.): *Program Evaluation in the Health Fields.* New York, Human Sciences Press, 1979, vol.II. pp. 319–334.
6. Bandura, A.: Self-efficacy mechanism in human agency. *American Psychologist, 37:*122–147, 1982.
7. Be patient in developing writing skills. *Communications Seminar.* Chicago, Dartnell, Feb. 15, 1982.
8. Bennett, E. C. and Weisinger, M.: *Program Evaluation: A Resource Handbook for Vocational Rehabilitation.* New York, ICD Rehabilitation and Research Center, 1974.
9. Biasco, F. and Redfering, D. L.: Effects of counselor supervision on group counseling: clients' perceived outcomes. *Counselor Education and Supervision, 15:*216–220, 1976.
10. Blanchard, K. and Johnson, S.: *The One Minute Manager.* New York, Berkley, 1982.
11. Brett, J. M.: Managing organizational conflict. *Professional Psychology: Research and Practice, 15:*664–678, 1984.
12. Broskowski, A.: Organizational controls and leadership. *Professional Psychology: Research and Practice, 15:*645–663, 1984.
13. Buhler, C. and Mossanik, F. (Eds.): *The Course of Human Life.* New York, Springer, 1968.
14. Chase, P. and Patrick, A.: *Management Control Project Final Report* (NIHR/ G008003051). Athens, University of Georgia, 1983.

15. Claiborn, W. L. Biskin, B. H. and Friedman, L. S.: CHAMPUS and quality assurance. *Professional Psychology: Research and Practice, 13:*40–49, 1982.
16. Commission on Accreditation of Rehabilitation Facilities: *Standards Manual for Organizations Serving People with Disabilities,* 1989 Edition. Tucson, Arizona, 1989.
17. Commission on Accreditation of Rehabilitation Facilities: *Program Evaluation: A First Step.* Tucson, Arizona, 1976.
18. Cooper, P., Harper, J., Vest, L. and Pearce, R.: *Case Weighting Systems in Vocational Rehabilitation: Selected Abstracts.* Arkansas Rehabilitation Research and Training Center, Arkansas Division of Rehabilitation Services, University of Arkansas, 1978.
19. Coulton, C. J.: *Social Work Quality Assurance Programs: A Comparative Analysis.* Washington, D.C., National Association of Social Workers, 1979.
20. Cronin, J. J.: REMAP: A theoretical framework for marketing analysis and planning in rehabilitation facilities. *Journal of Rehabilitation Administration, 11:*99–107, 1987.
21. CSAVR Committee on Program Evaluation: *CSAVR Position Paper on Program and Project Evaluation Standards* (unpublished manuscript). CSAVR (Council of State Administrators for Vocational Rehabilitation), 1984.
22. Cubelli, G. E.: *Community Organization and Planning for Rehabilitation Services.* Washington, D.C., American Hearing Society, 1965.
23. Cutlip, S. M. and Center, A. H.: *Effective Public Relations.* Englewood Cliffs, Prentice-Hall, 1978.
24. Dellario, D. J.: The relationship between mental health, vocational rehabilitation, interagency functioning and outcome of psychiatrically disabled persons. *Rehabilitation Counseling Bulletin, 28:*167–170, 1985.
25. Donnelly, J., Gibson, J. and Ivancevich, J.: *Fundamentals of Management,* 6th ed. Plano, Business Publications, Inc, 1987.
26. Donnelly, J., Gibson, J. and Ivancevich, J.: *Fundamentals of Management,* 5th ed. Plano, Business Publications, Inc., 1984.
27. Dreyfack, R and Bauer, E. G.: Overcoming resistance to change. *Communications Seminar.* Chicago, Dartnell, Dec. 6, 1982.
28. Dunnette, M. D., Campbell, J. P. and Hakel, M. D.: Factors contributing to job satisfaction and job dissatisfaction in six occupational groups. *Organizational Behavior and Human Performance, 2:*143–174, 1967.
29. Eighth Institute on Rehabilitation Issues: *Computer Assisted Rehabilitation Service Delivery.* Dunbar, West Virginia Research and Training Center, 1981.
30. Elliott, R. H.: *Public Personnel Administration: A Values Perspective.* Reston, Reston, 1985.
31. Emener, W. G and Stephens, J. E.: Improving the quality of working life in a changing (rehabilitation) environment. *Journal of Rehabilitation Administration, 6:*114–124, 1982.
32. English, R. W., Oberle, J. B. and Byrne, A. R.: Rehabilitation counselor supervision: a national perspective. *Rehabilitation Counseling Bulletin* (Special Issue), *22,* 1979.

33. Erikson, E. H.: *Childhood and Society.* New York, Norton, 1963.

34. Etzioni, A. (Ed.): *The Semi-professions and Their Organization — Teachers, Nurses, Social Workers.* New York, Free Press, 1969.

35. Feinberg, L. B.: Toward an integrated theory of rehabilitation supervision. In Emener, W. C. Luck R. S. and Smits, S. J. (Eds.): *Rehabilitation Administration and Supervision.* Baltimore, University Park Press, 1981, pp. 233–252.

36. Feldman, S, Sorensen, J. E. and Hanbery, G. W.: Budgeting and behavior. In Feldman, S. (Ed.): *The Administration of Mental Health Services,* 2nd ed. Springfield, Thomas, 1981, pp. 118–148.

37. Feroz, R. F. and Katz-Garris, L.: Incorporating theory Z into rehabilitation administration. *Journal of Rehabilitation Administration, 8:*84–91, 1984.

38. Fine, S. A. and Wiley, W. W.: *An Introduction to Functional Job Analysis.* Washington, D.C., W. E. Upjohn Institute for Employment Research, 1971.

39. Fisher, R. & Ury, W.: *Getting to Yes.* Boston, Houghton Mifflin, 1981.

40. Flanagan, J. C.: The critical incident technique. *Psychological Bulletin, 51:*327–358, 1954.

41. French, J. R. and Raven, B.: The bases of social power. In Cartwright, D. and Zander, A. F. (Eds.): *Group Dynamics.* Evanston, Row, Peterson, 1960, pp. 607–623.

42. French, W. L. and Bell, C. H.: *Organization Development: Behavioral Science Interventions for Organization Improvement.* Englewood Cliffs, Prentice-Hall, 1984.

43. Friedlander, F.: The relationship of task and human conditions to effective organizational structure. In Bass, B. M., Cooper, R. and Haas, J. A. (Eds.): *Managing for Accomplishment.* Lexington, Heath, 1970.

44. Fuller, G. T.: Basic negotiating strategy. *Better Communication* (No. 263). Stirling, New Jersey, Information Plus, 1981.

45. Gellerman, S. W.: *Motivation and Productivity.* New York, American Management Association, 1963.

46. Glisson, C. A. and Martin, P. A.: Productivity and efficiency in human services organizations as related to structure, size, and age. *Academy of Management Journal, 23:*21–37, 1980.

47. Georgopoulis, B. S.: *Hospital Organization Research: Review and Source Book.* Philadelphia, Saunders, 1975.

48. Gottlieb, A.: *A National Survey of Computer Use by Vocational Rehabilitation Facilities: A Final Report.* Albertson, New York, Employment Research and Training Center, National Center on Employment of the Disabled, Human Resources Center, 1986.

49. Gouldner, A.: Cosmopolitans and locals: toward an analysis of latent social roles: I. *Administrative Science Quarterly, 2:*281–306, 1958.

50. Greiner, L. E.: Patterns of organization change. *Harvard Business Review, 45:*119–130, 1967.

51. Hackman, J. and Oldham, G.: *The Diagnostic Survey: An Instrument for the Diagnosis of Jobs and the Evaluation of Job Redesign Projects (Technical Report*

No. 4). New Haven, Department of Administrative Sciences, Yale University, 1974.

52. Hackman, J., Oldham, G., Janson, R. & Purdy, K.: *A New Strategy for Job Enrichment (Technical Report No. 3).* New Haven, Department of Administrative Sciences, Yale University, 1974.

53. Hage, J.: *Communication and Organizational Control: Cybernetics in Health and Welfare Settings.* New York, Wiley, 1974.

54. Hamner, W.: Worker motivation programs: Importance of climate, structure and performance consequences. In Hamner, W. and F. Schmidt (Eds.): *Contemporary Problems in Personnel: Readings for the Seventies.* Chicago, St. Claire Press, 1974, pp. 280–401.

55. Hanbery, H. W. and Cattanach, R.: Quantitative techniques for planning and controlling. *Mississippi's Business,* August, 1972.

56. Hart, G.: *The Process of Clinical Supervision.* Baltimore, University Park Press, 1982.

57. Hergenhahn, B. R.: *An Introduction to Theories of Learning.* Englewood Cliffs, Prentice-Hall, 1976.

58. Hershenson, D. B.: Life stage vocational development system. *Journal of Counseling Psychology, 15:*23–30, 1968.

59. Herzberg, F., Mausner, B. and Snyderman, B.: *The Motivation to Work.* New York, Wiley, 1959.

60. Hogerty, G. E., Goldberg, S. C. and Schooler, N. R.: Drug and sociotherapy in the aftercare of schozophrenic patients: adjustment of nonrelapsed patients. In Schulberg H. C. and Baker, F. (Eds.): *Program Evaluation in the Health Fields.* New York, Human Sciences Press, 1979, vol. II, pp. 335–355.

61. Holland, J. L.: *Making Vocational Choices: A Theory of Careers.* Englewood Cliffs, Prentice-Hall, 1973.

62. Hollman, R. W.: Applying MBO research to practice. *Human Resource Management, 29:*28–36, 1976.

63. Huse, E. & Kay, E.: Improving employee productivity through work planning. In Blood, J. (ed.): *The Personnel Job in a Changing World.* New York, American Management Association, 1964, pp. 301–302.

64. Huse, E. F. and Cummings, T. G.: *Organization Development and Change,* 3rd ed. St. Paul, West, 1985.

65. Huse, E. F.: *Organization Development and Change.* St. Paul, West, 1975.

66. Just how important are writing skills. *Communications Seminar.* Chicago, Dartnell, Sept. 13, 1983.

67. Kazmier, L. J.: *Principles of Management.* New York, McGraw-Hill, 1974.

68. Kiresuk, T. J. and Lund, S. H.: Goal attainment scaling: Research, evaluation, and utilization. In Schulberg, H. C. and Baker, F. (Eds): *Program Evaluation in the Health Fields.* New York, Human Sciences Press, 1979, vol. II, pp. 214–237.

69. Klasson, C. R., Thompson, D. E. and Lubin, G. L.: How defensible is your performance appraisal system? *Personnel Administrator, 25:*69–73, 1980.

70. Korman, A. K.: *Organizational Behavior.* Englewood Cliffs, Prentice-Hall, 1977.

71. Kotler, P.: *Marketing Management.* Englewood Cliffs, Prentice-Hall, 1984.
72. Laird, D. A. and Laird, E. C.: *The Techniques of Delegation.* New York, McGraw-Hill, 1957.
73. Lakein, A.: *How to Get Control of your Time and Your Life.* New York, P.W. Wyden, 1973.
74. Laplace, M. A.: Communication: The key to higher productivity and morale. *Journal of Rehabilitation Administration, 7:*112–115, 1983.
75. Larsen, D. L., Attkisson, C. C., Hargreaves, W. A. and Nguyen, T. D.: Assessment of client/patient satisfaction in human service programs: Development of a general scale. *Evaluation and Program Planning, 2:*197–207, 1979.
76. Latham, G. P., and Yukl, G. A.: A review on the application of goal setting in organizations. *Academy of Management Journal, 18:*824–845, 1975.
77. Latta, J. A.: Excellence in rehabilitation: the leadership connection. *Journal of Rehabilitation Administration, 11:*53–59, 1987.
78. Lawrence, P., & Lorsch, J.: *Organization and Environment: Managing Differentiation and Integration.* Boston, Harvard University Graduate School of Business Administration, Division of Research, 1967.
79. Ledbetter, J. G.: *The Effects of Management Control System Training on the Rehabilitation Agencies Staffs' Perceptions of the Dysfunctionality of the Rehabilitation Service Delivery System.* Unpublished doctoral dissertation, University of Georgia, 1980.
80. Levinson, D. J., Darrow, C. M., Klein, E. B. Levinson, M. H. and Mcgee, B.: Periods in the adult development of men: Ages 18–45. *Counseling Psychologist, 6:*21–25, 1976.
81. LeVois, M., Nguyen, T. D., & Attkisson, C. C.: Artifact in client satisfaction assessment: Experience in community mental health settings. *Evaluation and Program Planning, 4:*1–12, 1981.
82. Lewin, K.: *Field Theory in Social Science.* New York, Harper and Row, 1951.
83. Likert, R.: From production- and employee-centeredness to systems 1–4. *Journal of Management, 5:*147–156, 1979.
84. Maslow, A. H.: *Motivation and Personality.* New York, Harper and Row, 1954.
85. Matkin, R. E., Sawyer, H. W., Lorenz, J. R. and Rubin, S. E.: Rehabilitation administrators and supervisors: their work assignments, training needs and suggestions for preparation. *Journal of Rehabilitation Administration, 6:*170–182, 1982.
86. Mayfield, E. C.: The selection interview-a re-evaluation of published research. *Personnel Psychology, 17:*239–260, 1964.
87. McCormick, E. J., Cunningham, J. W., and Thornton, G. C.: The prediction of job requirements by a structured job analysis procedure. *Personnel Psychology, 20:*431–440. 1967.
88. Meyer, H., Kay, E. and French, J.: Split roles in performance appraisal. *Harvard Business Review, 43:*123–129, 1965.
89. Miller, J. V., Lee, C., Wargel, J. and Won, H.: *Program Evaluation Approaches for State Rehabilitation Agencies: Current Status and Future Directions* (Michigan

Studies in Rehabilitation, Series 1, Monograph I). Ann Arbor, Rehabilitation Research Institute, School of Education, University of Michigan, 1977.

90. Moore, M. L.: *Designing Parallel Organizations to Support Organizational Productivity Programs.* Paper presented at Rehabilitation Mainframe, Kent State University, Kent, Ohio, June, 1985.

91. Morris, L. L. and Fitz-Gibbon, C. T.: Evaluator's handbook. In Morris, L. L. (Ed.): *Program Evaluation Kit.* Beverly Hills, Sage, 1978.

92. Morris, S.: Meet the press. *Better Communication* (No. 299). Stirling, New Jersey, Information Plus, 1982.

93. Morse, N. C. and Reimer, E.: The experimental change of a major organizational variable. *Journal of Abnormal and Social Psychology, 52:*120–129, 1956.

94. Mott, P. E.: *The Characteristics of Effective Organizations.* New York, Harper & Row, 1972.

95. Murphy, K. R. and Constans, J. I.: Behavioral anchors as a source of bias in rating. *Journal of Applied Psychology, 72:*573–577, 1987.

96. National Rehabilitation Administration Association. *Code of Ethics,* 1979.

97. Odiorne, G. S.: *Management by Objectives: A System of Managerial Leadership.* New York, Pitman, 1965.

98. Olmstead, J. A., and Christensen, H. E.: *Effects of Agency Work Contexts: An Intensive Field Study, Volume I, Report, National Study of Social Welfare and Rehabilitation Workers, Work and Organizational Contexts.* Washington, D.C., Social and Rehabilitation Service, U.S. Department of Health, Education, and Welfare, 1973.

99. Ouchi, W. G.: A conceptual framework for the design of organizational control mechanisms. *Management Science, 25:*833–848, 1979.

100. Ouchi, W. G.: *Theory Z.* New York, Avon, 1981.

101. Pascoe, G. C.: Patient satisfaction in primary health care: A literature review and analysis. *Evaluation and Program Planning, 6:*185–210, 1983.

102. Patrick, A. and Patterson, J. B.: The management control system: Counselor job satisfaction and work alienation. *Journal of Rehabilitation Administration, 10:*12–18, 1986.

103. Peters, T. J. and Waterman, R. H.: *In Search of Excellence.* New York, Warner, 1982.

104. Porter, L. W., Lawler, E. E., & Hackman, J. R.: *Behavior in Organizations.* New York, McGraw-Hill, 1975.

105. Porter, L.: Turning work into nonwork: the rewarding environment. In Dunnette, M. (Ed.): *Work and NonWork in the Year 2001.* Monterey, Brooks/Cole, 1973.

106. Porter, L. W. and Steers, R. M.: Organizational, work, and personal factors in employee turnover and absenteeism. *Psychological Bulletin, 80:*151–176, 1973.

107. Primoff, E. S.: *How to Prepare and Conduct Job-Element Examinations.* Washington, D.C., Personnel Research and Development Center, United States Civil Service Commission, 1974.

108. Reagles, K. W., Wright, G. N. and Butler, A. J.: *A Scale of Rehabilitation Gain for Clients of an Expanded Vocational Rehabilitation Program.* Wisconsin Studies in Vocational Rehabilitation, Monograph XIII, Series 2. Madison,

Regional Rehabilitation Research Institute, University of Wisconsin, 1970.

109. Rigger, T. F. and Matkin, R. E.: *Handbook for Management of Human Services Agencies.* Carbondale, Southern Illinois University Press, 1986.

110. Roark, A. E.: Interpersonal conflict management. *Personnel and Guidance Journal, 56:*400–402, 1978.

111. Roberts, R. E., Pascoe, G. C. and Attkisson, C. C.: Relationship of service satisfaction to life satisfaction and perceived well-being. *Evaluation and Program Planning, 6:*373–383, 1983.

112. Roesler, R. and Mack, G.: *Strategies for Interagency Linkages: A Literature Review.* Hot Springs, Arkansas Rehabilitation Research and Training Center, 1975.

113. Ross, C.: Supervision theory: a prescription for practice. *Journal of Rehabilitation Administration, 3:*14–19, 1979.

114. Rubin, S. E.: Designing state vocational rehabilitation agency evaluation research. In Rubin, S. E. (Ed.): *Issues in Program Evaluation Research in State Rehabilitation Agencies.* Symposium presented at the American Personnel and Guidance Association Convention, New Orleans, April, 1974.

115. Sample, J. A.: A model for the collaborative development and use of BARS in appraising the performance of rehabilitation supervisors and counselors. *Journal of Rehabilitation Administration, 8:*105–110, 1984.

116. Sampson, J. P.: Maximizing the effectiveness of computer applications in counseling and human development: The role of research and implementation strategies. *Journal of Counseling and Development, 63:*187–191, 1984.

117. Schwartz, J.: Computer headaches. *Newsweek,* July 6, 1987, pp. 34–35.

118. Scott, D.: *How to Put More Time in Your Life.* New York, Signet, 1980.

119. Shaw, M. E.: A comparison of two types of leadership in various communication nets. *Journal of Abnormal and Social Psychology, 50:*127–134, 1955.

120. Shaw, M. E.: *Group Dynamics: The Psychology of Small Group Behavior.* New York, McGraw-Hill, 1976.

121. Simon, S. E.: Productivity measurement and evaluation in rehabilitation and social service agencies. *Journal of Rehabilitation Administration, 6:*161–166, 1982.

122. Simon, S. E.: Work measurement methods: an approach to productivity management in the human services. *Journal of Rehabilitation Administration, 7:*151–161, 1983.

123. Simon, S. E.: A productivity optimizing model for rehabilitation agencies. *Journal of Rehabilitation Administration, 8:*119–126, 1984.

124. Simon, S. E.: Productivity, efficiency and effectiveness: simple indicators of agency performance. *Journal of Rehabilitation Administration, 11:*4–10, 1987.

125. Skinner, B. F.: *Science and Human Behavior.* New York, Macmillan, 1953.

126. Solomon, J. R.: The application of Japanese management strategies to rehabilitation administration. *Journal of Rehabilitation Administration, 8:*4–9, 1984.

127. Spaniol, L. A.: A program evaluation model for rehabilitation agencies and facilities. *Journal of Rehabilitation Administration, 1:*4–13, 1977.

128. Stein, C.: Objective management systems: two to five years after implementation. *Personnel Journal, 54:*525–528, 548, 1975.

129. Super, D. E., Starishevsky, R., Matlin, N. and Jordoan, J. P.: *Career Development: Self Concept Theory.* Princeton, College Entrance Examination Board, 1963.

130. Tannenbaum, A. S.: *Control in Organizations.* New York, McGraw-Hill, 1968.

131. Tannenbaum, R. & Hanna, R. W.: Holding on, letting go, and moving on: Understanding a neglected perspective on change. In Tannenbaum, R., Margulies, N., Massarik, F. and Associates (Eds.): *Human Systems Development.* San Francisco, Jossey-Bass, 1985.

132. Tannenbaum, R. & Schmidt, W. H.: How to choose a leadership pattern. *Harvard Business Review, 51:*162–180, 1973.

133. Thorndike, E. L.: *Animal Intelligence.* New York, McGraw-Hill, 1911.

134. Turner, R. R.: *Life Functioning Index.* Cambridge, Mass., Abt Associates, 1982.

135. Tyer, C. B. and Brabham, R. E.: Budgeting for rehabilitation in an age of accountability and scarce resources. In Emener, W. G., Luck, R. S. and Smits, S. J. (Eds.): *Rehabilitation Administration and Supervision.* Baltimore, University Park Press, 1981, pp. 45–61.

136. Uniform Guidelines on Employee Selection Procedures. *Federal Register,* August 25, 1978.

137. Vaillant, G. E.: How the best and the brightest come of age. *Psychology Today, 11:*34–39, 1977.

138. Van Maanen, J.: The process of program evaluation. Reprint from *The Grantsmanship Center NEWS.* The Grantsmanship Center, 1031 S. Grand Avenue, Los Angeles, CA 90015, (undated).

139. Veterans Administration. *Program Evaluation Project.* Washington, D.C., Vocational Rehabilitation and Education Service, 1986.

140. Vroom, V. H.: *Work and Maintenance.* New York, Wiley, 1964.

141. Wainwright, C. O. and Miner, K. R.: The supervision of human resources. In Emener, W. G., Luck, R. S. and Smits, S. J. (Eds.): *Rehabilitation Administration and Supervision.* Baltimore, University Park Press, 1981, pp. 333–353.

142. Walls, R. T. & Tseng, M. S.: Measurement of client outcomes in rehabilitation. In Bolton, B. (Ed.): *Handbook of Measurement and Evaluation in Rehabilitation.* Baltimore, Brookes, 1987, pp. 183–201.

143. Walz, G. W. and Benjamin, L.: *On Becoming a Change Agent.* Ann Arbor, ERIC Counseling and Personnel Services Information Center, School of Education, University of Michigan, 1977.

144. Westerheide, W. J. and Lenhart, L.: Development and reliability of a pretest-posttest rehabilitation services outcome measure. *Rehabilitation Research and Practice Review, 4:*15–23, 1973.

145. Whetten, D. A.: Coping with incompatible expectations: An integrated view of role conflict. *Administrative Science Quarterly, 23:*254–271, 1978.

146. Whittington, H. G.: People make programs: Personnel management. In Feldman, S. (Ed.): *The Administration of Mental Health Services.* Springfield, Thomas, 1980, pp. 41–77.

147. Wright, G. N.: *Total Rehabilitation.* Boston, Little Brown and Company, 1980.

148. Yates, B. T.: *Improving Effectiveness and Reducing Costs in Mental Health.* Springfield, Thomas, 1980.

INDEX